EARLY RECORDS OF BRITISH INDIA

EARLY RECORDS OF BRITISH INDIA

A HISTORY

OF THE

ENGLISH SETTLEMENTS IN INDIA,

AS TOLD IN THE GOVERNMENT RECORDS, THE WORKS OF OLD TRAVELLERS, AND OTHER CONTEMPORARY DOCUMENTS, FROM THE EARLIEST PERIOD DOWN TO THE RISE OF BRITISH POWER IN INDIA

J. TALBOYS WHEELER

GYAN

Published by

GYAN

Gyan Publishing House
5, Ansari Road
Daryaganj, New Delhi-110002
Phone: 011-47034999, 9811692060
E-mail: books@gyanbooks.com

Distribution Network
gyanbooks.com
India, USA, Canada, UK, Australia, France

ISBN: 978-81-212-9312-9 (PB)
First Published, 1878

2nd Impression 2023

Printed at: Gyan Press, Delhi.

EARLY RECORDS OF BRITISH INDIA

Author: J. TALBOYS WHEELER

EARLY RECORDS OF BRITISH INDIA:

A HISTORY

OF THE

ENGLISH SETTLEMENTS IN INDIA,

AS TOLD IN THE GOVERNMENT RECORDS, THE WORKS OF OLD TRAVELLERS, AND OTHER CONTEMPORARY DOCUMENTS, FROM THE EARLIEST PERIOD DOWN TO THE RISE OF BRITISH POWER IN INDIA.

BY

J. TALBOYS WHEELER,

LATE ASSISTANT SECRETARY TO THE GOVERNMENT OF INDIA IN THE FOREIGN DEPARTMENT; AUTHOR OF "A HISTORY OF INDIA FROM THE EARLIEST AGES;" "THE GEOGRAPHY OF HERODOTUS;" ETC.

LONDON:
PUBLISHED BY TRÜBNER AND COMPANY.
1878.

PREFACE.

THE subject-matter of the present volume is, perhaps, sufficiently told on the title-page. It may, however, be explained that the compiler was originally employed to report on the records of the Home Department in Calcutta, and intended to confine his extracts to the papers preserved there. As, however, he proceeded with the task it was discovered that the value of those records had been much overrated. They were incomplete in themselves, and not only overloaded with detail, but were mostly written in the verbose style of the eighteenth century. Those of an early date had been destroyed in the great storm of 1737, or were lost at the capture of Calcutta in 1756 by the Nawab of Bengal. Those of a later date throw considerable light upon the progress of affairs during the transition period, when the Company's servants were beginning to exercise a political power in India; but they do not furnish details as regards the social life of the early English settlers in Bengal, which is still a desideratum in Anglo-Indian history.

The extracts given will suffice to show to what extent these records possess an intrinsic interest. In order, however, to complete the usefulness of the volume, and render it of historical value, the compiler has been led to extend his researches over a wider field. He has collected extracts from the works of old travellers and other contemporary authorities, which bring out the workings of the English element amongst the native population, not only at Calcutta, but at Surat, Bombay, and Madras. Surat was perhaps scarcely a settlement; it was only a house or factory. But it was the first factory which the English established in India; and the pictures furnished by the old travellers, Mandelslo and Fryer, of English life at Surat in the reigns of Charles the First and Charles the Second, will probably have a charm for most readers. In like manner Fryer's description of Bombay, some twenty years after its cession to the English by the Portuguese, will excite imperial interest. It throws further light upon that indomitable spirit of English enterprise which has converted a pestilential island into one of the great commercial cities of the world.

As regards Madras, the compiler has had exceptional sources of information. The old records of the commercial period, which were wanting in Calcutta, have been preserved at Madras. In 1860

Sir Charles Trevelyan, then Governor of Madras, opened up the records of that Presidency to the compiler for the first time. The result was a publication of a series of extracts from the records; and these extracts were illustrated, or rather held together, by an explanatory narrative. The work was published in three volumes under the title of "Madras in the Olden Time."

That portion of the present volume which deals with Madras comprises a selection of such Madras records as are likely to interest general readers. Those which are only of local value, and likely to prove tedious to readers outside the Madras Presidency, have been generally excluded. Those which illustrate the primitive system of administration, the old English life within the walls of Fort St. George and Black Town, or the relations between the English residents and native population, have been reproduced *in extenso*, or in the form of an abridged summary. These again have been supplemented by extracts from the travels of Fryer and Hamilton. Something is thus opened up of the inner state of affairs during the seventeenth century, and early years of the eighteenth, and the way in which the Company's administration of Madras was regarded by strangers and interlopers.

In dealing with Calcutta the compiler has proceeded much on the same principle. The absence of records prior to the capture of Calcutta in 1756 has been supplied by extracts or summaries from contemporary authorities, such as Holwell, the Syar-ul-Mutakherin, Stewart's History of Bengal, and otherworks of a like character. The following documents are specially worthy of notice:—

1st.—The letters of certain English envoys who went on a mission from Calcutta to Delhi as far back as 1715. This correspondence was discovered at Madras during the investigations of 1860 and 1861.

2nd.—Extracts from Hamilton's Travels about 1720, which furnish graphic pictures of old Calcutta life, as well as sketches of all the European settlements in Bengal.

3rd.—Holwell's Narrative of the Tragedy in the Black Hole in 1756. Holwell was one of the sufferers in that terrible catastrophe, in which a hundred and twenty-three persons were stifled to death in a small dungeon, whilst only twenty-three lived till the next morning.

Of the remainder of the volume little need be said. It consists of extracts from the Calcutta records strung together by an explanatory narrative. There are some strange and lamentable episodes, such as the quarrel over the inland trade and the massacre at Patna. All, however, may be left to tell their own story.

The labour which has been spent upon this volume is beyond all calculation. It cannot be judged by the results, but only from the voluminous records which have been carefully searched but yielded nothing. The time expended, however, will never be regretted should it appear that the information now collected from original or half-forgotten sources has helped to throw more light upon the rise of British power in India.

J. TALBOYS WHEELER.

CALCUTTA,
The 26th December 1877.

CONTENTS.

CHAPTER I.

INDIA IN THE SEVENTEENTH CENTURY.

A. D. 1600 TO 1700.

CHAPTER II.

ENGLISH AT SURAT AND BOMBAY.

A. D. 1600 TO 1700.

CHAPTER III.

ENGLISH AT MADRAS.

A. D. 1600 TO 1677.

CHAPTER IV.

MADRAS UNDER GOLKONDA.

A. D. 1670 TO 1688.

CHAPTER V.

MADRAS UNDER THE MOGHULS.

A. D. 1688 TO 1750.

CHAPTER VI.

ENGLISH IN BENGAL.

A. D. 1640 TO 1750.

CHAPTER VII.

CALCUTTA AND ITS CAPTURE.

A. D. 1750 TO 1756.

CHAPTER VIII.

FIRST GOVERNMENT OF CLIVE.

A. D. 1757 TO 1760.

CHAPTER IX.

CALCUTTA RECORDS: CHANGING NAWABS.

A. D. 1760 TO 1763.

CHAPTER X.

CALCUTTA RECORDS: PRIVATE TRADE.

A. D. 1763.

CHAPTER XI.

CALCUTTA RECORDS: PATNA MASSACRE.

A. D. 1763.

CHAPTER XII.

SECOND GOVERNMENT OF CLIVE.

A. D. 1765 TO 1767.

CHAPTER XIII.

BEGINNING OF BRITISH ADMINISTRATION.

A. D. 1767 TO 1770.

EARLY RECORDS

OF

BRITISH INDIA.

CHAPTER I.

INDIA IN THE SEVENTEENTH CENTURY.

A. D. 1600 TO 1700.

THE three English Presidencies of Madras, Calcutta, and Bombay were founded in the seventeenth century, during the reigns of Charles the First, Oliver Cromwell, and Charles the Second. The records of British India consequently begin in the seventeenth century. Before describing their subject matter, it may be as well to glance at the existing state of India; to present, as it were, an outline picture of India in the seventeenth century. **Early English settlements.**

India is an inverted triangle. Its northern boundary is formed by the Himalayas; its western and eastern sides are washed by the Indian Ocean and the Bay of Bengal. It is divided into three belts or zones, which may be described as Hindustan, the Dekhan, and the Peninsula. Hindustan is in the north; the Dekhan in the middle; the Peninsula in the south. These three zones are separated from each other by lines running east to west, or west to **Division of India:—Hindustan, Dekhan, Peninsula.**

east, along two rivers, and reaching to the sea on either side. The line of the Nerbudda river separates Hindustan from the Dekhan; the line of the Kistna river separates the Dekhan from the Peninsula.[1]

Hindus under Muhammadan rule.

In the seventeenth century the people of India practically consisted of Hindus and Muhammadans. The bulk were Hindus; they were the subject race. The Muhammadans were comparatively few, but they were the ruling power. They had begun to invade India in the eleventh century. In the beginning of the seventeenth century they had established their dominion in Hindustan; they had founded kingdoms in the Dekhan; they had not as yet conquered the Peninsula. The Hindus were still masters in the Peninsula.

Afghans and Moghuls.

The Muhammadans were not all of the same race. They comprised Afghans and Moghuls; accordingly there was a race antagonism[2] between the two. The Afghans were bigoted Muhammadans; they were intolerant of Hindu idolatry; they had tried to force the Koran upon the people of India by war and persecution. In the sixteenth century their empire had been overturned by the Moghuls. The Moghuls were lax and indifferent in matters of reli-

[1] Politically the boundary between Hindustan and the Dekhan is formed by the Vindhya range of mountains. Geographically the line of the Nerbudda river is preferable. It has the Vindhya mountains on its northern bank, whilst its southern bank is formed by the Satpura range.

[2] Besides the Afghan element there was a Turkish element. There is no necessity in the present work to indicate any distinctive marks between Turks and Afghans, or between Turks and Moghuls.

gion; they called themselves Muhammadans, but many were Muhammadans only in name.

Moghul empire in India.

The Moghul empire in India had been the growth of the sixteenth century. Baber and Humáyun were the early Moghul conquerors. Their reigns are of no moment. The real founder of the Moghul empire was the celebrated Akbar. This semi-enlightened barbarian introduced a policy under which the discordant elements of Moghul, Afghan, and Hindu were quieted down, and the whole were moulded into one empire.

Akbar, 1556-1605.

The reign of Akbar has been regarded as a golden era in the history of India. He was a true Moghul, a descendant of Timur and Chenghiz Khan. He had the instincts of a warrior and a king. He established his empire over Hindustan, the Punjab, and Cabul; but he is best known by his policy. He abandoned the religious bigotry which had hitherto characterised Muhammadan rule in India. He was tolerant in religious matters, like the ancient Romans. At the same time he sought to be honoured as a deity, like the Roman emperors. This system of toleration was adopted by his son and grandson. During all three reigns it was the mainstay of the empire. It will be seen hereafter that it was abandoned by his great-grandson Aurungzeb for a policy of intolerance. The bigotry of Aurungzeb brought about the decline of Moghul rule.

Policy of Akbar.

The policy of Akbar and his immediate successors has rarely been understood. It was that of

Chenghiz Khan, the Moghul hero of the thirteenth century. According to the old laws of Chenghiz Khan, every religion was to be tolerated that acknowledged the worship of one God. Akbar acted on this policy. At the same time he was imbued with all the curiosity of a Moghul. He had a keen relish for religious discussion. He studied Brahmanism, Parsi worship, and Christianity. He broke up the authority of the Ulama, the collective body of Muhammadan lawyers and doctors, who often controlled the sovereign by appeals to the Koran. He threw off all the trammels of the Koran. He left men to follow their own religion, but wished them to pay him divine honours as a representative of deity. It is evident that he was a bad Muhammadan. But the result of his policy was that the Moghul empire was not endangered by religious antagonism. During the reigns of Akbar and his immediate successors, men of every religion dwelt in peace under Moghul rule. To all outward appearance the empire of the Moghul in India was as permanent as that of any European power.

Partiality for Hindus and Europeans.

Akbar carried his policy to an extreme. He made friends with Hindu princes; he appointed them to high commands; he took their daughters to be his wives. He entertained European gunners and artisans. These instincts have been common to Moghul princes from a very early period. Marco Polo tells of similar doings in the court of Kublai Khan; similar proclivities have long been at work in the present day at the court of the King of Burma.

But notwithstanding these outward signs of intelligence, the Moghul empire in India was politically weak. It was held together, not by common loyalty, but by mutual fear. There was much display of outward show and form; but there was no real strength in the body politic. It was always exposed to rebellions from within and invasions from without. These conditions are to be found in all Moghul empires. They are not distracted by religious antagonisms; but they are only held together by a system of intrigue and terrorism. They lack those bonds of patriotism and public spirit which alone secure the permanence of empires, whether Asiatic or European. The empires of Chenghiz Khan and Timur were of this type; so is the existing Moghul rule in Upper Burma; and so was the Moghul empire in India. Such empires may dazzle the world for a few generations; they generally perish in wars and revolutions. They leave nothing behind that can be called history. Family chronicles and court memoirs have been written to order by court scribes and parasites for the glorification of monarchs and their ancestors; but to this day our only reliable knowledge of the religion and civilisation of the Moghuls is to be derived from the testimony of contemporary European residents or travellers. Inherent weakness of Moghul rule.

The Moghul dominion in India was an absolute and irresponsible despotism. The will of the sove- Moghul despotism.

reign or Padishah[1] was law, and above all law. In theory, he was master of the life and property of every one of his subjects. He could imprison, flog, torture, mutilate, confiscate, or execute at will. There was no independent force to over-ride his whim; nothing but fear of rebellion or assassination. There were public Durbars, but no one ventured to dispute the will of the sovereign. There was no hereditary nobility, except amongst the Hindus. There was no public opinion worthy of the name; the voice of the people was rarely raised except in flattery of the Padishah. As far as the Moghul grandees were concerned, the Padishah was the sole proprietor of the soil, the sole inheritor of wealth, the sole fountain of honour. Hereditary rights were only possessed by Hindus, or by the lower classes. When the empire was at its zenith, all rights were often outraged or ignored; when the empire began to decline, rights began to harden into institutions.

Land tenures.

The following remarks of Robert Orme, the contemporary historian of British India, furnish such an exact insight into the tenure of land, and nature of property generally, under Moghul rule, that they are extracted at length:—

Renter and husbandman.

"We see in those parts of Hindustan, which are frequented by European nations, the customs or laws which regard lands

[1] The Moghul sovereign was known to Europeans as the King, the Emperor, or the Great Moghul. In India he was universally known as the Padishah. Abul Fazl gives the following meaning to the term Padishah: "'Pad,'" he says, "signifies stability and possession; 'Shah' means 'origin or lord." See preface to the Ain-i-Akbari, translated by Professor Blochmann, of Calcutta.

subject to contradictions, not easily reconcileable. The husbandman who possesses a few fields has the power of selling and bequeathing them, at the same time that the district in which these fields are included is annually let out by the Government to a renter who pays a certain sum of money to the lord of the country, and receives from the cultivator a certain part of his harvests. The renter sometimes quarrels with the husbandman, and displaces him from his possessions. Clamours as against the highest degree of injustice ensue. The prince interferes and generally redresses the poor man, who has so much need of support in such a cause of misery; and if he fails to give this proof of his inclination to justice, he is held in execration, and deemed capable of any iniquity.

Proprietory right of the Sovereign.

"In all the countries absolutely subjected, the Great Moghul styles himself proprietor of all the lands, and gives portions of them at will as revenues for life to his feudatories; but still these grants take not away from the cultivator the right of sale and bequest. The policy of all the Indian governments in Hindustan, as well as that of the Great Moghul, seems to consist more in a perpetual attention to prevent any one family from obtaining great possessions, than in the intention of multiplying oppressions upon the body of the people; for such slavery would soon leave the monarch little grandeur to boast of, and few subjects to command. As all acquisitions of land are subject to the inspection of the government, the man who should attempt to make himself proprietor of a large estate in land would be refused the certificates necessary to put him in possession, and would be marked as a victim necessary to be sacrified to the policy of the State. From what we see in the histories of this and other Eastern countries, the violences committed among the great lead us to think that the man of more humble condition is subject to still greater violences, when, on the contrary, this humility is the best of protections.

Rights of inheritance refused to office-holders.

"The feudatory, by the acceptance of a certain title and the pension which accompanies it, acknowledges the Great Moghul his heir. No man, from the Vizier downwards, has any trust of importance reposed in him but on these terms; and on his decease, the whole of his property that can be found is seized for the use of the Emperor, who gives back to the family what portion he pleases. The estates of all who are not feudatories descend to the natural heirs."

Life in public.

The Moghul Padishahs of Hindustan spent half their time in public; this was the one popular element in their rule. They received petitions and administered justice in public. They gave audiences in open Durbars. They publicly inspected horses, elephants, troops, arms, accoutrements, jewels, decorations, furniture, cattle and animals of all kinds, goods and chattels of every description. They delighted in hunting expeditions, after the old Moghul fashion which has prevailed since the days of Nimrod. They delighted in public fights between animals and gladiators, after the manner of the later Roman emperors. Akbar took great pains in the administration of justice; he was anxious for the welfare of the people. Neither his son Jehangir, nor his grandson Shah Jehan, cared anything for the people. They were greedy only of flattery and riches. They lavished enormous sums on harem establishments, jewels, palaces, mausoleums, and tented pavilions. Meanwhile they often hoarded up vast sums in the palace vaults of Delhi and Agra.

Government in the provinces.

The Moghul empire was divided into some twenty or thirty provinces. The governors of provinces collected revenue, administered justice, and kept the country under military command. The governor of a province was known as the Nawab or Subahdar. All appointments were supposed to be made direct by the Padishah; none were valid until they had been confirmed by the royal letters and insignia of investiture. It is scarcely worth while to map out the provinces. Their limits were sometimes changed at the will of the Padishah. Sometimes three or four were placed under a prince of the blood as viceroy. All, or nearly all, comprehended large tracts under Hindu Rajas. Sometimes the Moghuls invaded the territories of the Hindu Rajas. But many Hindu princes maintained their independence down to the last days of the empire.

The revenue system of the Moghuls was a series of struggles and compromises. In theory there was order and regularity; in practice there was disorder and uncertainty. The cultivators were known as Ryots; the middle man, who farmed or rented the land, was known as the Zemindar. From the Ryot to the Nawab or Subahdar there was a constant conflict of interests. The Ryots were often treated as serfs. The Ryot sought to appropriate the harvest without the knowledge of the Zemindar. The Zemindar's servants mounted guard over the Ryot and hoodwinked the Governor. The Governor played the same game in turn. The Padishah secured his own share of the revenue by appointing a Dewan to every province. The Dewan was supposed to keep the accounts; to remit the royal share to the imperial treasury. The Dewan was independent of the Subahdar; so far he was a check upon the Subahdar. Revenue system.

Generally, the Dewan was in collusion with the Subahdar. At spasmodic intervals he aspired after promotion, or reward, by a display of extraordinary zeal in behalf of the Padishah.

Presents.

Presents were as much an institution as the land revenue. No man appeared without a present before a revenue collector, a magistrate, or a local governor. Ryots made their presents to the Zemindar, and bribed his servants. Zemindars made their presents to the local Governor, and bribed his servants. Local Governors propitiated the Subahdar in like manner. On family occasions, such as the birth of a Subahdar's son, or the marriage of a son or daughter, extra presents were expected and demanded. All petitions were accompanied by presents. The gifts sent to court were enormous. Jewels and gold mohurs in sufficient abundance would purchase immunity from the grossest oppressions and the vilest crimes.[1]

Moghul court.

The Moghul court was nomadic. Its movements might be compared with the "royal progresses" of old English kings; they bore a closer resemblance to the migrations of the old Moghul Khans between summer and winter quarters. The Moghul Padishahs wandered to and fro over the conquered provinces of India in the same fashion that Chenghiz Khan and Timur wandered over the vast tracts

[1] Under British rule, return presents are generally given of equal value. Under Moghul rule, the most valuable jewels were often presented to the Padishah, whilst a piece of muslin, or an embroidered handkerchief, or a paltry medal, were given in return. Foreign ambassadors were treated differently, according to circumstances.

between China and Europe. Their encampments resembled great cities; they included streets of tents and pavilions; shops, bazars, fortifications, enclosures, and gateways of painted canvas. Sometimes the court left the camp, and was fixed for a while at Agra, Delhi, Lahore, or Ajmir; when the hot season began, it generally moved away to the cool mountains of Kashmir. The courts of Subahdars and Nawabs were all of the same type. They moved about their respective provinces in much the same fashion.

Rebellions.

The Moghul empire was always exposed to rebellion. Hindu Rajas rebelled against the Subahdar. Refractory Subahdars rebelled against the Padishah. The migrations of the court may have tended to preserve the peace of the provinces. At intervals the empire was convulsed by a war for the succession. The Padishah always had four sons and no more. This Moghul institution dates back to Chenghiz Khan. Other sons might be born; as a rule, only four were recognised. If one of the four died, another was taken to fill his room. The eldest was heir-apparent; he resided at court with his father. The three others were sent out to rule remote provinces as viceroys. When the Padishah died, or was about to die, the four brothers marched armies against each other; India was deluged with blood. When a prince had destroyed his three brothers, he ascended the throne and massacred all the males of the blood royal, excepting his own sons. After this India was tranquil.

Jehangir, 1605-1627.

Jehangir, son of Akbar, was an inferior man to his father. He is better known than any other of the Moghul Padishahs. Sir Thomas Roe was sent by James the First on a mission to Jehangir. The object was to procure the protection of the Padishah for an English factory at Surat. Roe saw a great deal of Jehangir. He describes him as a drunken sovereign, infatuated with a vindictive woman named Nurmahal. His reign was much disturbed by rebellions.

Shah Jehan, 1628-1658.

Shah Jehan, son of Jehangir, was selfish and sensual. His dominion extended over the same provinces as that of Akbar; it included Kabul, the Punjab, and Hindustan; it also extended over the Northern Dekhan.[1] His vices were a scandal to Asia. His court was utterly corrupt and depraved. There was a lax indifference to religion, morality, or public decency. The sons of Shah Jehan, with one exception, were men of the same stamp. The third son was the exception; his name was Aurungzeb.

Aurungzeb, 1658 to 1707.

Aurungzeb had little chance of the throne. He had two brothers older than himself; both were popular with Moghuls and Rajputs. Ambition fired his brain; it stimulated his genius; it im-

[1] Moghul dominion had been gradually encroaching upon the Dekhan ever since the reign of Akbar. In the reign of Shah Jehan, the conquered provinces in the Dekhan were formed into a viceroyalty, which was known as the "Dekhan." The Mussulman kingdoms of the Southern Dekhan were still unconquered. They were known as Bijapur and Golkonda. They extended southward to the River Kistna, or Krishna. India south of the River Krishna was distributed amongst a number of petty Hindu principalities, the relics of the old Hindu empire of Vijayanagar.

pelled him to form a policy. He abandoned the toleration of Akbar. He affected to be a strict Muhammadan. He curried favour with Muhammadans. He sought the support of all zealous Muhammadans throughout India. He made his religion a stepping-stone to the throne.

Bigotry and hypocrisy.

The early Padishahs were lusty men, sensual and jovial. Aurungzeb was lean and spare. His eyes were sunk in his head; they were bright and piercing. He abstained from wine and flesh meat; he lived chiefly on rice and vegetables. He was always talking of the Koran. He was ostentatious in the performance of his religious duties. He was never a sincere zealot. His religion never interfered with his pleasures or policy. He had a weak digestion; his abstinence from wine and meat was therefore a necessity. He was heterodox in his marriages. His favourite wife was a Christian from Georgia. Another favourite was a Rajput lady. He flattered Rajput Rajas to win them to his cause. He flattered Sivaji, the Mahratta leader in the Western Dekhan. Sivaji might help him in the coming struggle for the throne. Sivaji might give him a refuge in the event of defeat and disaster. He ceded territory to Sivaji; he made a treaty of friendship with the Mahratta.

War between the four princes.

The war between the four brothers began whilst Shah Jehan was still alive. In the end Aurungzeb obtained the mastery. His brothers were slaughtered or poisoned with all their male descendants. His father Shah Jehan was deposed and imprisoned in the palace at Agra. Aurungzeb ascended the throne at Delhi. He began his reign with caution. He disguised his hatred of Hindus. He trimmed between Muhammadans and Rajputs. Occasionally he sent armies against the Mahrattas; but many years passed away before he waged war against Hinduism and Hindus.

Reign of Aurungzeb.

The reign of Aurungzeb lasted from 1658 to 1707. It covered half a century,—the interval between the death of Oliver Cromwell and the opening years of Queen Anne. The great characteristic of the reign was the restoration of the Koran as the supreme law throughout Hindustan. Apart from this revival of Islam, there are three prominent events in his reign, namely: the rise and growth of the Mahratta power; the persecuting wars against the Hindus; the development of three English factories into presidency towns.

Rise of the Mahrattas.

Aurungzeb became alarmed at the growing power of Sivaji and the Mahrattas. Sivaji was becoming a thorn in the side of the Moghul empire. He was thirty years of age when Aurungzeb became Padishah. He had been brought up amongst the precipices and defiles of the Western Ghâts. His head-quarters were at Poona. He had numerous fortresses on the mountains. He had founded a kingdom on a basis of plunder. Every year during the dry season his Mahratta horsemen scoured the plains in search of booty. When the rains began they carried off the spoil to their mountain fortresses. Sivaji established a system of black mail;

it consisted of one-fourth of the revenue; it was known as *chout*. Whenever the inhabitants paid the chout, their district or village was spared. Whenever they withheld the chout, they were plundered every year until they yielded to the demand.

Sivaji was unscrupulous and perfidious. In his early years he inveigled a Muhammadan general into a private interview; he slaughtered him with a secret weapon ringed to his fingers, known as "tigers' claws." When Aurungzeb came to the throne, he broke his treaty with Sivaji; he took back the territory he had ceded to Sivaji. In revenge, Sivaji plundered Surat. He tried to plunder the English factory at Surat, but the English beat him off. Sivaji, the Mahratta.

Aurungzeb regarded Sivaji with contempt. He referred to Sivaji as "the mountain rat." He sent his uncle Shaista Khan to subdue "the mountain rat." Shaista Khan captured Poona, and Sivaji retired to his hill fortresses. One night, whilst Shaista Khan was asleep at Poona, his house was attacked by Mahrattas. His eldest son was slaughtered on the spot. He himself escaped through a window with the loss of a finger. Amidst the panic, Sivaji and his Mahrattas went out of the city. They were seen in the distance ascending a hill fortress amidst the glare of torches. War against Sivaji.

Aurungzeb next set a trap for "the mountain rat." Sivaji was invited to Delhi under pretence of being appointed viceroy of the Moghul Sivaji at Delhi.

conquests in the Dekhan. He went to Delhi; he found himself deceived, insulted, and a prisoner. He was in danger of assassination, but escaped out of the city in an empty hamper. He was fortunate enough to reach Poona in safety.

Death of Sivaji, 1680.

It is needless to dwell on the wars of Aurungzeb against the Mahrattas. It will suffice to say that Sivaji escaped from every toil and danger; he founded a kingdom and a dynasty. He died about 1680.

Aurungzeb takes the field.

When Sivaji was dead, Aurungzeb took the field. Possibly he had been afraid of Sivaji; afraid that Sivaji would circumvent him or assassinate him. Henceforth, and until his last illness twenty-seven years afterwards, Aurungzeb remained in camp. Throughout this period he was constantly warring against the Hindus. He began the war in the vain hope that he could dethrone the Hindu gods and establish the Koran from sea to sea.

Persecuting wars against Hindus.

The fire of persecution began with the destruction of pagodas in Hindustan. A large pagoda was burnt down near Delhi. Orders were issued to the governors of provinces to destroy all heathen temples throughout the empire. Idols were cast down; temples were converted into mosques. Hindu penitents, known as Yogis and Saniasis, were driven out of Hindustan. All the great officers of the Crown, who refused to become Muhammadans, were deprived of their posts. The celebration of Hindu festivals was prohibited. Worst of all, the hateful poll-tax, known as the Jezya, was levied on all who refused to embrace Islam. This tax pressed heavily upon the Hindus. Merchants paid a yearly Jezya of thirteen rupees and a half per head; artizans paid six rupees and a quarter; the poorer classes paid three rupees and a half. It is difficult to conceive how such a tax could have been levied without a rebellion.

Wars in Rajputana.

There was danger in Rajputana. Aurungzeb moved all the forces of the empire against Rajputana. Jaipur consented to pay the Jezya. Marwar refused at first, but afterwards came to a compromise; the tax was redeemed by the cession of territory. The Rana of Udaipur resolutely set his face against the demand. Most of his territory was walled in by mountains. He abandoned all the country outside the mountains. The whole nation was in arms; strong guards were posted in every gorge and defile. Aurungzeb was baffled. At one time he was lost in a labyrinth of defiles. His favourite wife was taken prisoner. His force was nearly starved out. At last he retired to Ajmir. The remainder of his reign is devoid of all interest. It was wasted in wars with Rajputs, Mahrattas, and Afghans. He died in 1707.[1]

Having thus reviewed the condition of the Moghul empire during the seventeenth century, it may be advisable to glance at the early history of the English settlements in India during the same period.

---

[1] Elliot's History, Vol. VII. Catron's Moghuls.

CHAPTER II.

ENGLISH AT SURAT AND BOMBAY.

1600—1700.

Early settlement at Surat.

THE early history of the English in India is a tedious detail of voyages, personal adventures, fights with the Portuguese, or quarrels with the Moghul Governor of Surat. In the first instance the English effected a lodgment at Surat. This town is seated on the western coast of India, the side nearest to Europe. The port of Surat had been famous from a remote antiquity. It was situated about a hundred and eighty miles to the north of Bombay. It was the first place in India where the English and Dutch established a trade.

Hostility of the Portuguese.

The Portuguese had already been a century in India. The Pope had given them the sovereignty of the East. They denied the right of the English to come there at all. They hated the English as heretics. They told the Moghul Governor of Surat that the English were pirates. The details of such squabbles have lost all their interest. It will suffice to say that between the years 1610 and 1620 both English and Dutch were permitted to establish factories at Surat.

Pomp of the President.

The trade with India must have been most profitable. In 1623, the English and Dutch Presidents were living in state in large houses like palaces; the senior merchants were furnished with chambers in the same mansion. Whenever the President went abroad, a banner was carried before him, and he was followed by merchants on horseback, as well as by native attendants armed with swords, bucklers, and bows and arrows.[1]

Visit of Mandelslo.

In 1638 a young gentleman of Holstein paid a visit to Surat. His name was Albert de Mandelslo.[2] He has left a curious account of his visit; it furnishes a graphic picture of the English factory:—

Surat Custom House.

"Within a league of the Road we entered into the river upon which Surat is seated, and which hath on both sides a very fertile soil, and many fair gardens, with pleasant country-houses, which being all white, a colour it seems the Indians are much in love with, afford a noble prospect amidst the greenness whereby they are encompassed. But this river, which is the Tapte, called by others Tynde, is so shallow at the mouth of it, that barks of 70 or 80 ton can hardly come into it. We came ashore near the Sulthan's Palace,[3] and went immediately to the Custom-house to have our things searched by the officers there: which is done with such exactness in this place, that they think it not enough to open chests and portmantles, but examine people's clothes and pockets. The Sulthan or Governour, nay the Customers[4] themselves, oblige merchants and passengers to part with, at the price they shall think fit to put upon them, those goods and commodities which they had brought for their own private use. Accordingly the Sulthan himself, who came to the Custom-house as soon as we were got thither, having found among my things a bracelet of yellow amber, and a diamond, would needs buy them both of me: whereto when I made him answer, that I

[1] Travels of Pietro della Valle in 1623 and 1624. London: 1665.

[2] Travels of J. Albert de Mandelslo in 1638 and 1639. London: 1669.

[3] The local Governor of Surat was called Sultan out of courtesy.

[4] The Custom House Officers are always termed Customers by old travellers. After the English established themselves in India and levied duties, the Collector was always known as the Customer.

was no merchant, and that I valued those things only for their sakes who had bestowed them on me, he was pleased to return me the diamond, but detained the bracelet, telling me I should have it again when I honoured him with a visit.

Entertainment at the English house.

"While we were in this contestation, came to the place an Indian coach, drawn by two white oxen, which the English President had sent to bring me to their house; so that leaving the Sulthan with the bracelet, I went into it. At the entrance of the house I met the President, with his Second, that is to say, he who commands under him, and in his absence, whose name was Mr. Fremling, who received me with extraordinary kindness, and very civilly answered the compliment I made them, upon the freedom I took to make my advantage thereof. The President, who spoke Dutch very well, told me I was very welcome; that in the country where we then were, all Christians were obliged to assist one another, and that he was the more particularly obliged thereto as to what concerned me, in respect of the affection I would have expressed towards some of his nation at Ispahan. He thereupon brought me to his chamber, where there was a collation ready. It consisted of fruits and preserves, according to the custom of the country. As soon as we were set, he asked me what my design was, and understanding that I intended to return for Germany within twelve months, he told me I was come too late to get away that year, by reason no more ships would come that way, but that if I would stay with him five or six months, till there were a convenience of passage, he would take it kindly: that during that time he would contribute all he could to my divertisement: that he would find out a means how I might see the most eminent places in the country—nay, that he would send some of his own nation along with me, who should find me those accommodations I could not otherwise hope for. This obliging discourse soon prevailed with me to accept of these proffers, so that he shewed me all the house that I might make choice of a convenient lodging, which I took near his Second's chamber. In the evening, some merchants and others belonging to the President, came and brought me from my chamber to supper into a great hall, where was the Minister with about a dozen merchants, who kept me company, but the President and his Second supped not, as being accustomed to that manner of life, out of a fear of overcharging their stomachs, digestion being slowly performed, by reason of the great heats which are as troublesome there in the night time as in the day. After supper the Minister carried me into a great open gallery, where I found the President and his Second taking the coolness of the sea-air. This was the place of our ordinary rendezvous, where we met every night; to wit, the President, his Second, the principal merchant, the Minister and myself; but the other merchants came not but when they were invited by the President. At dinner he kept a great table of about fifteen or sixteen dishes of meat, besides the desert.

"The respect and deference which the other merchants have for the President was very remarkable, as also the order which was there observed in all things, especially at Divine Service, which was said twice a day, in the morning at six, and at eight at night, and on Sundays thrice. No person in the house but had his particular function, and their certain hours assigned them as well for work as recreation. Our divertisement was thus ordered. On Fridayes after Prayers, there was a particular assembly, at which met with us three other merchants, who were of kin to the President, and had left as well as he their wives in England, which day being that of their departure from England, they had appointed it for to make a commemoration thereof, and drink their wives' healths. Some made their advantage of this meeting to get more than they could well carry away, though every man was at liberty to drink what he pleas'd, and to mix the Sack as he thought fit, or to drink *Palepuntz*, which is a kind of drink consisting of *aqua vitæ*, rose-water, juice of citrons and sugar.[1]

Order of the English Factory.

[1] It is a curious fact, not generally known, that punch was an Indian drink invented by the convivial Factors at Surat. It was called punch from the Hindustani word signifying five ingredients, *viz.*, brandy, sugar, limes, spice, and water.

Tea.

"At our ordinary meetings every day, we took only *Thé*, which is commonly used all over the Indies, not only among those of the country, but also among the Dutch and English, who take it as a drug that cleanses the stomach, and digests the superfluous humours, by a temperate heat particular thereto. The Persians instead of *Thé* drink their *Kahwa*, which cools and abates the natural heat which *Thé* preserves.[1]

English Garden.

"The English have a fair Garden without the city, whither we constantly went on Sundayes after Sermon, and sometimes also on other dayes of the week, where our exercise was shooting at Butts, at which I made a shift to get a hundred Mamoudis (or five pound sterling) every week. After these divertisements, we had a collation of fruit and preserves, and bathed our selves in a tanke or cistern which had five foot water. Some Dutch gentlewomen served and entertained us with much civility. What troubled me most was, that my little acquaintance with the English tongue made me incapable of conversation, unless it were with the President, who spoke Dutch.

Amusements at Surat.

"During my abode at Surat I wanted for no divertisement; for either I walked down to the Haven, or found company in the city, especially at the Dutch President's, who had his family there, and with whom it was the easier for me to make acquaintance, in as much as I could converse with them in my own language. But understanding that the English ships, with which I intended to return into Europe, would not be ready for their departure under three or four months, I resolved to take a journey into the country, to the

Journey to Ahmadabad.

[1] This is a curious allusion to tea and coffee. In China tea is called Cha; so it is in India. Olearius, in his travels through Muscovy, Tartary, and Persia, makes the following remarks :—

"The Persians are great frequenters of the taverns or tipling houses, which they call Tazri Chattai Chane, in regard there they may have Thé, or Cha, which the Usbegues Tartars bring thither from Chattai. It is an herb which hath long and narrow leaves, about an inch in length and half an inch in breadth. In order to the keeping and transportations of it, they dry it, so that it turns to a dark grey colour, inclining to black, and so shrivelled up, that it seems not to be what it really is; but as soon as it is put into warm water, it spreads and re-assumes its former green colour."

Great Mogul's Court, taking my advantage of a Caffila, or Caravan, of thirty wagons loaden with quicksilver, roenas, which is a root that dies red, spices, and a considerable sum of money, which the English were sending to Ahmadabad. The President had appointed four merchants, certain Banians, twelve English soldiers, and as many Indians, to conduct and convoy this small Caravan; so that confident I might undertake this journey without any danger, (which it had not been safe for me to attempt without this convenience, by reason of the Rajputs, and their robberies upon the high-way,) I took the President's advice, and put my self into their company.

"These Rajputs are a sort of high-way men, or tories, who keep in the mountains between Baroda and Baroche, which are called Champenir, where they have their fortified places and retreats, wherein they sometimes make their party good against the Mogul himself. Not long before he had taken one of their strongest places, and by that means kept them a long time in subjection; but they revolted again, and exercised their robberies with greater cruelty then ever." Rajput outlaws.

The journey of Mandelslo from Surat to Ahmadabad is too long for extract. At Ahmadabad he paid a visit to the Moghul Governor. His account of this visit is very graphic. Areb Khan, the Governor, was a type of the Governors of provinces in the reigns of Jehangir and Shah Jehan. Ahmadabad.

"The city of Ahmadabad maintains for the Mogul's service, out of its own revenue, twelve thousand horse and fifty elephants, under the command of a Khan, or Governor, who hath the quality of Raja, that is to say, Prince. He who commanded there in my time, was called Areb Khan, and about sixty years of age. I was credibly informed, that he was worth in money and houshold-stuffe, ten Crore, which amount to fifty millions of crowns, the Crore being accounted at a hundred Lacs of Rupees, each Lac being worth fifty thousand crowns. It was not long before, that his daughter, Amadabad maintains 12,000 horse. The Governor's wealth.

one of the greatest beauties in the country, had been married to the Mogul's second son; and the Khan, when she went to the Court, had sent her attended by twenty elephants, a thousand horse, and six thousand wagons, loaded with the richest stuffs, and whatever else was rare in the country. His Court consisted of above 500 persons, 400 whereof were his slaves, who served him in his affairs, and were all dieted in the house. I have it from good hands, that his expence in housekeeping amounted to above five thousand crowns a month, not comprehending in that account that of his stables, where he kept five hundred horse and fifty elephants. The most eminent persons of his retinue were very magnificently clad, though as to his own person, he was nothing curious, and was content commonly with a garment of cotton, as are the other Indosthans, unless it were when he went abroad into the city, or took a journey into the country; for then he went in great state, sitting ordinarily in a rich chair, set upon an elephant, covered with the richest tapistry, being attended by a guard of 200 men, having many excellent Persian horses led, and causing several standards and banners to be carried before him.

His Court.

His expence.

"I went along with the English merchant to visit the Governor, whom we found sitting in a pavilion or tent which looked into his garden. Having caused us to sit down by him, he asked the merchant who I was: He told him in the Indosthan language, that I was a gentleman of Germany, whom a desire to see foreign countries, and to improve himself by travel, had obliged to leave his own. That coming into Persia, upon occasion of an Embassy sent thither by the Prince my master, I took a resolution to see the Indies, as being the noblest country in the world; and being come to that city, that I hoped he would not take it ill if I aspired to the honour of waiting upon him. The Governor made answer, I was very welcome, that my resolution was noble and generous, and that he prayed God to bless and prosper it. He thereupon asked me, whether during my abode in Persia, I had learnt ought of the

Mandelslo visits the Governor of Ahmadabad.

Their discourse.

language. I reply'd that I had a greater inclination to the Turkish language, and that I understood it so far as to make a shift to express my self in it. The Governor, who was a Persian born, made answer, that it was true indeed, the Turkish language was much more commonly spoken in the Shah's Court then that of the country, and thereupon asked me my age, and how long it was since I left Germany. I told him I was 24 years of age, and that I had travelled three years. He replied that he wondered very much my friends would suffer me to travel so young, and asked me whether I had not changed my habit by the way; whereto having made answer that I had not, he told me, that it was an extraordinary good fortune, that I had travelled in that costume through so many countries, without meeting with some unhappy accident, and that the Dutch and English, to prevent any such misfortune, clad themselves according to the fashion of the country.

"After about an hour's discourse, we would have risen and taken our leaves of him, but the Governor intreated us to stay and dine with him. He caused some fruit to be brought, while his people were laying the cloth, which was of cotton, laid upon a large carpet of red Turkie-leather. The dinner was very noble, and served up and drest according to the Persian way, the meat being laid in dishes, all porcelane, upon rice of several colours, in the same manner as we had seen at the Court at Ispahan. Presently after dinner we came away, but as I was taking my leave of the Governor he told me in the Turkish language, *Senni dahe kurim,* that is to say, we shall see you again, giving me thereby to understand, that he would be glad of some further discourse with me. Dinner

"Accordingly we went thither again, but I had clad my self according to the mode of the country, upon the design I had to travel into Cambaya, which I could hardly do without changing habit. We found him in the same apartment where we had seen him the time before. He was clad in a white vestment, according to the Indian mode, A second visit to the Governor.

over which he had another that was longer, of brocade, the ground carnation lined with white satin, and above, a collar of sables, whereof the skin were sewed together, so as that the tails hung down over the back. As soon as he saw us come in, he made us sit down by the Lords that were with him. He was about some business, which hindered him for a while from discoursing with us, yet could I not but observe that he was pleased at my change of habit. He dispatched several orders, and sometimes writ himself; yet did not his business take him up, so as to hinder him from taking tobacco, which he took after the same manner, there standing near him a servant, who with one hand held the pipe to his mouth, and set fire to it with the other. He quitted that exercise to go and take a view of certain troops of horse and companies of foot, which were drawn up in the court. He would see their arms himself, and caused them to shoot at a mark, thereby to judge of their abilities, and to augment the pay of such as did well at the cost of the others, out of whose pay there was so much abated. So that seeing him thus employed we would have taken our leaves, but he sent us word that we should dine with him, causing in the mean time fruit to be sent us, whereof by his order we sent the best part to our lodging.

Opium. "Soon after he called for a little golden cabinet, enriched with precious stones, and having taken out two drawers, out of one he took Offion, or Opium, and out of the other Bengi, a certain drug, or powder, made of the leaves and seed of hemp, which they use to excite luxury. Having taken a small spoonful of each, he sent the cabinet to me, and told me, that it could not otherwise be, but that, during my abode at Ispahan, I must needs have learnt the use of that drug, and that I should find that as good as any I had seen in Persia. I told him, that I was no competent judge of it, in regard I had not used it often, however I would then take of it for the honour's sake of receiving it from his hands. I took of it, and the English merchant did the like, though neither of us had ever taken any before, nor did much like it then.

"The Governor of Ahmadabad was a judicious understanding man, but hasty, and so rigorous, that his government inclined somewhat to cruelty. It happened one day, that the two principal Directors of the English and Dutch trade there, being invited by him to dinner; a young gentleman that waited upon the former, comes into the hall to attend upon his master. He had on a slashed doublet, much after the fashion which was worn about thirty years since, which the Governor thought so ridiculous, that he could not forbear laughing at it, and asked the English President, in what quality that slashed gallant served him, since that according to his habit, he conceived he kept him for his Fool. The President made answer, not without some confusion, that he waited on him in his chamber, and that he had opened his doublet in that manner to make way for the air, the better to avoid the excessive heats of the country, which the Europeans could not well endure. Whereto the Governor replied, that that reason gave some satisfaction, but what he most wondered at was that the Christians, who are a wise and understanding people, had not yet found out the way to make their doublets of several shreds, rather then cut and mangle whole pieces of stuffes to put themselves into that mode. This jesting with the English merchant put him into so good an humour, that he would needs devote the remainder of the day to sport and divertisement, and thereupon sent for twenty women-dancers, who as soon as they were come into the room fell a singing and dancing, but with an activity and exact observation of the cadence, much beyond that of our dancers upon the ropes. They had little hoops or circles, through which they leaped as nimbly as if they had been so many apes, and made thousands of postures, according to the several soundings of their musick, which consisted of a *tumbeck*, or timbrel, a haw-boy, and several tabours. Having danced near two hours, the Governor would needs send into the city for another band of dancers, but the servants brought word, that they were sick and could not come. This excuse being not taken, he sent out the same servants, with express order to

Character of the Governor of Ahmadabad.

bring those women away by force; but they returning the second time with the same excuse, he ordered they should be cudgelled. Upon that, the women came and cast themselves at the Governor's feet, and acknowledged that it was indeed true, they were not sick, and that they denied to come, because they knew well enough he would not pay them. He laught at it, but immediately commanded out a party of his guard to bring them to him, and they were no sooner entered into

His cruelty. Mandelslo leaves Ahmadabad.

the hall ere he ordered their heads to be struck off. They begged their lives with horrid cries and lamentations; but he would be obeyed and caused the execution to be done in the room before all the company, not one of the Lords then present daring to make the least intercession for those wretches, who were eight in number. The strangers were startled at the horror of the spectacle and inhumanity of the action; which the Governor taking notice of, fell a laughing, and asked them what they were so much startled at. Assure your selves Gentlemen, said he, that if I should not take this course, I should not be long Governor of Ahmadabad. For should I connive once at their disobedience, these people would play the Masters, and drive me out of the City. 'Tis but prudence in me to prevent their contempt of my authority, by such examples of severity as these are."

Visit of Fryer.

Thirty-six years passed away. In 1674, Dr. Fryer visited Surat.[1] He was a Surgeon in the service of the East India Company. He has left the following description of the English factory at Surat. It indicates a considerable increase in the Company's establishment at Surat, as well as a large extension of their trade.

The English Factory.

"The house the English live in at Surat, is partly the King's gift, partly hired; built of stone and excellent

[1] Fryer's Travels in India and Persia between 1672 and 1681. London: 1698.

timber, with good carving, without representations; very strong, for that each floor is half a yard thick at least, of the best plastered cement, which is very weighty. It is contrived after the Moor's buildings, with upper and lower galleries, or terrace-walks; a neat Oratory, a convenient open place for meals. The President has spacious lodgings, noble rooms for counsel and entertainment, pleasant tanks, yards, and an hummum to wash in; but no gardens in the city, or very few, though without the city they have many, like wildernesses, overspread with trees. The English had a neat one, but Sevaji's coming, destroyed it: It is known, as the other Factories are, by their several flags flying.

"Here they live (in shipping-time) in a continual hurly-burly, the Banians presenting themselves from the hour of ten till noon; and then afternoon at four till night, as if it were an Exchange in every row; below stairs, the packers and warehouse-keepers, together with merchants bringing and receiving musters, make a meer Billinsgate; for if you make not a noise, they hardly think you intent on what you are doing. Full of noise.

"Among the English, the business is distributed into four offices; the Accomptant, who is next in dignity to the President, the general accompts of all India, as well as this place, passing through his hands; he is quasi Treasurer, signing all things, though the broker keep the cash. Next him is the Warehouse-keeper, who registers all Europe goods vended, and receives all Eastern commodities bought; under him is the Purser Marine, who gives account of all goods exported and imported, pays Seamen their wages, provides wagons and porters, looks after tackling for ships, and ships' stores. Last of all is the Secretary, who models all Consultations, writes all letters, carries them to the President and Council to be perused and signed; keeps the Company's seal, which is affixed to all passes and commissions; records all transactions, and sends copies of them to the Company; though none of these, without the President's approbation, can act or do any thing. The affairs of India are solely under his regulation; The Four Chief Offices.

from him issue out all orders, by him all preferment is disposed; by which means the Council are biassed by his arbitrament.

The Company's Servants, and their Salaries.

"The whole mass of the Company's servants may be comprehended in these classes, *viz.*, Merchants, Factors, and Writers; some Bluecoat Boys also have been entertained under notion of apprentices for seven years, which being expired, if they can get security, they are capable of employments. The Writers are obliged to serve five years for 10*l.* *per Ann.* giving in a bond of 500*l.* for good behaviour, all which time they serve under some of the forementioned Offices: After which they commence Factors, and rise to preferment and trust, according to seniority or favour, and therefore have a 1,000*l.* bond exacted from them, and have their salary augmented to 20*l.* *per Ann.* for three years, then entering into new indentures, are made Senior Factors; and lastly, Merchants after Three Years more; out of whom are chose Chiefs of Factories, as places fall, and are allowed 40*l.* *per Ann.* during their stay in the Company's service, besides lodgings and victuals at the Company's charges.

The under Factories modelled by this.

"These in their several Seigniories behave themselves after the fundamentals of Surat, and in their respective Factories live in the like grandeur; from whence they rise successively to be of the Council in Surat, which is the great Council; and if the President do not contradict, are sworn, and take their place accordingly, which consists of about five in number, besides the President, to be constantly resident.

The Presidency.

"As for the Presidency, though the Company interpose a deserving man, yet they keep that power to themselves, none assuming that dignity till confirmed by them: His salary from the Company is 500*l.* a year; half paid here, the other half reserved to be received at home, in case of misdemeanor to make satisfaction; beside a bond of 5,000*l.* sterling of good securities.

"The Accountant has 72*l.* *per annum*, fifty pound paid here, the other at home: All the rest are half paid here, half at home, except the Writers, who have all paid here.

"Out of the Council are elected the Deputy-Governor of Bombay, and Agent of Persia; the first a place of great trust, the other of profit; though, by the appointment from the Company, the Second of India claims Bombay, and the Secretary of Surat the Agency of Persia, which is connived at, and made subject to the will of the President, by the interest of those whose lot they are; chusing rather to reside here, where consignments compensate those emoluments; so that none of the Council, if noted in England, but makes considerably by his place, after the rate of five in the hundred, commission; and this is the Jacob's ladder by which they ascend. The advantage of being at the Council.

"It would be too mean to descend to indirect ways, which are chiefly managed by the Banians, the fittest tools for any deceitful undertaking; out of whom are made brokers for the Company, and private persons, who are allowed two *per cent.* on all bargains, besides what they squeeze secretly out of the price of things bought; which cannot be well understood for want of knowledge in their language; which ignorance is safer, than to hazard being poisoned for prying too nearly into their actions: Though the Company, to encourage young men in their service, maintain a master to learn them to write and read the language, and an annuity to be annexed when they gain a perfection therein, which few attempt, and fewer attain. The baseness of the Banians.

"To this Factory belongs twenty persons in number, reckoning Swally Marine into the account; a Minister for Divine Service, a Surgeon, and when the President is here, a guard of English soldiers, consisting of a double file led by a Serjeant. Number of persons in the Factory.

"The present Deputy has only forty Moor-men, and a flagman, carrying St. George his colours swallow-tailed in silk, fastened to a silver partisan; with a small attendance of horse with silver bridles, and furniture for the gentlemen of the house, and coaches for Ladies and Council.

"The President besides these has a noise of trumpets, and is carried himself in a Palenkeen, a horse of state led before State of the President.

him, a Mirchal (a fan of ostriches' feathers) to keep off the sun, as the Omrahs or great men have, none but the Emperor have a Sumbrero among the Moguls: Besides these, every one according to his quality has his menial servants to wait on him in his chamber, and follow him out.

All places in India subject to the Presidency, with their Commodities.

"The Presidency of Surat is esteemed superior to all in India, the Agency of Bantam being not long since subordinate to it, but since made independent; though the South Sea trade is still maintained from hence to Bantam with such cloth as is vendible there, from thence with dollars to China for sugar, tea, porcelane, laccared ware, quicksilver, tuthinag and copper; which with cowreys, little sea-shells, come from Siam and the Phillipine Islands; gold and elephants' teeth from Sumatra, in exchange of corn. From Persia, which is still under the Presidency, come drugs and Carmania wool; from Mocha, cohar, or coffee. The Inland Factories subject to it, are Ahmadabad, whence is provided silks, as atlases wrought with gold; Agra, where they fetch indico, chuperly, course cloth, Siring chints, Broach baftas, broad and narrow; dimities, and other fine calicuts; Along the coasts are Bombay, Rajapore for salloos; Carnear for dungarees, and the weightiest pepper; Calicut for spice, ambergreez, granats, opium, with salt petre, and no cloth, though it give the name of Calicut to all in India, it being the first port from whence they were known to be brought into Europe: All which, after the Europe ships have unladen at Surat, they go down to fetch; and bring up time enough before the Caffilas out of the country come in with their wares.

The Investment set on foot in the Rains.

"The places about Surat afford variety of Calicuts, but not such vast quantities as are yearly exported, and moreover not so cheap; which is the reason at every place the factors are sent to oversee the weavers, buying up the cotton-yarn to employ them all the rains, when they set on foot their investments, that they may be ready against the season for the ships: or else the chief broker imploys Banians in their steads, who are responsible for their fidelity.

This trade managed by a Company better than Free-Traders.

"On these wheels moves the traffick of the East, and has succeeded better than any Corporation preceeding, or open trade licensed in the time of Oliver Cromwell; though how much more to the benefit of England than a free commerce, may be guessed by their already being over-flocked with Europe merchandise, which lowers the price. What then would a glut do, which certainly must follow, but debase them more, and enhance these?

Their Freemen greater Slaves than their Servants.

"But lest the New Company should be exclaimed against as too greedy monopolizers, they permit free traders on their Island Bombay; when, to speak truth, they are in a far worse condition than their servants; being tied up without hopes of raising themselves: so that in earnest they find out that to be but a trick.

The Charges of the English Company not so great as the Hollanders.

"However, to confess on the Company's behalf, the trade (I mean on this coast) for some years lately passed has hardly ballanced expences. They employing yearly forty sail of stout ships to and from all parts where they trade, out and home; manning and maintaining their Island Bombay, Fort St. George, and St. Helens; besides large sums expended to bear out the port of their Factors; which notwithstanding by impartial computation has been found inferior to the costs of the Hollanders, and therefore more to the profit of the English East India Company, than theirs, in the few years they have adventured; so that I should mightily blame them should they prove ungrateful to His Majesty, who by his gracious favour has united them in a society, whereby they are competitors for riches (though not strength) with the notedest Company in the universe.

Their Charter put in force.

"This Charter was granted presently after the happy restoration of our Gracious Sovereign, when order began to dawn, and dispel the dark chaos of popular community: Then was sent out a President, to put their Charter in force, and establish a graduation among their servants, which before was not observed; only for order's sake, they did nominate an Agent; the rest being independent, made no distinction. When as now, after a better model, they commence according to their standing, and are under a collegiate manner of restraint.

The Course of the Presidents.

"The last Agent was Agent Rivinton, who was abolished by the Company's sending out President Wynch, who lived not much more than two years: President Andrews took his place; and he resigning, Sir George Oxendine held it till his death; in whose time Sevaji plundered Surat; but he defended himself and the merchants so bravely, that he had a khillut or Serpaw, a robe of honour from head to foot, offered him from the Great Mogul, with an abatement of customs to Two and an half *per cent.* granted to the Company: For which his masters, as a token of the high sense they had of his valour, presented him a medal of gold, with this device:

'*Non minor est virtus quam quærere parta tueri.*'

The English defend themselves with honour against Sevaji a second time.

"After whose decease, the Honourable Gerald Aungier took the chair, and encountered that bold mountaineer a second time, with as great applause; when the Governor of the town and province durst neither of them shew their heads:

"*Fluctum enim totius Barbariæ ferre urbs una non poterat.*

"The enemies by the help of an Europe engineer had sprung a mine to blow up the castle; but being discovered, were repulsed; for though he had set fire to the rest of the city, they retained the castle, and the English their house.

The Power of he President.

"The extent of the Presidency is larger in its missions than residency; in which limits may be reckoned an hundred Company's servants continually in the country; besides the annual advenues of ships, which during their stay are all under the same command: Therefore what irregularities are committed against only the Presidency or Company, in case of non-submission, the persons offending are to be sent home, and dismissed their employments for refractoriness; but if an higher Court lay hold of them in case of murder or any capital crime, then they are to be sent to Bombay, there to have a legal trial, according to the laws of England, as the President is created Governor of His Majesty's Island.

Ill success of the first Adventures.

"The ill-managing of which penalties formerly, or the invalidity to inflict them, may be the true cause of the unprosperousness of the ancient undertakers; who had this inconveniency still attending, to wit, the incorrigible stubbornness of their own men, after they had overcome all other difficulties, occasioned by the grant of the East to the Portugal, and West-Indies to the Spaniard. Nevertheless this fairy gift was the ground of a long and tedious quarrel in each of the world's ends; so that our ships encountring with their Carracks, seldom used to part without the loss of one or both. Nay, the long-lived people yet at Swalley, remember a notable skirmish betwixt the English and Portugals there, wherein they were neatly intrapped; an ambuscado of ours falling upon them behind in such sort, that they were compelled between them and the ships in the road, to resign most of their lives; and gave by their fall a memorable name to a Point they yet call Bloody Point, for this very reason. But since these sores are fortunately bound up in that conjugal tye betwixt our sacred King and the sister of Portugal, laying all foul words and blows aside, let us see how the affairs stand betwixt them and the Dutch, who followed our steps, and got in at the breach we made. They made them more work, not only beating them out of their South-Sea trade, but possessed themselves of all their treasures of spice, and have ever since kept them, with all their strong-holds, as far as Goa; they only enjoying the gold trade of Mosambique undisturbed; the Japanners having banished both their commerce and religion. War with Portugal.

"Wherefore our ships almost alone, were it not for a little the French of late, lade Calicuts for Europe: The Dutch have a Factory here, that vend the spices they bring from Batavia, and invest part of the money in coarse cloth, to be disposed among their Planters, or sold to the Malayans, and send the rest back in rupees: So that we singly have the credit of the Port, and are of most advantage to the inhabitants, and fill the Custom-House with the substantialest incomes. But not to defraud the French of their just commendations, whose Factory is better stored with Monsieurs than with cash, they live well, borrow money, and make a show: Here are French Capuchins, who have a Convent, and live in esteem." The Company enrich this Port.

Dr. Fryer furnishes a curious account of the relations between the English and the Muhammadans at Surat:—

Rudeness of the Mussulman mendicants.

"Going out to see the city of Surat, I passed without any incivility, the better because I understood not what they said; for though we meet not with boys so rude as in England, to run after strangers, yet here are a sort of bold, lusty, and most an end, drunken beggars, of the Mussulman cast, that if they see a Christian in good clothes, mounted on a stately horse, with rich trappings, are presently upon their punctilios with God Almighty, and interrogate him, Why he suffers him to go a foot, and in rags, and this Kafir (Unbeliever) to vaunt it thus? And are hardly restrained from running a *Muck* (which is to kill whoever they meet, till they be slain themselves), especially if they have been at Hadji, a pilgrimage to Mecca, and thence to Juddah, where is Mahomet's Tomb; these commonly, like evil spirits, have their habitations among the tombs. Nor can we complain only of this libertinism, for the rich Moormen themselves are persecuted by these rascals.

Seamen.

"As for the rest, they are very respectful, unless the seamen or soldiers get drunk, either with toddy or bang (a pleasant intoxicating seed, mixed with milk); then are they monarchs, and it is madness to oppose them; but leave them to themselves, and they will vent that fury, by breathing a vein or two with their own swords, sometimes slashing themselves most barbarously."

Subordination of Bombay to Surat.

The allusions to Bombay in the foregoing extracts show that it was considered at this period to be a subordinate place to Surat. It had been given to the English in 1661 as a portion of the dowry of Donna Infanta Catherina, sister to the King of Portugal, when she was given in marriage to Charles the Second. Some years elapsed before the English effected a settlement at Bombay. Dr. Fryer visited the Island about 1674, and has left the following description of Bombay and its surroundings :—

"Let us walk the rounds. At distance enough lies the town, in which confusedly live the English, Portugueze, Topazes, Hindoos, Moors, Cooly Christians, most fishermen. The Town of Bombay.

"It is a full mile in length, the houses are low, and thatched with oleas of the cocoe-trees, all but a few the Portugals left, and some few the Company have built, the Custom-house and Ware-houses are tiled or plastered, and instead of glass, use panes of oyster-shells for their windows (which as they are cut in squares, and polished, look gracefully enough). There is also a reasonable handsome Bazar.

"At the end of the town looking into the field, where cows and buffoloes graze, the Portugals have a pretty house and Church, with orchards of Indian fruit adjoining. The English have only a Burying-place, called Mendam's-Point, from the first man's name there interred, where are some few tombs that make a pretty show at entring the Haven, but neither Church or Hospital, both which are mightily to be desired.

"There are no fresh water rivers, or falling streams of living water: The water drank is usually rain-water preserved in tanks, which decaying, they are forced to dig wells into which it is strained, hardly leaving its brackish taste; so that the better sort have it brought from Massegoung, where is only one fresh spring. Fresh Water-springs scarce.

"On the backside of the towns of Bombay and Maijm, are woods of cocoes (under which inhabit the Banderines, those that prune and cultivate them), these Hortoes being the greatest purchase and estates on the Island, for some miles together, till the sea break in between them: Over-against which, up the Bay a mile, lies Massegoung, a great fishing town, peculiarly notable for a fish called bumbelo, the sustenance of the poorer sort, who live on them and batty, a course sort of rice, and the wine of the cocoe, called toddy. The ground between this and the great breach Woods of Cocoes.

is well ploughed, and bears good batty. Here the Portugals have another Church, and Religious House belonging to the Franciscans.

Parell. "Beyond it is Parell, where they have another Church, and demesnes belonging to the Jesuits; to which appertains Siam, manured by Columbeens, husbandmen, where live the Frasses, or porters also; each of which tribes have a Mandadore, or superintendent, who give an account of them to the English, and being born under the same degree of slavery, are generally more tyrannical than a stranger would be towards them; so that there needs no other task-master than one of their own Tribe, to keep them in awe by a rigid subjection.

Salt-Pans. "Under these uplands the washes of the sea produce a lunary tribute of salt left in pans or pits made on purpose at spring-tides for the overflowing; and when they are full are incrustated by the heat of the sun. In the middle, between Parell, Maijm, Sciam, and Bombay, is an hollow, wherein is received a breach running at three several places, which drowns 40000 acres of good land, yielding nothing else but samphire; athwart which, from Parell to Maijm, are the ruins of a stone causeway made by penances.

Maijm. "At Maijm the Portugals have another complete Church and House; the English a pretty Custom-house and Guard-house: The Moors also a Tomb in great veneration for a Peor, or Prophet, instrumental to the quenching the flames approaching their Prophet's Tomb at Mecha (though he was here at the same time) by the fervency of his prayers.

Salvasong. "At Salvasong, the farthest part of this Inlet, the Franciscans enjoy another Church and Convent; this side is all covered with trees of cocoes, jawks, and mangoes; in the middle lies Verulee, where the English have a watch.

Malabar-hill. "On the other side of the great inlet, to the sea, is a great point abutting against Old Woman's Island, and is called Malabar-hill, a rocky, woody mountain, yet sends forth long grass. A-top of all is a Parsee Tomb lately reared; on its declivity towards the sea, the remains of a stupendous

Pagoda, near a tank of fresh water, which the Malabars visited it mostly for.

"Thus have we compleated our rounds, being in the circumference twenty miles, the length eight, taking in Old Woman's Island, which is a little low barren Island, of no other profit, but to keep the Company's antelopes, and other beasts of delight. **Bigness of the Island.**

"The people that live here are a mixture of most of the neighbouring countries, most of them fugitives and vagabonds, no account being here taken of them: Others perhaps invited hither (and of them a great number) by the liberty granted them in their several religions, which here are solemnized with variety of fopperies (a toleration consistent enough with the rules of gain), though both Moors and Portugals despise us for it; here licensed out of policy, as the old Numidians to build up the greatest empire in the world. Of these, one among another, may be reckoned 60000 souls; more by 50000 than the Portugals ever could. For which number this Island is not able to find provisions, it being most of it a rock above water, and of that which is overflowed, little hopes to recover it. However, it is well supplied from abroad both with corn and meat at reasonable rates; and there is more flesh killed for the English alone here in one month, than in Surat for a year for all the Moors in that populous city. **Mixt people.**

"The Government here now is English; the soldiers have martial law: The freemen, common; the chief arbitrator whereof is the President, with his Council at Surat; under him is a Justiciary, and Court of Pleas, with a Committee for regulation of affairs, and presenting all complaints. **English Government.**

"The President has a large commission, and is *Vice-Regis*: he has a Council here also, and a guard when he walks or rides abroad, accompanied with a party of horse, which are constantly kept in the stables, either for pleasure or service. He has his chaplains, physician, surgeons, and domesticks; his linguist, and mint-master: At meals he has his trumpets usher in his courses, and soft music at the table; **Power and state of the President.**

If he move out of his chamber, the silver staves wait on him; if down stairs, the guard receive him; if he go abroad, the Bandarines and Moors under two standards march before him. He goes sometimes in the coach, drawn by large milk-white oxen, sometimes on horseback, other times in palenkeens, carried by Cohors, Mussulman porters: Always having a Sumbrero of state carried over him: And those of the English inferior to him, have a suitable train.

Unhealthiness of Bombay.

"But for all this gallantry, I reckon they walk but in charnel-houses, the climate being extremely unhealthy; at first thought to be caused by Bubsho, rotten fish; but though that be prohibited, yet it continues as mortal: I rather impute it to the situation, which causes an infecundity in the earth, and a putridness in the air, what being produced seldom coming to maturity, whereby what is eaten is undigested; whence follows fluxes, dropsy, scurvy, barbiers (which is an enervating the whole body, being neither able to use hands or feet), gout, stone, malignant and putrid fevers, which are endemial diseases: Among the worst of these, Fool Rack (brandy made of blubber, or carvil, by the Portugals, because it swims always in a blubber, as if nothing else were in it; but touch it, and it stings like nettles; the latter, because sailing on the waves it bears up like a Portugal Carvil: It is, being taken, a jelly, and distilled causes those that take it to be fools).

English women.

"To support their colony, the Company have sent out English women; but they beget a sickly generation; and as the Dutch well observe, those thrive better that come of an European father and Indian mother: which (not to reflect on what creatures are sent abroad) may be attributed to their living at large, not debarring themselves wine and strong drink, which immoderately used, inflames the blood, and spoils the milk in these hot countries, as Aristotle long ago declared. The natives abhor all heady liquors, for which reason they prove better nurses.

Longevity of natives and Portuguese.

"Notwithstanding this mortality to the English, the country people and naturalized Portugals live to a good old age, supposed to be the reward of their temperance; indulging themselves neither in strong drinks, nor devouring flesh as we do. But I believe rather we are here, as exotic plants brought home to us, not agreeable to the soil: For to the lustier and fresher, and oftentimes the temperatest, the clime more unkind; but to old men and women it seems to be more suitable.

"Happy certainly then are those, and only those, brought hither in their nonage, before they have a gust of our Albion; or next to them, such as intoxicate themselves with Læthe and remember not their former condition: When it is expostulated, Is this the reward of an harsh and severe pupilage? Is this the Elysium after a tedious wastage? For this, will any thirst, will any contend, will any forsake the pleasures of his native soil, in his vigorous age, to bury himself alive here? Were it not more charitable at the first bubbles of his infant-sorrows, to make the next stream over-swell him? Or else if he must be full grown for misery, how much more compassionate were it to expose him to an open combat with the fiercest duellists in nature, to spend at once his spirits, than to wait a piecemealed consumption? Yet this abroad and unknown, is the ready choice of those to whom poverty threatens contempt at home: What else could urge this wretched remedy? For these are untrodden paths for knowledge, little improvement being to be expected from barbarity, custom and tradition are only venerable here; and it is heresy to be wiser than their forefathers; which opinion is both bred and hatched by an innate sloth; so that though we seem nearer the heavens, yet bodies here are more earthy and the mind wants that active fire that always mounts, as if it were extinguished by its *Antiparistasis:* Whereby society and communication, the characteristic of man, is wholly lost. What then is to be expected here, where sordid thrift is the only science? After which, notwithstanding there is so general an inquest, few there be acquire it: For in five hundred, one hundred survive not; of that one hundred, one quarter get not estates; of those that do, it has not

Misery and mortality of the English.

been recorded above one in ten years has seen his country: And in this difficulty it would hardly be worth a sober man's while, much less an ingenuous man's, who should not defile his purer thoughts, to be wholly taken up with such mean (not to say indirect) contemplations; however, a necessary adjunct, wealth, may prove to buoy him up on the surface of repute, lest the vulgar serve him as Æsop's frogs did their first revered deity."

English embassy to Sivaji.

Dr. Fryer visited Bombay in stirring times. Sivaji had established his Mahratta kingdom in the Konkan. He was preparing for his coronation as Raja. The English at Bombay sent an embassy to the Raja in the hope of opening up a trade through his dominions into the Dekhan. Fryer describes the progress of the embassy. Sivaji held his head-quarters at the great hill fortress of Rairee. At this time he was absent on a pilgrimage. Accordingly the English ambassador halted at Puncharra, a town situated at the foot of the hill. Here he had an interview with Narainji Pundit, one of the Mahratta ministers. He begged the Pundit to persuade Sivaji of the profit that would accrue to him by the opening up of the trade; for, as the Raja had been a soldier from his infancy, it was possible that he paid no attention to such matters. The Mahratta minister replied to the following effect:

Officiousness of a Chief Minister of State to the English.

"That he doubted not but it would be effected in a short time; for that the King of Bijapur, who is owner of those countries (from whence most sorts of wares come) being weary of wars with his master, had sent several embassies to conclude a peace with him; which he thought would be made up in two or three months, and then the ways would be free, and the merchants have egress and regress as formerly.

That the Rajah, after his coronation, would act more like a Prince, by taking care of his subjects, and endeavouring the advancement of commerce in his dominions; which he could not attend before, being in perpetual war with the Great Mogul, and King of Bijapur. This is the substance of his (the ambassador's) discourse with Narainji Pundit, who seemed to him to be a man of prudence and esteem with his master: so after a little sitting he took his leave of him, having first presented him with a diamond ring, for which he expressed a liking; and his eldest son a couple of Pamerins, which are fine mantles.

"They continuing under their tent, found it very hot and incommodious; wherefore they were glad when they heard the Rajah was returned from Purtabghur, when the ambassador solicited Narainji Pundit to procure his leave to pass up the Hill into Rairee Castle: the next day they received order to ascend the hill into the castle, the Rajah having appointed a house for them; which they did; leaving Puncharra about three in the afternoon, they arrived at the top of that strong mountain, forsaking the humble clouds about sun-set. Rairee.

"Rairee is fortified by nature more than art, being of very difficult access, there being but one avenue to it, which is guarded by two narrow gates, and fortified by a strong wall exceeding high, and bastions thereto: all the other part of the mountain is a direct precipice, so that it is impregnable, except the treachery of some in it betray it. On the mountain are many strong buildings, as the Rajah's Court, and houses of other Ministers, to the number of about 300. It is in length about two miles and an half, but no pleasant trees or any sort of grain grows thereon. Their house was about a mile from the Rajah's Palace, into which they retired with no little content. The hill.

"Four days after their ascent, by the solicitation of Narainji Pundit, the Rajah gave them audience, though busily employed by many other great affairs, relating to his coronation and marriage. Our ambassador presented him, and his son Sambaji Rajah, with the particulars appointed for them; Audience with Sivaji.

which they took well satisfied with them; and the Rajah assured them we might trade securely in all his countries without the least apprehension of ill from him, for that the peace was concluded. Our ambassador replied, that was our intent; and to that intent the President had sent him to this Court to procure the same articles and privileges we enjoyed in Indostan and Persia, where we traded. He answered, it is well, and referred our business to Moro Pundit his Peshwa, or Chancellor, to examine our articles, and give an account what they were. He and his son withdrew into their private apartments, to consult with the Brahmans about the ceremonies preparatory to his enstalment; which chiefly consisted in abstinence and purifying; till which be over, he will hear no farther of business. They likewise departed to their lodgings.

Sivaji weighed in gold.

"About this time the Rajah, according to the Hindu custom, was weighed in gold, and poised about 16,000 Pagodas, which money, together with an 100,000 more, is to be distributed among the Brahmans after the day he is enthroned, who in great numbers flock hither from all parts of his territories.

Grants the request of the English.

"Being earnest to press on his errand he came for, the ambassador sent to Narainji Pundit to know what was transacted in the articles; but was returned for answer:—The Rajah stopt his ears to all affairs, declaring he had granted all the demands, except those two articles, expressing our money shall go current in his dominions, and his on Bombay; and that he shall restore whatever wrecks may happen on his coasts belonging to the English, and inhabitants of Bombay: the first he accounted unnecessary to be inserted, because he forbids not the passing of any manner of coins: nor on the other side, can he force his subjects to take those monies whereby they shall be losers; but if our coin be as fine an allay, and as weighty as the Mogul's, and other Princes, he will not prohibit it. To the other he says, that it is against the laws of Konkan to restore any ships, vessels, or goods, that are driven ashore by tempest, or otherwise; and that should he grant us that privilege, the French, Dutch, and other merchants, would claim the same right; which he could not grant without breaking a custom has lasted many ages: the rest of our desires he willingly conceded, embracing with much satisfaction our friendship, promising to himself and country much happiness by our settlement and trade: notwithstanding Narainji Pundit did not altogether despair of obtaining our wrecks, because we enjoyed the same privilege in the Mogul and Deccan country.

The Ambassador summoned to the Coronation.

"Near a month after they had been here, Narainji Pundit sent word, that to-morrow about seven or eight in the morning, the Rajah Sevaji intended to ascend his throne; and he would take it kindly if they came to congratulate him thereon; that it was necessary to present him with some small thing, it not being the custom of the Eastern parts to appear before a Prince empty-handed. The ambassador sent him word, according to his advice he would wait on the Rajah at the prescribed time.

Coronation of Sivaji.

"Accordingly next morning he and his retinue went to Court, and found the Rajah seated on a magnificent throne, and all his nobles waiting on him in rich attire; his son Sambaji Rajah, Peshwa Moro Pundit, and a Brahman of great eminence, seated on an ascent under the throne; the rest, as well officers of the army as others, standing with great respect. The English made their obeisance at a distance, and Narainji Pundit held up the diamond ring that was to be presented him: He presently took notice of it, and ordered their coming nearer, even to the foot of the throne, where being vested, they were desired to retire; which they did not so soon, but they took notice on each side of the throne there hung (according to the Moor's manner) on heads of gilded lances many emblems of dominion and government; as on the right-hand were two great fishes' heads of gold, with very large teeth; on the left, several horses' tails, a pair of gold scales on a very high lance's head, equally poised, an emblem of justice; and as they returned, at the Palace gate stood two small elephants on each side, and two fair horses with gold trappings, bridles, and rich furniture; which made them admire how they brought them up the hill, the passage being both difficult and hazardous.

The Rajah marries a fourth Wife.

"Two days after this, the Rajah was married to a fourth wife, without state; and doth every day bestow alms on the Brahmans.

Sivaji signs the Articles.

"Some days after, Narainji Pundit sent word the Rajah had signed their articles, all but that about money. Then the rest of the Ministers of State signed them, and they went to receive them of Narainji Pundit, who delivered them to the ambassador with expressions of great kindness for our nation, and offered on all occasions to be serviceable to the English at the Court of the Rajah."

Value of the foregoing description.

The description of the reception by Sivaji of an English ambassador is very valuable; it brings the English reader face to face with the court of the once famous Mahratta. Strangely enough it is not noticed in Grant Duff's History of the Mahrattas.

CHAPTER III.

ENGLISH AT MADRAS

1600—1677.

WHILST the English were establishing themselves at Surat on the western side of India, they made many futile attempts to effect a settlement on the eastern side, known as the Coast of Coromandel. The trade on the Coromandel Coast was very valuable. The natives in this quarter had brought the art of painting or dyeing calicoes to the highest pitch of perfection. They were in great demand in Europe. Above all, they were in great demand in the countries further to the eastward; in Burma, Siam and the Indian Archipelago; especially in what were known as the Spice Islands. *Attempts at a settlement on the eastern side of India.*

The English, however, wanted something more than a factory. They wanted a territory which they could fortify. No such territory could be obtained in the Moghul dominions. The Moghuls would neither grant territory nor allow of any fortifications. *Want of a territory and fortification.*

It would be tedious to narrate the many abortive attempts that the English made in this direction. *Purchase of Madras.*

At last they succeeded in buying a piece of land from a Hindu Raja. It was in the remote Peninsula, far away to the south and far away from the Moghul frontier. It was afterwards known as Madras. It was the first territory which the English secured in India.

Madras founded, 1639. Madras was founded in 1639. A site was chosen on the sandy shores of the Coast of Coromandel. The spot was hard by the Portuguese city of St. Thomé. In the sixteenth century St. Thomé was famous throughout the world of Christianity. St. Thomas the Apostle was said to have been martyred there. His bones were found, or were said to have been found, in a neighbouring mount. The city and cathedral of St. Thomé were built to commemorate the legend.[1]

Territory and island. The English territory of Madras was a mere strip of land to the north of St. Thomé. It ran six miles along the shore and one mile inland. It was exposed to the heavy surf which rolls in from the Bay of Bengal; but it possessed one crowning advantage. There was a small island in the strip facing the sea; it was formed on the land side by the river Koum. It was only four hundred yards long and about a hundred yards wide; but it could be easily rendered secure against the predatory attacks of native horsemen.

---

[1] The story of St. Thomas is told in the tenth book of the "Lusiad" of Camoens. The "Lusiad" is a Portuguese epic composed in the sixteenth century. It is known to English readers through the poetical translation of William Mickle.

A certain Mr. Day bought the strip from the Hindu Raja of Chandragheri.[1] The English agreed to pay a yearly rent of twelve hundred pagodas, or nearly six hundred pounds sterling, for this piece of land. They built a wall round the island. They laid out the enclosure in little streets and alleys, with a fortress in the centre. No one but Europeans were allowed to live on the island. It was accordingly known as "White Town." White Town.

There was soon a large native settlement outside the island. It was inhabited by weavers and other people of the country; hence it was known as "Black Town." White Town and Black Town were both included under the name of Madras. White Town was also called Fort St. George.[2] Black Town.

[1] The Hindu Raja of Chandragheri deserves a passing notice. His name was Sri Ranga Raja. He was a descendant of the old Rajas of Vijayanagar, who had been driven out of the western table-land in the previous century. He affected to live in state at the fortress of Chandragheri, about seventy miles to the south-west of Madras. His suzerainty was still respected by some of the local governors round about. The governors were called Naiks or deputies of the Raja. The strip of seaboard, afterwards called Madras, was within the government of the Naik of Chingleput.

Sri Ranga Raja was a genuine Hindu. Like all Hindus, he was ardently desirous of perpetuating his family name to future ages. In granting the land to the English, he expressly stipulated that the English town should be called Sri Ranga Raja-patanam, or "the town of Sri Ranga Raja." The grant was engraved on a plate of gold. The English kept the plate for more than a century. It was lost in 1746 at the capture of Madras by the French.

The Raja of Chandragheri was outwitted by the Naik of Chingleput. The father of the Naik was named Chinnapa. The Naik set the Raja defiance. He ordered the town to be called Chinna-patanam, or "the town of Chinnapa." The Raja was helpless. The Muhammadans were pressing towards the south. In 1646 the Raja fled away to Mysore. The English gave the name of Madras to their town on the Coast of Coromandel. To this day the native people call it by the old name of Chinna-patanam.

[2] The accompanying drawing of Fort St. George in 1677 is taken from Fryer's Travels.

Early perils.

The English at Madras were at first exposed to great danger. The Hindu Raja was soon conquered by the Muhammadans of the neighbouring kingdom of Golkonda. The officer of the Sultan of Golkonda who commanded the country round about Madras was known as the Nawab. He was never contented with the yearly rent; he wanted presents and exacted fines. Sometimes he laid an embargo upon all goods and supplies going to Madras until the money was paid. Sometimes he besieged the place. After the walls were finished, no native army ever captured Fort St. George.

Rise of Madras.

For some years the houses in White Town were very few in number. The Europeans were few. There were twenty or thirty servants of the Company, and a few soldiers. The Portuguese at St. Thomé were invited to build houses at Madras; and many were glad to come and live under the protection of the English guns.

Absence of records prior to 1670.

Little or nothing is known of Madras in those early days. There are no records at Madras before 1670. The times, however, were very bad. In England there was civil war, followed by the Common wealth and the restoration of Charles the Second. In India the advance of the Sultan of Golkonda into the Peninsula, and the occasional inroads of Mahrattas, were a great hindrance to the trade.

Capture of St. Thomé by the Muhammadans of Golkonda.

About 1662 a general of Golkonda captured the city of St. Thomé. Numbers of Portuguese were driven out of the town. Many took refuge in

Fort St. George, and built houses there. This Portuguese population strengthened the place for a time, but caused much inconvenience in after years.

Madras in 1672.

In the year 1672 Madras was an important place. White Town contained about fifty houses laid out in twelve streets. In the midst was the large house of the Governor, where all the Company's servants took their early dinners. Some of the older servants were married, and lived in separate houses; but all were expected to be present at dinner, and to maintain order and decorum.

European establishment.

The establishment at Madras was on the same plan as that at Surat, which has already been described. The Governor or Agent was of course the first member of Council. The Book-keeper was second in Council; the Warehouse-keeper was third; and the Customer was fourth. The duties of these officers may be gathered from their names. The duties of Customer were peculiar to the English settlements. He collected all customs, rents, and other taxes; he also sat as Justice of the Peace in Black Town. The administration of justice will be brought under consideration hereafter.

Consultations and general letters.

The Council met every Monday and Tuesday at eight o'clock for the transaction of business. Everything was discussed and decided in Council. All that concerned the Company or their servants down to the most trifling point was duly laid before the Council. The Secretary was always in attendance. He kept a diary of all proceedings and consultations. A copy of the diary was sent home every year, together with a general letter reviewing the proceedings; in reply a general letter was received from the Court of Directors. These records have been preserved either in India or in England down to our own time.

Merchants, Factors, Writers, and Apprentices.

The members of Council were known as Merchants. Those under them were graded as Factors, Writers, and Apprentices. The salaries were very small. The Governor of Madras drew only three hundred pounds a year; the second in Council drew one hundred; the third drew seventy; and the fourth only fifty. Factors were paid between twenty and forty; Writers received only ten pounds, and Apprentices only five. But all were lodged and boarded at the expense of the Company.

Private trade and presents.

The salaries were very low. They were mere fractions of the real incomes. Fortunes were sometimes acquired by private trade. Every servant of the Company was allowed to trade to any port in the East, so long as he paid the custom duties levied by the Company, and did not interfere with the trade between India and Europe. Again, it was impossible to prevent the receipt of presents from native merchants and others who sold goods to the Company. Throughout the whole period of the Company's monopoly there were always suspicions and complaints under this head.

Chaplain and Schoolmaster.

In addition to the foregoing, there was a Chaplain, on a hundred a year, who read prayers every day and preached on Sundays. There was also a Schoolmaster, on fifty pounds a year, who taught the children in White Town. He was directed to teach Portuguese and native children, provided they were also taught the principles of Christianity according to the Church of England.

The administration of justice by the Collector of Customs was of a primitive character. As far as natives were concerned there was no difficulty. As Magistrate in Black Town, he flogged, imprisoned, or fined at discretion. But Europeans were dealt with in a different manner. The Governor and Council became the judges; and twelve men were summoned to serve as jurors. Administration of justice.

In the White Town the public peace was maintained by the Agent, as commander of the garrison. In the Black Town it was kept by a native public officer known as the Pedda Naik. In the early days of the settlement, twenty native servants, known as peons, sufficed to keep the peace. Subsequently the number was increased to fifty. In return the Pedda Naik was granted some rice-fields rent free; also some petty duties on rice, fish, oil, and betel-nut. The office of Pedda Naik soon became hereditary after native fashion. It also drifted into native ways. The Pedda Naik and his peons came to an understanding with the thieves. They suffered thieves to escape on condition of receiving half of the stolen goods. They imprisoned the people who were robbed, in order to prevent their complaining to the Agent. Native police.

The discovery led to a change. The Pedda Naik was bound over to make good all losses by theft; and the new system seems to have worked satisfactorily.

Morals. The neighbourhood of Black Town was not conducive to the morals of the Fort. The younger men would climb over the walls at night time, and indulge in a round of dissipation. There were houses of entertainment known as punch houses. They are still called punch houses. They took their name from the Indian drink concocted by the convivial Factors at Surat. As already shown, it was an essentially Indian drink called by the Hindustani name which signifies "five."

Fryer's visit about 1674. Dr. Fryer visited Madras about the year 1674. He thus describes the place and its surroundings:—

Went ashore in a boat called a Mussoola. "I went ashore in a *Mussoola*, a boat wherein ten men paddle, the two aftermost of whom are the steers-men, using their paddles instead of a rudder: The boat is not strengthened with knee-timber, as ours are; the bended planks are sowed together with rope-yarn of the cocoe, and calked with *dammar* (a sort of rosin taken out of the sea) so artificially, that it yields to every ambitious surf, otherwise we could not get ashore, the Bar knocking in pieces all that are inflexible: Moving towards the shore, we let St. Thomas, which lies but three miles to the south of Maderas, and Fort St. George in the midway Maderas river in great rains opens its mouth into the sea; having first saluted the banks of Fort St. George on the west: Towards the sea the sand is cast up into a rampire, from whence the fluid artillery discharges itself upon us, and we on the shoulders of the blacks must force our way through it.

Landed, are well wetted at Fort St. George. "Though we landed wet, the sand was scalding hot, which made me recollect my steps, and hasten to the Fort. As it looked on the water, it appeared a place of good force. The outwork is walled with stone a good heighth, thick enough to blunt a cannon-bullet, kept by half a dozen ordnance at each side the water-gate, besides an half-moon of fire-guns. At both points are mounted twelve guns eying the sea, Maderas, and St. Thomas; under these in a line stand pallisadoes, reaching from the wall to the sea; and hedge in at least a mile of ground. On the south side they have cut a ditch of sufficient depth and breadth to prevent scaling the wall, which is a quarter of a mile in length afore it meets with a third point or bastion, facing St. Thomas, and the adjacent fields; who suffer a deluge when the rains descend the hills. From this point to the fourth, where are lodged a dozen guns more that grin upon Maderas, runs no wall, but what the inhabitants compile for their gardens and houses planted all along the river parallel with that, that braces the sea. From the first point a curtain is drawn with a parapet; beneath it are two gates, and sally ports to each for to enter Maderas; over the gates five guns run out their muzzels, and two more within them on the ground.

"Over all these the Fort it self lifts up its four turrets, every point of which is loaded with ten guns alike: On the south-east point is fixed the standard; the forms of the bastions are square, sending forth curtains fringed with battlements from one to the other; in whose interstitiums whole culverin are traversed. The Governor's house in the middle overlooks all, slanting diagonally with the court. Entering the garrison at the out-gate towards the sea, a path of broad polished stones spreads the way to pass the second guard into the Fort at an humble gate; opposite to this, one more stately fronts the High-street; on both sides thereof is a court of guard, from whence, for every day's duty, are taken two hundred men: There being in pay for the Honourable East India Company of English and Portuguez 700, reckoning the Montrosses and Gunners. The Fort described.

Neat Dwellings. "The streets are sweet and clean, ranked with fine mansions of no extraordinary height (because a garrison-town) though beauty, which they conciliate, by the battlements and terrace walks on every house, and rows of trees before their doors, whose Italian porticos make no ordinary conveyance into their houses, built with brick and stone.

Portuguese Chapel. "Edifices of common note are none, except a small Chapel the Portugals are admitted to say Mass in.

"Take the town in its exact proportion, and it is oblong.

The English masters of Madras. "The true possessors of it are the English, instaled therein by one of their Naiks or Prince of the Hindoos 90 years ago, 40 years before their total subjection to the *Moors*;[1] who likewise have since ratified it by a patent from Golconda, only paying 7000 *pagods* yearly for royalties and customs that raises the money fourfold to the Company; whose Agent here is Sir William Langhorn, a gentleman of indefatigable industry and worth. He is Superintendent over all the Factories on the Coast of Coromandel, as far as the Bay of Bengala, and up Huygly river (which is one of the falls of Ganges, viz., Fort St. George *alias* Maderas, Pettipolee, Mechlapatan, Gundore, Medapollon, Balisore, Bengala, Huygly, Castle Bazar, Pattana. He has his Mint, and privilege of coining; the country stamp is only a *Fanam*, which is 3*d*. of gold; and their *Cash*, twenty of which go to a *Fanam*. Moreover he has his Justiciaries; to give sentence, but not on life and death to the King's liege people of England; though over the rest they may. His personal guard consists of 300 or 400 Blacks; besides a band of 1500 men ready on summons: He never goes abroad without fifes, drums, trumpets, and a flag with two balls in a red field; accompanied with his Council and Factors on horseback, with their Ladies in palenkeens.

Sir William Langhorn Agent.

---

[1] Dr. Fryer is mistaken in his chronology. Madras was founded about thirty-five years before his visit. He is also mistaken about the rent paid to Golkonda, which was only twelve hundred pagodas.

"The English here are Protestants, the Portugals Papists, who have their several Orders of Fryers; who, to give them their due, compass sea and land to make proselytes, many of the natives being brought in by them.

"The number of English here may amount to three hundred; of Portuguez as many thousand, who made Fort St. George their refuge, when they were routed from St. Thomas by the Moors about ten years past, and have ever since lived under protection of the English.

Number of English and Portugals.

"Thus have you the limits and condition of the English town: Let us now pass the pale to the heathen town, only parted by a wide parade, which is used for a bazar, or market-place.

"The Native town of Maderas divides itself into divers long streets, and they are chequered by as many transverse. It enjoys some Choultries for Places of Justice; one Exchange; one Pagoda, contained in a square stone-wall; wherein are a number of Chapels (if they may be comprehended under that class, most of them resembling rather monuments for the dead, than places of devotion for the living), one for every Tribe; not under one roof, but distinctly separate, though altogether, they bear the name of one entire Pagoda. The work is inimitably durable, the biggest closed up with arches continually shut, as where is supposed to be hid their Mammon of unrighteousness (they burying their estates here when they die, by the persuasion of their priests, towards their *viaticum* for another state) admitting neither light nor air, more than what the lamps, always burning, are by open funnels above suffered to ventilate: By which custom they seem to keep alive that opinion of Plato, in such a revolution to return into the world again, after their transmigration, according to the merits of their former living. Those of a minuter dimension were open, supported by slender straight and round pillars, plain and uniform up to the top, where some hieroglyphical portraiture lends its assistance to the roof, flat, with stones laid along like planks upon our rafters. On the walls of good sculpture were

Black Town.

Visited a Pagoda or Heathen Temple.

many images: The floor is stoned, they are of no great altitude; stinking most egregiously of the oil they waste in their lamps, and besmear their beastly gods with: Their outsides shew workmanship and cost enough, wrought round with monstrous effigies; so that *oleum et operam perdere*, pains and cost to no purpose, may not improperly be applied to them. Their gates are commonly the highest of the work, the others concluding in shorter piles.

The English Tombs.

"Near the outside of the town the English Golgotha, or place of sculls, presents variety of tombs, walks and sepulchres; which latter, and they stand in a line, are an open cloyster; but succinctly and precisely a *Quadragone* with hemispherical apartitions; on each side adorned with battlements to the abutment of every angle, who bear up a coronal arch, on whose vertex a globe is rivited by an iron wedge sprouting into a branch; paved underneath with a great black stone, whereon is engraved the name of the party interred. The buildings of less note are low and decent; the town is walled with mud, and bulwarks for watch-places for the English Peons; only on that side the sea washes it, and the Fort meets it. On the north are two great gates of brick, and one on the west, where they wade over the river to the washermen's town.

The English Gardens.

"Without the town grows their rice, which is nourished by the letting in of the water to drown it: Round about it is bestrewed with gardens of the English; where, besides gourds of all sorts for stews and pottage, herbs for sallad, and some few flowers, as jassamin, for beauty and delight; flourish pleasant topes of plantains, cocoes, guiavas, a kind of pear, jawks, a coat of armour over it like an hedge-hog's, guards its weighty fruit, oval without for the length of a span, within in fashion like squils parted; mangos, the delight of India, a plum, pomegranets, bananas, which are a sort of plantain, though less, yet much more grateful; betel, which last must not be slipt by in silence: It rises out of the ground to twelve or fourteen feet heighth, the body of it green and slender, jointed like a cane, the boughs flaggy and spreading, under whose arms it brings forth from its pregnant womb (which bursts when her month is come) a cluster of green nuts, like wallnuts in green shells, but different in the fruit; which is hard when dried, and looks like a nutmeg.

"The Natives chew it with *Chinam* (lime of calcined oyster-shells) and *Arach*, a convolvulus with a leaf like the largest ivy for to preserve their teeth, and correct an unsavoury breath: If swallowed, it inebriates as much as tobacco. Thus mixed, it is the only Indian entertainment, called Pawn. What Pawn is.

"These plants set in a row, make a grove that might delude the fanatic multitude into an opinion of their being sacred; and were not the mouth of that grand impostor hermetically sealed up, where Christianity is spread, these would still continue, as it is my fancy they were of old, and may still be the laboratories of his fallacious oracles: For they masquing the face of day, beget a solemn reverence, and melancholy habit in them that resort to them; by representing the more inticing place of zeal, a Cathedral, with all its pillars and pillasters, walks and choirs; and so contrived, that whatever way you turn, you have an even prospect.

"But not to run too far out of Maderas before I give you an account of the people; know they are under the bondage with the Moors, were not that alleviated by the power of the English, who command as far as their guns reach: To them therefore they pay toll, even of cowdung (which is their chiefest fireing), a prerogative the Dutch could never obtain in this kingdom, and by this means acquire great estates without fear of being molested. Their only merchants being Gentues, forty Moors having hardly cohabitation with them, though of the natives 30,000 are employed in this their monopoly. Nature of the people.

"The country is sandy, yet plentiful in provisions; in all places topes of trees, among one of which, on the top of a withered stump sate perching a Chamelion, clasping with its claws its rotten station, filling himself with his aerial food, The country.

a banquet which most other creatures else arise an hungered from: But to be confirmed in the truth of what we have only by tradition, I caused a Black who had a bow there, to fell him with an earthen pellet, which when he had, and after a small time he revived, and making a collar of straw for his neck, he carried him to my lodgings, where I dieted him a month on the same provant. That he changes his colours at a constant time of the day, is not to be contradicted; but whether he live by the air alone, I will not stand to it, unless there were a dearth of flies in the country: though for my part I never did see him eat any. In shape he comes nearest a newt; with his lungs his body does agitate itself up to its neck; he crawls on all four, and has a tail longer than his body, which all together was no more than half a foot; he has teeth, and those sharp."

St. Thomé.

Dr. Fryer also furnishes the following curious particulars respecting St Thomé:—

History of St. Thomas.

"St. Thomas is a city that formerly for riches, pride, and luxury, was second to none in India; but since, by the mutability of fortune, it has abated much of its adored excellencies.

"The sea on one side greets its marble walls, on the other a chain of hills intercepts the violence of the inflaming heat; one of which, called St. Thomas his Mount, is famous for his sepulture (in honour of whom a chapel is dedicated, the head priest of which was once the Metropolitan Bishop of India), and for a tree called *Arbor Tristis*, which withers in the day, and blossoms in the night.

St. Thomas Christians.

"About this Mount live a cast of people, one of whose legs is as big as an elephant's; which gives occasion for the divulging it to be a judgment on them, as the generation of the assassins and murtherers of the blessed Apostle St. Thomas, one of whom I saw at Fort St. George.

"Within the walls seven Churches answer to as many gates; the rubbish of whose stupendous heaps do justify the truth of what is predicated in relation to its pristine state.

"The builders of it were the Portugals."

Such was the condition of Madras between 1670 and 1677, as told by Dr. Fryer. It may now be as well to glance at the general daily life of the English at Madras, as it is told in the Government records.

CHAPTER IV.

MADRAS UNDER GOLKONDA.

1670—1688.

"Madras in the Olden Time."

THE Madras records were investigated by the present writer seventeen years ago. At that time he published a number of extracts in three volumes under the title of "Madras in the Olden Time." The mass of these extracts has but little interest outside the Madras Presidency. It will be easy to indicate their subject matter by the following narrative, which has been drawn up from the earlier records, and in which a selection of the more interesting extracts will be found incorporated.

Government of Sir William Langhorn, 1670—1677.

Sir William Langhorn was Governor of Madras from 1670 to 1677. He was present at Madras at the time of Fryer's visit. He is indeed duly noticed by Fryer. The times were stormy. Charles the Second had been ten years on the throne of England. There was an alliance between England and France against the Dutch.

French invasion.

A French fleet arrived in India. A French force landed at St. Thomé, and took the place by storm. The Muhammadan army of Golkonda, under the command of a General named Bobba Sahib, was endeavouring to recover St. Thomé from the French.

Madras in danger.

Sir William Langhorn was thus hemmed around with dangers. He dared not help the French lest he should provoke the wrath of Bobba Sahib. Meanwhile, Bobba Sahib was angry because the English would not join him with men and guns to fight against the French. All this while a Dutch fleet was cruising off the coast of Coromandel. The Dutch fleet had attacked the French at St. Thomé, but was repulsed. It was daily expected that the Dutch would attack Fort St. George.

At this juncture Sir William Langhorn resolved in Council to propitiate Bobba Sahib by sending him a present of scarlet broadcloth and looking-glasses. Bobba Sahib, however, was still as angry as ever. In after years Bobba Sahib had cause to regret this exhibition of hostility, as will be seen by the following extract from the consultations of the Agency, dated 6th May 1678:— Bobba Sahib.

"Bobba Sahib, formerly General of the King of Golconda's force against the French at St. Thomé, and in those days a bitter enemy to the English, but now in disgrace and debt, has been some days here trying all ways to borrow money, and to have an interview with the Governor, which is refused him by reason of his former unkindnesses when he was in power, and he in despair quits the place for Pullimalee, intending to go to his own country."

A year and a half passed away, and the French still remained in possession of St. Thomé. Within that time they had established a camp at Triplicane, the Muhammadan quarter of Madras; and fortified it far more strongly than the English were fortified at Fort St. George. Sir William Langhorn and his Council were at one time contemplating the advisability of abandoning Madraspatanam altogether; Proposed abandonment of Madras.

but afterwards decided on more energetic measures. At a Consultation held on the 2nd February 1674, it was recorded that the interests of the Honorable Company, as well as the lives of the residents at the Presidency, were staked upon the issue of the siege. Their enemies at sea and land were within musket-shot; their walls were slight and tottering; they were pestered with the great native town close to them; and the Dutch Governor-General was daily expected with a large fleet. Under these circumstances they resolved, after mature consideration, to enlarge and strengthen their fortifications as much as possible; but their efforts in this direction do not seem to have much increased their strength, or to have rendered them more independent of the belligerent powers. Four Frenchmen from Java were staying in Fort St. George; and in May, the Dutch and Mussulmans peremptorily demanded their removal. For a long time Sir William Langhorn refused to comply, because of the English alliance with France; but at last the Muhammadan army fairly laid siege to Fort St. George, and would hear of no further delay. The Frenchmen, on their part, refused to leave the place unless they were permitted to go to St. Thomé, and there the Dutch and Muhammadans would not allow them to proceed. At last, the President in Council resolved to send them under passports and an escort to Bijapore, another Muhammadan kingdom in the Western Dekhan. There they seem to have gone, loudly protesting, however, against the proceeding, inasmuch as they were subjects of the King of France, a friend and ally of the Crown of England.

Surrender of the French.

For two years the French held possession of St. Thomé. At length, on the 26th August 1674, they surrendered to the Dutch, on the condition that the garrison should be transported to Europe.

Peace with the Dutch.

Fortunately for the Madras Agency, at that moment the news arrived from Europe that in the preceding January peace had been concluded between England and Holland. But for the happy peace, the Dutch would have followed up the capture of St. Thomé with the siege of Fort St. George; and there can be little doubt that the fall of the place would have followed, for the fortifications were still but weak, and there were only two hundred and fifty men in garrison.

Moral rules at Madras.

Sir William Langhorn was a disciplinarian in his way. He tried to promote public morals by laying down the following rules. As far as drinking was concerned they were certainly liberal; but those were the days of Merrie King Charles.

No one person was to be allowed to drink above half a pint of arrack or brandy and one quart of wine at one time, under a penalty of one pagoda upon the housekeeper that supplied it, and twelve fanams upon every guest that had exceeded that modest allowance. Drunkenness was to be punished by a fine and the stocks. All persons addicted in any way to the social evil were to be imprisoned at the discretion of the Governor, and if not reclaimed were to be sent back to England. All persons telling a lie, or absenting themselves from morning or evening prayers, were to be fined four fanams for each offence. Persons being out of White Town after eight o'clock, would be punished; and any one committing the heinous offence of getting over the walls of White Town upon any pretence whatever, was to be kept in irons until the arrival of the ships, and then to be sent to England to receive further condign punishment on his arrival. It was also ordained that all persons swearing, cursing, banning or blaspheming the sacred name of Almighty God should pay a fine of four fanams for each offence; that any two persons who should go out into the fields to decide a quarrel between them by the sword or fire-arms should be imprisoned for two months on nothing but rice and water; that any soldier giving another the lie should be made fast to a gun, and there receive ten blows with a small rattan, well laid on by the man to whom he had given the lie; and that any officer who should in any way connive at the offence, or at any mitigation of the punishment, should forfeit a month's wages.

Low state of morals.

Notwithstanding these and other similar rules, public decorum was often outraged. Brawlings were not unfrequent, and were by no means confined to the barrrcks, the punch shops, or the warehouse, but even were to be occasionally heard in the Council chamber itself. One little circumstance which took place during the meeting of Council on 6th June 1676, is singularly illustrative of the disturbances which occasionally arose. Nathaniel Keeble, buyer of jewels, uttered some provocative words concerning the wife of Mr. Herries, a member of Council. Herries was of course present, and a fight took place in the Council chamber. The combatants were soon parted by the Governor and Council; but Keeble had received a bloody nose from the clenched fist of the indignant husband, and swore to be revenged upon him though he were hanged for it. Herries then swore the peace against Keeble, and the Governor ordered the latter to be confined to his chamber until he had furnished security that he would keep the peace for the future. The same day, however, Keeble broke from his arrest, leaped down the Fort walls, and sprained his leg; and was accordingly ordered to be confined in the "Lock house" until the arrival of the ships, when he could be dispatched to England. The next day, however, the whole matter was arranged. Nathaniel Keeble sent in his humble submission and promised amendment, and the Government mercifully forgave him. Incidents such as these are sufficient to prove that, however strict rules might be laid down, yet the times were as lawless in Fort St. George as they were in Covent Garden or the Strand. That they were not worse is abundantly proved by the character of the literature and condition of the people of England during the reign of the second Charles.

Rev. Patrick Warner.

About this period a certain Reverend Patrick Warner was Chaplain at Fort St. George. He was much shocked at the low state of the morals in the settlement. He was also alarmed at the countenance which Sir William Langhorn had given to the Roman Catholics. It appears that the Portuguese had built and consecrated a new church within the Fort, and that Sir William Langhorn had ordered salutes to be fired in honour of the ceremony. Under these circumstances Mr. Warner wrote the following letter to the Court of Directors. It is dated 31st January 1676.

"Right Worshipfuls,

Letters to the Directors.

"It is my trouble that I have so little acquaintance with your Worships, because of this I could not take the confidence of writing to you, nor had I anything worth the writing, having then remained so short a while in this place; but now having been a servant under you in the ministry of the Gospel some considerable time, I have to my grief met with that which maketh me, contrary to my inclination, break off my silence, and give you the trouble of these lines.

Vicious lives.

"I have the charity to believe that most of you have so much zeal for God, and for the credit of religion, that your heads would be fountains of water, and eyes rivers of tears, did you really know how much God is dishonoured, his name blasphemed, religion reproached amongst the Gentiles, by the vicious lives of many of your servants. Did I not therefore complain of them, I should not be faithful either to God or you, or to their own souls. And if it be not a desire to approve myself in some measure faithful unto all those, God the searcher of hearts and tryer of reins will one day discover, if it be not, I say, such a desire that moves me to the present undertaking.

Drunkenness.

"It may be for a lamentation to hear and see the horrid swearing and profanation of the name of God, the woful and abominable drunkenness and uncleanness that so much reign and rage among the soldiery; and these not secretly or covertly, but as it were in the sight of the sun, and men refuse therein to be ashamed, neither can they blush."

* * * * *

Popery.

"Most of those women are popish christians; and if those that marry them do not fall into the former inconveniences, they hardly escape being seduced by their wives and wives' families into popery. There have not been wanting instances of this also. Since I entered into this place, I have constantly refused to celebrate any such marriages except one that I was urged into, and this not before she had solemnly and before several witnesses renounced popery, and promised to attend upon ordinances with us; but she had not been many weeks married when at the instigation of some popish priests here she perfidiously fell from those promises.

Evil marriages.

"I wish your Worships may consider it be not requisite to inhibit such marriages, for the children turn either infidels or popish. I do also earnestly wish there may be more inspection taken what persons you send over into these places; for there come hither some thousand murderers, some men stealers, some popish, some come over under the notion of single persons and unmarried, who yet have their wives in England, and here have been married to others, with whom they have lived in adultery; and some on the other hand have come over as married persons, of whom there are strange suspicions they were never married. These and other abuses there are among the soldiery. There are also some of the Writers who by their lives are not a little scandalous to the Christian religion, so sinful in their drunkenness that some of them play at cards and dice for wine that they may drink, and afterwards throwing the dice which shall pay all, and sometimes who shall drink all, by which some are forced to drink until they be worse than beasts. Others pride themselves in making others drink till they be insensible, and then strip them naked and in that posture cause them to be carried through the streets to their dwelling place. Some of them, with other persons whom they invited, once went abroad to a garden not far off, and there continued a whole day and night drinking most excessively, and in so much that one of the number died within a very few days after, and confessed he had contracted his sickness by that excess. A person worthy of credit having occasion to go the next day into the same garden could number by the heads 36 bottles, and the best of his judgment they were all pottles, for it is their frequent custom to break bottles as soon as they have drunk the wine, and this they have done sometimes within the walls of the Fort, and withal, sing and carouse at very unseasonable hours. And this their drunkenness is not alone, but in some attended with its ordinary concomitant uncleanness."

* * * * *

Neglect of public worship.

"They can find time and leisure for these things, but cannot find any time or leisure for the worship of God, which is exceedingly neglected by all, notwithstanding your orders to the contrary. I have sometimes, having waited long enough, been forced at length to begin duty with only three or four persons present, and when we have done there hath not been above twelve or thirteen in all; but who amongst the Writers are most guilty in this, your Worships may know by the enclosed list of their absence taken by me indifferently, some appointed thereunto by the Governors; of others no account is taken.

Immorality of the few.

"But because it is no less a sin to condemn the just than to justify the wicked, I must bear witness for most of the young men, that they cannot, to the best of my knowledge, be accused of the former enormities. There are but a few of them that are guilty in the manner before described; whose names I would have inserted, that so I might clear the others, but that they have been lately sick, and some small hopes there are that they may amend; they have given some ground to expect it. But if they shall return with the dog to the vomit, I will, if it please God to spare me so long, give your Worships a more full account thereof by word of mouth, upon my arrival with the next ships; for as you have already been informed, I intend to return with them, and I hope with your good leave so to do. Therefore what I have written may in charity be supposed, not to proceed from expectation of any advantage to myself, but from respect to the glory of God, and their good, and the encouragement of succeeding ministers.

"I did write, what the last year's ships give an account, in a letter to Captain Broockman, upon the civil usage I met with from the Governor and others of Council, and indeed generally from all as to mine own person, which I do not now retract, only I could wish they were more zealous. When I have complained of those former abuses, I have been told by several that persons here are a good deal more civilised than formerly they have been. If it be so, there is a great cause to admire the patience and long suffering of God, but withal cause to fear that if those things be not reformed He will not always keep silence. The Governor I understand hath refused to listen to any that would prevent his firing of great guns, and then vollies of small shot by all the soldiers in garrison, at the consecration of a popish church within the walls; if he be therein acquitted by you I have no more to say, but pray that God himself would discountenance that idolatry and superstition so much countenanced by others, and prevent the hurt that may redound to the place and to your interests thereby. Salute at a Catholic Church.

"One Mr. Mallory, formerly Surgeon's mate in the President and now Surgeon's mate in this place, and another, Barnes, who formerly went to sea as master of some small vessel, but having wasted the money entrusted to him, lives now idly and out of any employment. These two are constant companions with any of the young men in whatever Mallory and Barnes.

debaucheries they were guilty of, and it gives ground for suspicion that they may be guilty of enticing them thereunto.

Warner's return.

"There are some other things that I would humbly have remonstrated to your Worships, but because I intend, if it shall so please God, to see you with the next ships, at which time if it be acceptable it may more conveniently be done. I do therefore at present forbear, only praying that God would continue to prosper your undertaking and enable you faithfully to design His glory therein, and lead you to the reasonable means that may conduce to His glory, in the encouragement of godliness, and restraint of sin in these places where your power reacheth. I am or desire to be,

Right worshipfuls,
Your faithful servant,
According to my station,
PATRICK WARNER.

MADRAS,
January 31st 1676."

Change of Governors at Madras.

Sir William Langhorn left Madras in 1677. He was succeeded by a gentleman named Mr. Streynsham Masters. It was at this period that Sivaji, the founder of the Mahratta empire, attained the height of his power. He had assumed all the insignia of a great Raja; and, as already seen, an English deputation from Bombay had been present at his coronation. Suddenly he entered upon a campaign which is a marvel in history. It was more than equivalent to marching an army from Bombay to Madras. He set out from his country in the Western Ghâts; marched through the Dekhan from the north-west to the south-east; and entered the Peninsula and went to Tanjore. On his way he passed by Madras. The entries in the diary or consultation books of the Madras Presidency will show the general state of alarm:—

"*14th May 1677.*—Having this day received a message and a letter from Sevaji Raja by a Brahmin and two others of his people, requesting some cordial stones and counter poisons, we resolved to send him some, together with a civil letter, by a messenger of our own, as a small present, together with some such fruit as these gardens afford, and to bestow upon his Brahmin three yards of broad cloth and some sandalwood, not thinking it good to require the money for so small trifles, although offered in his letter; considering how great a person he is, and how much his friendship does already and may import the Honorable Company as he grows more and more powerful and obvious to them." Sivaji, the Mahratta.

The value of the present thus sent to Sivaji is stated in the records at Madras; the cost of the whole was something like sixty pagodas.

A few days afterwards Sivaji sent for more cordials and medicines. The English gladly responded to his request. Indeed, Sivaji was the terror of India. Madras was constantly alarmed with rumours that he was about to attack the English and Dutch settlements. After a while the English were gladdened by the news that the Mahrattas had retired to their own country after having some bloody battles with the Naik of Mysore. Departure of Sivaji.

The Mysore ruler was at this period a sovereign of the same type as Sivaji. His army, like the Mahratta army, was composed of bandits. They committed atrocities worse than those of the Mahrattas. The following extract from the Consultation Condition of Mysore.

book of January 1679 shows the general character of their warfare:—

"Their custom is not to kill, but to cut off the noses with the upper lips of their enemies; for which they carry an iron instrument with which they do it very dexterously, and carry away all the noses and lips they despoyle their enemys of, for which they are rewarded by the Naik of Mysore according to the number, and the reward is the greater, if the beard appear upon the upper lip. This way of warfare is very terrible to all that those people engage with, so that none care to meddle with them; they being also a resolute people, and have destroyed many that have attempted them, for though they kill them not outright, yet they die by lingering deaths, if they make not themselves away sooner, as for the most part they do that are so wounded, the shame and dishonor of it being esteemed greater than the pain and difficulty of subsisting."

The nose-cutting Raja of Saranpatan.

The account in the Madras records is fully confirmed by Dr. Fryer. He refers to the Mysore ruler as the Raja of Saranpatan, which is doubtless the same as Seringapatam. The extract is curious:—

"The Raja of Saranpatan must not be slipped by in silence, because his way of fighting differs from his neighbours; he trains up his soldiers to be expert at a certain instrument to seize on the noses of his enemies with that slight either in the field or in their camps, that a budget-full of them have been presented to their Lord for a breakfast; a thing, because it deforms them, so abashing, that few care to engage with him; and this he makes use of, because it is against his religion to kill any thing. He enjoys a vast territory on the back of the Zamerbin."

The following miscellaneous extracts will explain themselves. They also serve to illustrate the character of the early Madras records.

Thursday, 28th October, 1680.—"The new church was dedicated by virtue of commissions directed to the Government, and to Mr. Richard Portman the minister, from his Lordship the Bishop of London. The solemnity was performed in very good order, and concluded with vollies of small shot fired by the whole garrison drawn out, and the cannon round the Fort. The church named St. Mary's as at first intended, and from this day forward all public service to be there performed. Foundation of a Protestant church at Madras.

"It is observable that at the dedication of a new church by the French Padres and Portuguese in 1675, Sir William Langhorn, then Agent, had fired guns from the Fort; and yet at this time neither Padre nor Portuguese appeared at the dedication of our church, nor so much as gave the Governor a visit afterwards to wish him joy of it."

Monday, 22nd March, 1680.—"It fell under consideration whether it consisteth with our religion and interest to admit of marriages between Protestants and Roman Catholics in this place, and upon the debate resolved :— Marriages of Protestants and Catholics.

"1st, That it is not against the law of God in Holy Scripture, nor the laws of England, and hath frequently been practised in England for Protestants to marry Roman Catholics.

"2nd, That the Roman Catholics of this place, being the offspring of foreign nations chiefly Portuguese, and born out of England, and not liable to the laws of England provided against Roman Catholics, they always owning themselves vassals to the King of Portugal.

"3rd, That it is our interest to allow of marriages with them, especially our men with their women, to prevent wickedness, and in regard there is not English women enough for the men, and the common soldiers cannot maintain English women and children with their pay, as well as they can the women of the country, who are not so expensive and not less modest than our ordinary or common people are, and in matter of marriages we have already gained by them many hopeful children brought up in the Protestant religion.

"It is also further to be remembered that these Roman Catholics of the Portuguese nation were invited hitherto upon our first settlement; ground was given them to build upon; a church and French Priests were allowed, to encourage them to come in and inhabit here; and they have been loyal and serviceable in the defence of the place in time of war, and are a great security to us on that account. Moreover, our greatest income arises from the customs upon their commerce."

Offspring of mixed marriages.

The Protestant feelings which prevailed at the time were far too strong to permit these rules to be carried out. Two Chaplains were consulted by the Governor and Council. The following rules were then added, for the maintenance of Protestantism:—

Thursday, 25th March, 1680.—"The marriages of Protestants with Roman Catholics being again taken into consideration, the Honorable Company's two Chaplains, Mr. Richard Portman and Mr. Richard Elliot, were sent for into the Council, and upon the debate it is concluded, resolved, and ordered,

"That upon the marriage of a Protestant with a Roman Catholic, both the parties to be married shall solemnly promise before one of the Chaplains of the place by themselves, or some for them, before the Banns shall be published, and also in the Chapel or Church by themselves in person, upon the day of marriage and before the parties shall be married, that ALL the children by them begotten and born, shall be brought up in the Protestant religion, and herein due care shall always be taken by the overseers of the orphans and the poor."

Oppression of Lingapa.

In 1680 the English settlement suffered much from a Golkonda general, named Lingapa, who had been appointed to the command of the district.[1] His object was to raise the yearly rental from twelve hundred pagodas to two thousand; or rather to threaten to raise it in the hope of procuring a present for himself. The records are too voluminous for extract. A native officer entered Black Town with drums beating and a flag flying, as though he had been high in command. He declared that he had been appointed to take the command of the town for the Sultan of Golkonda. The Governor sent three files of soldiers after him and brought him into the Fort. After a short examination the man was sent out of the town.

It was soon discovered that Lingapa was at the bottom of these proceedings. He placed an embargo upon the English settlement. For months no goods or provisions were procurable from the surrounding villages. Matters grew so serious that the English garrison was forced to make raids into the country to procure provisions and fuel. The English Governor contemplated leaving Madras altogether, and removing to the country of some Hindu Rajah further south. The embargo was broken through, but Lingapa continued to be very troublesome. To make matters worse, he protected certain objectionable ship captains, who carried on a trade with India in defiance of the Company's charter. The Company had always regarded these interlopers

Embargo on Madras.

[1] The Sultan of Golkonda was a Shiah Muhammadan. The name of Lingapa shows that he was a Hindu.

as pirates. The Governor of Madras was at last forced to come to terms with Lingapa. Seven thousand pagodas were sent to Lingapa, equivalent to about three thousand pounds sterling. Matters quieted down at once. Lingapa ceased to protect the interlopers; the yearly rent of Madras was again fixed at twelve hundred pagodas. The Sultan of Golkonda sent a firman to the Governor of Madras; and it will be seen from the following extract that the firman was received with every honour:—

Firman from Golkonda.

Monday, 12th November, 1683.—"This afternoon at four o'clock, the Agent and Council (being attended with the Factors and Writers, the Company's Merchants and two companies of soldiers) went to the Hon'ble Company's new Garden-house to receive the King of Golconda's firman; after which, at the drinking of the King of Golconda's health, there was fired three vollies of small shot, and thirty-one great guns. When the ceremony was ended, the messenger that brought the firman attended upon the Agent to the Fort, where after drinking a health to Madana and Accana, the Chief Ministers of State, there was one volley more of small shot fired, and so the messenger was dismissed for the present."

Troubles at Madras.

Not long afterwards there were internal troubles at Madras. There was a strike about taxes amongst the men who dyed the native calicoes and were known by the name of painters. The whole body left the Company's jurisdiction and went away to St. Thomé. They threatened to murder all the native servants of the Company who refused to join them. They also stopped all provisions and goods coming to the town. The Governor and Council took strong measures. They entertained a hundred black Portuguese to keep guard over the washers, to prevent them following the evil example. The wives and children of the mutineers were taken out of their houses in Black Town, and driven into the pagoda. At last it was proclaimed by beat of drum that unless the mutineers delivered themselves up within ten days, all their houses, goods, and chattels within the jurisdiction of the Company would be confiscated. Eight days afterwards the ringleaders were arrested at St. Thomé, and brought within the Company's territories. They were at once committed to prison; the same evening all the rest came into the town and made their submission.

Meanwhile a new Governor was appointed to Madras. His name was Mr. William Gyfford. In after years, the Directors referred to him as "our too easy Agent Gyfford." The origin of this epithet involves a story. Mr. William Gyfford.

At this period Mr. Josiah Child was Chairman of the Court of Directors. Child was a man of mark, but hard and overbearing in his ways. The Court of Directors had been anxious to raise a quit rent from all the householders in Madras, native and European. They hoped by so doing to defray the yearly charge for repairs and fortifications. Mr. Josiah Child.

Mr. Masters had succeeded in raising such a tax; not for repairs or fortifications, but for promoting the sanitation of Black Town. On his departure all the native inhabitants of Black Town petitioned against the tax; and "our too easy Agent Gyfford" abolished the tax. Local taxes.

Resolution of the Directors.

On the 20th September 1682, the Directors wrote to the Government of Madras as follows:—

"Our meaning as to the revenue of the town is that one way or another, by Dutch, Portuguese, or Indian methods, it should be brought to defray at least the whole constant charge of the place, which is essential to all governments in the world. People protected ought in all parts of the universe, in some way or other, to defray the charge of their protection and preservation from wrong and violence. The manner of raising which revenue we shall leave to your discretion, as may be most agreeable to the humour of that people."

Inundation at Madras.

Meantime there had been a great inundation of the sea at Madras. The circumstance is described in the following entry:—

Tuesday, 11th July.—"The sea having for about 10 days past encroached upon this town, and we, hoping as it is usual, that it would retreat again of itself, forbore any remedies to keep it off; but now that instead of its losing it mightily gains ground upon us, and that without a speedy course be taken the town will run an apparent hazard of being swallowed up, for it has undermined even to the very walls, and so deep that it has eaten away below the very foundation of the town,—and the great bulwark next to the sea side, without a speedy and timely prevention, will certainly, in a day or two more, yield to its violence: it is therefore ordered forthwith that the drum be beat to call all coolies, carpenters, smiths, peons, and all other workmen, and that sufficient materials be provided, that they may work day and night to endeavour to put a stop to its fury: for without effectual means be used in such an eminent danger and exigency, the town, garrison, and our own lives, considering all the foregoing circumstances, must needs be very hazardous and insecure."

On the 31st May 1683 the Directors remarked on the event in the following terms :— **Directors insist on local taxation.**

"We take notice of the great inundation that endangered our Town and Fort, and we would have you endeavour to prevent such future accidents by laying such a deep and strong foundation with chunam, as you mention, that may be sufficient in all human probability to prevent damage by any such accident hereafter. And in all other respects we would have you to strengthen and fortify our Fort and Town by degrees, that it may be terrible against the assault of any Indian Prince and the Dutch power of India, if we should happen to have any difference with them hereafter. But we must needs desire you so to contrive your business (but with all gentleness) that the inhabitants may pay the full charge of all repairs and fortifications, who do live easier under our Government than under any Government in Asia, or indeed under any Government in the known part of the world. Their saying they pay customs is a frivolous objection, and relates only to their security at sea under our Passes, and under the guns of our Fort in port; but the strong fortifying of the town, etc., and the raising new works is a security to their lives, houses, wives, and children, and all that belongs to them."

These orders were frequently repeated from home. The results are set forth in the following extracts from the Madras Consultations :— **Petition of Natives of Madras.**

Monday, 4th January 1686.—"This morning the heads of the several Castes appeared before the President and Council, to be heard according to their desire; and after begging pardon for the great crime they had committed in raising such a mutiny, delivered in their Petition, translate whereof is as follows :—

"'*To the Hon'ble Governor and Council.*

"'The inhabitants of this town declare, that it is now forty years and upwards, from the foundation of this Fort, and that they were invited to people and increase the town upon the word and favour of the English, under whom they have till now lived, receiving many honours and favours without paying any tribute or rent. Only in the time of the past Governor Mr. Master, who imposed a tax upon arrack, and upon paddy, and causing us to pay for cleansing the streets; also increasing the Choultry customs of goods imported and exported; also the rents of the fields of paddy, and ordered that double custom should be received of tobacco which came from other places, and because the owners could not pay said custom, they carried their tobacco to St. Thomé, by which means the Choultry hath been hindered of the customs formerly paid. Also the close siege this Town suffered, which upon your Honour's arrival was taken off, whereby this Town was newly revived from death to life, hoping that your Honour would have relieved us from all tributes and rents; but instead thereof we find you go about to impose and increase other new tributes upon our houses, which can in no wise be, nor ought your Honour to do it. Wherefore we beg your Honour for the sake of the most high God, and in the name of the most serene King of England and of the Hon'ble Company, that you will free this Town from so heavy a yoke, as is this tax laid upon our houses, seeing we are a poor people, and live upon our labour and trouble; this Town having the fame, and is called place of Charity, and we shall live confident in your favours and assistances, and the whole Town lightened by your goodness, as they hope from your Honour.

"'Signed by the heads of the several Castes underwritten, *viz.*, chuliars, painters, tailors, husbandmen, coolies, washers, barbers, pariahs, comities, oilmakers, fruiterers, shepherds, potmakers, muckwas, patanava, tiaga, cavaree, nugabunds, pally, goldsmiths, chitties, weavers.'

Proceedings of the Madras Government.

"Upon perusal of said Petition, the President and Council told them, that it did not lie in their power totally to excuse them from contributing towards the charges of this Garrison, in regard it was the Right Honorable Company's positive orders, they commanding to have the Black Town walled round at the charge of the Inhabitants; and there was no remedy but that they must be conformable thereunto, it being a very small matter, only three fanams a year for a small house, six fanams for a middle size house, and nine fanams for a great house, which could be no burthen to them. But they continued very obstinate, and declared themselves unwilling and unable to pay, for reasons given in their Petition; and further that it would breed a custom, and they feared it would be increased hereafter. But it was still replied it must be done, and they as positive on the other hand refused, offering two of their heads, if that would satisfy, to excuse them from this tribute and heavy yoke, as they call it. After which they were one by one asked whether they would leave the town, make war upon us, or submit to our orders and government; to which they every one answered they would submit, but on a sudden all at once denied what they had said, and that they would not pay do what we would to them; which forced us to cause the drum to beat, and declare our resolution that we would execute our orders declared to them yesterday by beat of drum of pulling down their houses, selling their lands, and banishing them the place. Which when they perceived us so much in earnest, at last submitted, promising to be obedient to our government, and that they would take off the prohibition laid upon their people and our prohibitions, and that all things should be at peace and quiet. So they were dismissed, and after awhile, the shops were opened, provisions brought in, and the washer-men, muckwas, catamaran-men, coolies, and servants returned to their several businesses; and now it only remains that they be obedient in paying their contributions."

There are various entries in the Madras Consultation Books respecting slaves. They are printed together in the present place, as they throw considerable light upon the public opinion of the time as regards slaves:— Slave trade at Madras.

Monday, 18th September 1683.—"There being great number of slaves yearly exported from this place, to the great grievance of many persons whose children are very commonly privately stolen away from them, by those who are constant traders in this way, the Agent and Council, considering the scandal that might accrue to the Government, and the great loss that many parents may undergo by such actions, have ordered that no more slaves be sent off the shore again."

Monday, 13th November 1683.—"An Order in English, Portuguese, Gentoo [*i. e.*, Tamil], and Malabar, for the preventing the transportation of this country people by sea and making them slaves in other countries, was read and past and ordered to be hung up in four public places of this town. The contents are as followeth :—

"Whereas formerly there hath been an ill custom in this place of shipping off this country people, and making them slaves in other strange countries. We, therefore, the present Governor and Council of Fort St. George, have taken the same into our serious consideration, and do hereby order that, for the future, no such thing be done by any person whatsoever, resident in this place. And we do hereby also strictly command all our officers by the water side, whether they be English, Portuguese or Gentoos [*i. e.*, Tamil-speaking Hindus], to do their utmost endeavours to prevent the same ; or else suffer such punishment, either in body or goods, as we shall think fit to inflict upon them. And if any person, being an inhabitant of this Town of Madraspatanam, shall hereafter presume clandestinely to do anything contrary to this our order, by shipping such slaves of this country and it be proved against him,—he shall pay for every slave so shipped off or sent away, fifty pagodas, to be recovered of him in the Choultry of Madraspatanam ; one-third for the use of the Honorable East India Company, one-third to the poor, and one-third to the informer."

Monday, 1st August 1683.—"The trade in slaves growing great from this Port, by reason of the great plenty of poor, by the sore famine, and their cheapness,—it is ordered for the future that each slave sent off this shore pay one pagoda custom to the Right Honorable Company, and that the Justices do receive no more for the usual fee for registering and passport, than two fanams a head till the Council shall think fit to alter it as formerly."

Thursday, 29th September 1687.—"We do now order that Mr. Fraser (who being Land Customer has the best opportunity for it) do buy forty young sound slaves for the Right Honorable Company, and dispose them to the several Mussoola Boats, two or three in each, in charge of the Chief man of the Boat, to be fed and taught by them; and to encourage their care therein, it is ordered a short red broad cloth coat be given to each Chief man; and that the Right Honorable Company's mark be embroidered with silk on their backs, with the number of their rank and the boat, which are also to be so numbered, whereby we shall have them at better command, our business go more currently on, and easier thereby discover their thieveries."

Thursday, 2nd February 1688.—"In consideration of the several inconveniences that have happened by the exportation of children stolen from their parents, to prevent which for the future,—it is ordered that no slaves shall be shipped off or transported, except such who are first examined by the Justices of the Choultry, and their several names registered in a book for that purpose; for which the Justices are to receive two fanams for each slave. And whosoever shall offend against this same rule, and shall be convicted of stealing people, are to pay for the first fault five pagodas, and for the next to lose their ears in the pillory. And this order shall be fixed upon the several gates and in the Choultry."

Monday, 14th May 1688.—"The custom by the exportation of slaves here, being now of little advantage to the Right Honorable Company by their scarcity, and it having brought upon us great complaints and troubles from the country government, for the loss of their children and servants spirited and stolen from them, which being likely to increase, by the new government of the Mogul's who are

Final prohibition of the slave trade.

very averse, and prohibit all such trade in his dominions, and has lately expressed his displeasure therein against the Dutch for their exporting of slaves from Metchlepatam. To prevent which prejudice and mischiefs for the future, and we having received a late letter from the Seer Lascar about it,—it is agreed and ordered that, after the 20th instant, no person inhabitant of this place, either Christian or other, do directly or indirectly buy or transport slaves from this place or any adjacent Port (whereby the Government may be any ways troubled or prejudiced) upon the penalty of fifty pagodas for each slave bought and transported against this our order. But in consideration that several persons in town have formerly bought slaves which still remain by them, by reason of their sickness or want of opportunity to transport them:—It is agreed that they be permitted to ship off such slaves, provided they give a list of them to the Justices of the Choultry, and produce them publicly there, to be duly examined and registered. And the better to prevent any demands upon them hereafter, the Justices are ordered to proclaim the same by beat of drum; that no person may pretend ignorance thereof, and that all may come and make their demands for children and slaves stolen, and upon due proof, they be delivered to them free of charge."

Golkonda threatened by Aurungzeb.

Meanwhile there had been a great change in the political horizon. In 1685, the Sultan of Golkonda was assailed by the Moghul Emperor Aurungzeb. The details of the war are of no interest. The Sultan, however, was in sore extremity; he called upon the English at Madras to help him against the Moghul. The point is only important from its having elicited the following remarks from the Court of Directors; they are evidently penned by Mr. Josiah Child:—

Instructions of the Directors.

"We know the King of Golconda is rich enough to pay for any assistance you give him, either in diamonds or pagodas; and therefore we intend to be at no charge for his assistance against the Mogul, but what he shall pay us for beforehand, or put diamonds into your hands for the security of our payment, both principal and interest.

English defy the Sultan of Golkonda.

"For the King of Golconda's writing to you, you may acquaint him in a decent and friendly manner, that we are none of his subjects; wherein we would have you be guided by the old Proverb, "suaviter in modo fortiter in re." But if nevertheless he pretend to any dominion over your city, you may, when you are in a good condition, tell him in plain terms that we own him for our good friend, ally, and confederate and sovereign and lord paramount of all that country, excepting the small territory belonging to Madras, of which we claim the sovereignty, and will maintain and defend against all persons, and govern by our own laws, without any appeal to any prince or potentate whatsoever, except our Sovereign Lord the King, paying unto him the King of Golconda our agreed tribute of 1200 pagodas per annum. And if ever he break with you upon these terms, we require you to defend yourselves by arms, and from that time renounce paying him any more tribute. It being strange to us that while he is oppressed by the Mogul on one hand, and by a poor handful of Dutchmen on the other, you should make yourselves so timorous and fearful of asserting our own King's just right and prerogative to that important place."[1]

[1] It may be as well to specify that a pagoda is equivalent to three rupees eight annas, and that its English value varied from seven shillings to half a sovereign. A fanam was a small coin worth about twopence.

CHAPTER V.

MADRAS UNDER THE MOGHULS.

1688—1720.

Golkonda conquered by Aurungzeb.

ABOUT 1688 there was a great change in the fortunes of Madras. The Sultan of Golkonda was conquered by Aurungzeb, and consequently the English settlement at Madras was brought under the paramount power of the Great Moghul.

Destruction of the English Factory at Hughli.

The change was effected at a remarkable crisis. The English in Bengal had been allowed to establish a factory at Hughli. They had been prohibited from building any walls or fortifications, like those which they possessed at Madras; they had consequently been exposed to the oppressions and exactions of the Nawab of Bengal; and on one occasion, Mr. Job Charnock, the Governor at Hughli, was imprisoned and scourged by the Nawab.[1] The result was that James the Third made war upon the Emperor Aurungzeb. A squadron of English men-of-war was sent into the eastern seas to capture and destroy the ships of the Moghul. Aurungzeb was soon in alarm. Every complaint was redressed. The war was brought to a close, but was never forgotten. It sufficed to keep the peace between the English and the Moghul authorities for a period of seventy years.

---

[1] Orme's Hindustan, Vol. II. The Nawab of Bengal was afterwards known as the Subahdar. Charnock is often spelt Channock.

The light in which the war was regarded by the Court of Directors may be gathered from the following remarks, which appear in a general letter, dated 27th August 1688:— War between the English and Moghuls.

"The subjects of the Moghul cannot bear a war with the English for twelve months together, without starving and dying by thousands, for want of work to purchase rice; not singly for want of our trade, but because by our war we obstruct their trade with all the Eastern nations, which is ten times as much as ours, and all European nations put together. Therefore we conclude Fort St. George is now much more worth and secure to us, than ever it was in the mean King of Golconda's time; for he had little at sea for us to revenge ourselves upon; but now if new injuries should be offered us, we have a fat enemy to deal with, from whom something is to be got to bear our charges. Therefore we conclude that the Moghul's governors will never give us fresh provocations, nor deny you St. Thomé, or anything else you shall reasonably and fairly request of him.

"No great good was ever attained in this world without throes and convulsions: therefore we must not grudge at what is past."

The following extracts from the Consultation Books will suffice to tell the story of one result of the war in Bengal:— Mr. Charnock at Madras.

Thursday, 7th March 1689.—"Agent Charnock, his Council and the several Factors and Writers to the number of twenty-eight persons, being arrived from Bengal, who, having from their disturbances and sudden surprising departure thence, laden the Right Honorable Company's concerns and remains in great confusion upon the several ships, of which we have received neither Invoices nor Bills of Lading: it is therefore ordered that each Commander shall give a list of what they have on board."

Nawab of Bengal invites the English to return.

Monday, 7th October 1689.—"The "Pearl" frigate arriving yesterday from Vizagapatam, and by her came Bengal peons, who brought us several letters and a firman from the new Nawab of Bengal, Ibrahim Khan, to the President, dated 2nd July, very kindly inviting us to return and resettlement, with assurance of a just and fair usage to the Right Honorable Company's servants and trade, and upon the former privileges, and to assist us in the recovery of our debts owing to us in those parts; much blaming the late Nawab's injustice and cruelty to our people: which notwithstanding it is most acceptable news to us as we doubt not it will also be to the Right Honorable Company; but our resettlement being a matter of great weight and importance, it is ordered and agreed that the Agent, etc., of the Bengal Council be summond to a Council with us."

Thursday, 10th October.—"Agent Charnock and Council being this day joined with us in Council, the Nawab's letters and firman from Bengal to the President were perused and long debated on, and being concluded to be a happy good opportunity to return and settle in Bengal, that Government being under that famously just and good Nawab Ibrahim Khan, who has so kindly invited us to it, and faithfully engaged our peace and safety, of his honour the Agent has had long experience at Patna; . . . but the war continuing still at Bombay . . . it is agreed that the General of Surat be advised as soon as possible thereof, and copies of the firman and letters sent him, with our opinion thereof, desiring his advice and orders therein, and that a small vessel be fitted for that purpose, the overland passage being very uncertain and dangerous."

Madras, a Sovereign State.

During the latter years of the seventeenth century Madras underwent a great change. It was no longer a fortified factory; it had become a sovereign state. Accordingly other qualifications were necessary in men holding the higher appointments than had been necessary in the earlier days of the settlement. The following remarks in a general letter from the Court respecting the appointment of a Mr. Higginson to be Second Member of Council are worthy of preservation. They are as applicable now as they were two centuries ago. It is difficult perhaps to say who penned them; but from all that is known of Mr. Josiah Child, it might be safely inferred that he was the author:—

"Let none of you think much or grudge at the speedy advancement of Mr. Higginson. We do not do it out of any partiality to him, for he has no relation here to speak for him, nor ever had the ambition to think of such a thing himself; neither have we done it out of any ill feeling or disrespect to any others now being of our Council, but sincerely as we apprehend for the public good; knowing him to be a man of learning, and competently well read in ancient histories of the Greeks and Latins, which with a good stock of natural parts, only can render a man fit for Government and Political Science, martial prudence, and other requisites for ruling over a great city. This, we say, with some experience of the world and knowledge of the laws and customs of nations, can alone qualify men for such a Government, and for treaties of peace or war, or commerce with foreign Princes. It is not being bred a boy in India, or studying long there and speaking the language, understanding critically the trade of the place, that is sufficient to fit a man for such a command as the Second of Fort St. George is, or may be in time; though all these qualifications are very good in their kind, and essentially necessary to the well carrying on of the trade; and little science was not necessary formerly, when we were in the state of mere trading merchants. But the case is altered from that, since his Majesty has been pleased, by his Royal Charters and during his Royal will and pleasure, to form us into the condition of a Sovereign State in India, that we may

Qualifications for a Second in Council.

offend, or defend ourselves, and punish all that injure us in India as the Dutch do.

Difficulties between the Directors and the Council.

"The great trouble we labour under is, that you cannot get out of your old forms, and your cavilling way of writing, or perverting or misconstruing, procrastinating or neglecting our plain and direct orders to you; as if you were not a subordinate but a co-ordinate power with us; which has and will (till you conform to our known minds and intentions) force us to make more changes in your Council than anything else could have induced us to; of which we hope we shall have no more hereafter, but that your well understanding and performance of our orders will cause us to change the style of our letters to you, as we hoped to have done before this, for which we more earnestly desire a fit occasion than you can yourselves."

Form of Municipal Government: Natives mixed with Europeans.

The Court of Directors at this period were anxious to form a municipal corporation, in which natives were mixed with English freemen. The question is an interesting one. The following paragraphs are extracted from the original instructions sent out from England :—

"If you could contrive a form of a corporation to be established, of the Natives mixed with some English freemen, for aught we know some public use might be made thereof; and we might give the members some privileges and pre-eminencies by Charter under our seal, that might please them (as all men are naturally with a little power); and we might make a public advantage of them, without abating essentially any part of our dominion when we please to exert it. And it is not unlikely that the heads of the several castes, being made Aldermen and some others Burgesses, with power to choose out of themselves yearly their Mayor, and to tax all the inhabitants for a Town Hall, or any public buildings for themselves to make use of,—your people would more willingly and liberally disburse five shillings towards the public good, being taxed by themselves, than sixpence imposed by our despotical power (notwithstanding they shall submit to when we see cause), were Government to manage such a society, as to make them proud of their honour and preferment, and yet only ministerial, and subservient to the ends of the Government, which under us is yourselves.

"We know this can be no absolute platform for you. You may make great alterations according to the nature of the place and the people, and the difference of laws, customs, and almost everything else, between England and India; but this will serve as a foundation from whence to begin your considerations and debates concerning this affair, which will require great wisdom and much thinking and foresight, to create such a Corporation in Madras, as will be beneficial to the Company and place, without the least diminution of the sovereign power his Majesty has entrusted us with, and which we are resolved to exercise there during his Majesty's royal pleasure and confidence in us." Discretionary powers.

All this while, however, Madras was exposed to great perils. The English were often threatened by the Mahrattas. They were also threatened by the Moghuls, who had conquered the Sultan of Golkonda and were taking possession of all his dominions in the Dekhan and Peninsula as far south as the river Koleroon. Madras in danger.

The following extracts will serve to show the early relations between the English and the Moghuls and Mahrattas. It should be explained that the Sivaji, here mentioned, was not the celebrated founder of the Mahratta Empire; for he had died as far back as 1680. The name was applied to his son Ram Raja, who was generally known as Sivaji, and sometimes as the "New Sivaji." Relations between the English and the Moghuls and the Mahrattas.

Saturday, 29th October 1687.—"Having received a letter from Potty Khan, commissioned by the Mogul to be Souba- Moghuls capture Golkonda. Madras submits to the Moghul.

dar of this part of the country, and Governor of Chingleput Fort as formerly, who advises us that the Mogul has certainly taken Golconda Castle, and the Sultan prisoner; and that all the considerable Forts and Towns in this country have already admitted the Mogul's colours and government, the Towns of Pulicat and St. Thomé, our nearest neighbours, having also submitted thereto; he also intimating to us the ceremony and solemnity that was generally performed at the news of the conquest, implicitly desiring and expecting the same from us; which being a matter of no great weight or charge, and may oblige them, and the neglect do us a prejudice:—It is agreed and ordered that the servant that brought the letter be presented with perpetuanos, and that 15 guns be fired at the delivery of the President's letter to them, and 20 marcalls of paddy given among the poor, in respect to their customs in such cases."

Application of a Moghul's Life Guardsman.

Saturday, 7th January 1688.—This evening the Right Honorable Company's Chief Merchant acquainted the President that one of the Mogul's Life Guards, sent down into these parts to receive his rents, desired to wait upon him to-morrow; but doubting he might be too prying and inquisitive of the garrison, the President excused his coming then, as being Sunday, and desired it may be at nine this night. Three other Members of Council were sent for and were present at his coming, when after a long discourse of the Court and Government, he declared the occasion of his coming was, that he had received about a lakh of rupees and 6000 pagodas for the Mogul's account, and had left it at Poonamallee; but in regard Sivaji's flying army was foraging those parts and robbing and plundering, desired our assistance, supply him with 300 horses, 500 soldiers and 500 peons to guard it as far as Kistna River; which he pressed hard, and that it would be most acceptable to the King (Aurungzeb). But the Governor considering the unreasonableness and dangerous consequence of undertaking such a charge, or intermeddling with things of that nature, returned him for answer, that we should be always ready to serve the Mogul, but that he well knew Sivaji's forces, and that he had lately taken three Forts and a hundred Towns very near us, and done many other mischiefs in the country, and that this place was also threatened by him, and that he was within twenty-four hours of us: therefore we could not spare our forces from our guard. Besides, that three or four hundred horse would signify little to Sivaji's three or four thousand in the field, though we feared not ten times so many here; but there it would turn the King Aurungzeb's money and our people into great danger. Thereupon desired him (the Mogul's Life Guard) to consider well of it. Whereupon he desired permission to bring it into Town; but hearing of our war in Bengal he requested that the President would give him his word and hand that he and his treasure should be safe, and have liberty to carry it away when he thought convenient. Which being agreed to by all, he was told by the President that the Town was free to all persons, and that no prejudice should be done to him by the English, but that they should fare as we did, and that he might choose what place he pleased to reside in; desiring him to send no more people than necessary, and those to be sober and civil. Whereupon he was dismissed with rosewater and betel, and seemed pleased with the discourse and the entertainment."

Friday, 13th January.—" Letters last night advise that Sivaji's forces had plundered Conjeveram, killed about 500 men, destroying the Town, and put the inhabitants to flight, dispersing themselves about the country, and many of them run hither; and about twelve this day came a letter from Chingleput advising the Governor that they had certain news from the Mahratta camp, that they had drawn out a party of about 2000 horse and 5000 foot under the command of a General, to assault this place, giving them encouragement that the plunder should be their own. Upon which advice the Governor and Council ordered that the Portuguese and Gentoos [*i. e.*, Hindus] should be summoned to their arms; one man from each family that had two therein, and

Mahratta ravages.

two from each family that had six and many therein, from 15 to 60 years of age."

Affairs at Golkonda.

Sunday, 6th May 1688.—"Letters from Mr. Chardin at Golconda to the Governor, of April last, give the following account. That the Mogul would free his son Shah Allum from his long confinement, but the Prince generously refused it except he would also enlarge Abul Hassan, the Sultan of Golconda, because he (the Prince) was instrumentally the ruin of the Sultan; having formerly engaged his word that neither the Mogul, nor he, should ever come with power to trouble him; and that he would rather choose to lose his life, than break his faith and word with the Sultan of Golconda, which was confirmed by his faith. That Sivâji's troops, joined with Siddee Masson's, are within six leagues of Golconda burning and destroying all before them, they expect them there in a little time. That Nabob Rowalloo Khan had sent his jewels and treasure into the castle, and he and his family are on the following thereof. That there are no soldiers in the Fort (of Golconda), nor provisions fit to withstand an enemy, so that if the enemy comes, he may with great facility take the Fort. That the Dutch and the French are much in the Mahratta's favour, and all roads are full of robbers. That the King of Persia marcheth in person with a great army after Sultan Akbar,[1] to give him help, in case the 60,000 horsemen he hath already sent be not sufficient; and sworn upon his beard that he will set him upon the Indostan throne."

Moghul negotiations.

Monday, 18th March.—"Letters from the Mogul's Dewan [*i. e.*, Finance Minister] wherein he descants upon the smallness of our rent and present, in consideration of the great profits and revenues we made of the place, which now was under the Mogul's dominion, and therefore not to be as in the Sultan of Golconda's time. His chief design herein being to get a great present from us, which being well considered of, it is resolved not to concede to, since it can do us little kindness and may encourage their exactions.

[1] Akbar was a rebel son of Aurungzeb, who had fled to Persia.

"The Dewan's messenger, a great Moorman that was sent with the letter and to discourse more particularly in this occasion, was sent for and civilly treated; who, after many stories and magnifying his Master's interest and power in the Mogul's Court and this country; the President told him that we were and should be very desirous to continue the Dewan's friendship, which we hope he would not deny us, in consideration of the many great advantages our settlement and trade brought to the country; and that he was misinformed of our profits by it, the Revenues not defraying half the charge we were at in maintaining it and the poor; however it was our own, given us by the grant of several sovereigns, and solely raised and built by the Right Honorable Company's charge from a barren sand; which we should defend against all opposers of our right; and so dismissed the Moor with calmer thoughts and expectations than he brought."

Presents to the Mahratta Raja.

Monday, 4th December 1689.—"Having received certain advice that Rama Raja, king of the Mahrattas, is come over land from his kingdom and army at Poona to the government and castle at Ginjee, and that the French and Dutch have already sent persons with considerable presents to congratulate him into the country, each reported to be to the amount of nearly 1400 pagodas; and it being also expected that we should likewise pay our respects to him in the same nature, as well for the favourable assistance done the Right Honorable Company at Bombay, as also for the protection of our Garrison and trade in his country; and though he may expect to be visited by one of our Council, yet lest that should give suspicion to the Mogul government and army in these parts and exasperate them against us, which they seem now inclined to from the late news and troubles at Bombay:—we therefore conclude it more safe and expedient that the Chief of Conimere,[1] with a suitable retinue, do go and visit Rama Raja at Ginjee, with a present from thence, wherein not much to exceed the amount of pagodas 600. Since the French circum-

[1] Conimere was a small English factory near Ginjee or Jinjee. It was withdrawn shortly afterwards.

stances and ours in those parts are different, where they having their chief residence and settlement in that government, and lately built a considerable Fort at Pondicherry."

Mahrattas besiege Pondicherry.

Tuesday, 10th December 1689.—"This day came news from Conimere that the Mahrattas had besieged the French at Pondicherry, demanding great sum of money from them, notwithstanding they had lately received a considerable present from them; and that the Conimere Government and the Dewan's peons have likewise been very pressing with our merchants there for 1,000 or 500 pagodas a man loan from them."

Moghul Carnatic and Mahratta Carnatic.

The country between the rivers Kistna and Koleroon is known by the general name of the Carnatic. Politically it was divided into a northern and a southern region, which may be distinguished as the Moghul Carnatic and the Mahratta Carnatic. The Moghul Carnatic had been previously a province of Golkonda; it had now become a province of the Moghul; it included the English settlement at Madras. The Mahratta Carnatic comprised the southern region which had been conquered by Sivají the Mahratta; it included the French settlement at Pondicherry.

Frontier fortress of Ginjee or Jinjí.

The frontier between Moghul and Mahratta dominion was formed at this period by the celebrated fortress of Ginjee or Jinjí. This notable fortress was seated on three precipitous hills or rocks about six hundred feet high. They were connected by lines of works, and enclosed a large triangular plain inside. For ages this fortress had been regarded as the strongest in the Carnatic. It had been the stronghold of the old Rajas of Chola. In 1677 it had been captured by the first Sivají.

In 1689, as already seen, it was in the possession of his son Ram Raja. It was the frontier fortress of the Mahrattas against the Moghuls.

Zulfikar Khan, first Nawab of the Carnatic.

In 1690 Zulfikar Khan commanded the Moghul army in the Carnatic. He laid siege to Jingí. A rebellion broke out in the Moghul army. Mr. Elihu Yale was Governor of Madras. He supplied Zulfikar Khan with powder and rendered other services. As a reward he obtained a firman from the Moghul general, confirming the English Company in the possession of all their settlements in Golkonda territory and Jinjí territory.

English settlement at Fort St. David.

In 1691 the Mahrattas were still masters of Jinjí. Ram Raja was sovereign over the whole country from Jinjí to the river Koleroon. So firmly was his power established, that the English purchased the site of Fort St. David[1] from the Mahratta Raja.

Siege of Jinjí by the Moghuls.

In 1692 Zulfikar Khan was still besieging Jinjí. He was accompanied by the youngest son of the Emperor Aurungzeb, named Kámbakhsh.[2] The Moghul army before Jinjí was in wretched plight. In December 1692 the Moghuls were defeated by the Mahrattas; many of the Moghul officers fled to Madras in disguise, and were well entertained.

Privations of the Moghuls.

In January 1693 an English soldier in the service of Zulfikar Khan returned to Madras. He

---

[1] Fort St. David was about a hundred miles to the south of Madras, and sixteen miles to the south of Pondicherry.

[2] This prince was known to our forefathers as Cawn Bux. In Herodotus and Xenophon the name appears as Cambyses.

brought a budget of news from the Moghul camp. Kámbakhsh had tried to go over to Ram Raja; he was seized and imprisoned by Zulfikar Khan. The camp was reduced to starvation from want of provisions. Zulfikar Khan made a peace for twenty-four hours with Ram Raja, and then retired to Wandiwash, leaving most of his baggage at the discretion of the Mahrattas.

Troubles at the Moghul camp.

In 1694 there was more news from the Moghul camp. Zulfikar Khan was quarrelling with his officers; it was said that Aurungzeb had sent orders to arrest him. The Moghul horse were plundering the country. Zulfikar Khan sent ten camels loaded with rupees to Ram Raja; they were intercepted by another Moghul general named Dáúd Khan. The Moghul officers were waiting an opportunity to arrest Zulfikar Khan. The Mahrattas had poisoned the water; they mixed milk hedges in some of the tanks, which killed abundance of people.

Mahratta successes.

In 1696 the Mahrattas were increasing in strength at Jinjí. The English at Fort St. David were warned to be on good terms with Ram Raja and his officers. The Mahrattas would certainly continue masters of the country, unless a considerable army was sent to reinforce Zulfikar Khan.

Zulfikar Khan straitened for money.

In the following March, Zulfikar Khan was in such straits for money that he sent to Madras to borrow a hundred thousand pagodas, equivalent to above thirty-five thousand pounds sterling. Mr. Nathaniel Higginson was Governor of Madras. He sent a present, but declined to lend the money. It was feared that Zulfikar Khan would resent the refusal. He, however, distributed a small sum amongst his army, and ostentatiously praised the liberality of the English at Madras. His only object had been to gain time; to amuse the soldiery with prospects of pay.

In the following November, it was feared that Zulfikar Khan would attack Madras. The following extract from the "Consultations" shows the feeling which prevailed at Fort St. George:— **Nawab expected to attack Madras.**

Thursday, 5th November 1696.—"It may be objected that it is very probable that the Nawab Zulfikar Khan cannot make war against this place without the King's [*i. e.*, Emperor's] order. But it may be also considered that the Nawab hath frequently done greater things than that, not only without but against the King's order. He has imprisoned Kámbakhsh the King's son; and though the King for a time did express resentment, yet there followed no effect. He hath been frequently ordered to take Ginjee, and it hath been in his power to do it and destroy all the Mahrattas in the country; but instead of that it appears plain that he hath joined council with them, and notwithstanding all the endeavours of his enemies, his father Vizier Asad Khan still prevails at court to keep the Nawab in his Government. And if he hath an interest to defend himself against so potent enemies, he can more easily baffle any complaints that we can make to the King. And it is in his power, if he be so inclined, to trouble and plague us, and to raise new impositions to the stopping all business; and it will not be in our power to procure a remedy at last, but by the same means that he and his officer now aim at, that is by a more considerable present."

In 1697 Zulfikar Khan had grown more formidable. He had defeated the Mahrattas near Tanjore. In 1698 he captured Jinjí. **Moghuls capture Jinjí.**

Nawab's friendship for the English.

Zulfikar Khan was one of the most distinguished grandees of his time. He was not only in command of the Moghul army in Jinjí, but exercised a powerful influence at court. He was the adopted son of Asad Khan, the Vizier. He was inclined to favour the English at Madras. He had already granted firmans confirming them in the possession of their territorial settlements in Golkonda and Jinjí. He now procured them firmans from the Vizier in the Emperor's name. The English were told that the firmans were ready on the payment of ten thousand pagodas, nearly four thousand pounds sterling. There was some demur, but the money was paid.

Dáúd Khan, second Nawab of the Carnatic.

In 1701 Zulfikar Khan was succeeded by Dáúd Khan as Nawab of the Carnatic. The English sent him letters and presents. A present valued at seventeen hundred pagodas was given in public; and a donation of three thousand rupees was given in private. The proceedings are sufficiently explained in the following extracts:—

Friday, 17th January 1706.—"Dáúd Khan being ordered by the King (Aurungzeb) Nawab of the Carnatic and Ginjee countries who has been several months on his march from the King's Camp. Two days ago we were advised, by people that we keep in his Camp to give us intelligence, that he was come to Arcot above four days' march from hence. We have had several letters of compliment from him, wherein he has desired sundry sorts of liquors, which accordingly have been sent him; and it being the custom of all Europeans to present all Nawabs and Governors when they come first to their Government in order to procure a confirmation of their privileges, besides at present we are carrying on a great investment here and at Fort St. David, and have a great deal of money spread up and down the country; further a few days ago we have advice from Surat by Armenian letters that our affairs are embroiled there; all of which induces us to consider of a considerable present for the Nawab and Dewan and their officers, and fitting persons to send with it; though before we heard the news from Surat, we intended to have sent two Englishmen, but altered our resolution, not knowing but that the troubles there may affect us here. So there being one Senor Nicholas Manuch, a Venetian and an inhabitant of ours for many years, who has the reputation of an honest man, besides he has lived at the King's Court upwards of thirty years, and was a servant to one of the Princes, and speaks the Persian language excellently well; for which reasons we think him the properest person to send at this time with our Chief Dubash Ramapah; and have unanimously agreed with the advice of all capable of giving it, to send the presents."

The Nawab sent back the presents. It was discovered that he was in a rage. He was bent upon having ten thousand pagodas like Zulfikar Khan. He threatened to ruin Madras and set up St. Thomé in its room. More demands for money.

Mr. Thomas Pitt was Governor of Madras. He is said to have been the grandfather of the famous Earl of Chatham. At any rate, he had the Chatham spirit. He utterly refused to pay the money. Ten thousand pagodas had been paid to Zulfikar Khan on account of the firmans; but no firmans were wanted from Nawab Dáúd Khan. A new Nawab might come every month, and demand ten thousand pagodas in like manner. Governor Pitt prepared to resist to the last; landed Resolution of Governor Pitt.

quotas of men out of the Europe ships; increased the train bands; and raised a force of Portuguese.

Nawab Dáúd Khan gives way.

Nawab Dáúd Khan began to give in. His officers expressed their fears that something would happen to their good friends the English unless the ten thousand pagodas were paid up. Governor Pitt was obdurate. At last the Nawab condescended to receive the present which he had previously refused. The Nawab now became friendly and cordial.

Governor Pitt's hospitality.

The following extracts from the "Proceedings" describe an entertainment that was given by Mr. Pitt to the famous Nawab Dáúd Khan:—

Preparation for entertaining the Nawab Dáúd Khan.

Friday, 11th July 1701.—"This day the Nawab sent us word that to-morrow himself, the Dewan, and Buxie would dine with us, and desired to know with what attendance we would admit him.[1] We would fain have evaded it, but the messenger he sent, pressing us so hard for a direct answer, we sent him word that the honour was too great to desire it, and greater than we expected; and if he pleased to come, he should be very welcome, and we be ready to receive him in the Garrison with one hundred horse. So all imaginable preparation is ordered to be made, and Messrs. Marshall and Meverell (two of the Council), attended with ten Files of Grenadiers, ordered to meet and receive him at Mr. Ellis's Garden to conduct him into town."

---

[1] These three officials—the Nawab, the King's Dewan, and the Buxie or Bakkshi—were appointed to every province in the Moghul empire.

The Nawab held the military command of the province, and enforced obedience to the laws.

The King's Dewan took charge of the revenues in the name of the King, Padishah, or Emperor. He paid the salaries of all the higher officials, including the Nawab. He remitted the surplus revenue to the Moghul Court as the King's due. Sometimes the Dewan also held the post of Nawab.

The Buxie, properly Bakhshi, was Paymaster of the Army, but often held the rank of General.

Saturday, 12th July 1701.—"About twelve this noon, the Nawab, the King's Dewan, and Buxie were conducted into town by Messrs. Marshall and Meverell; the streets being lined with soldiers from St. Thomé Gate up to the Fort, and the works that way manned with the Marine Company handsomely clothed with red coats and caps, and the curtain of the Inner Fort with our Train Bands, all which made a very handsome appearance. The Governor, attended with the Council, the Mayor, the Commanders of the Europe ships, and some of the Principal Freemen, received him (the Nawab) a little way out of the Gate of the Fort; and after embracing each other, the Governor presented him with a small ball of Ambergrease cased with gold and a gold chain to it, and then conducted him into the Fort and carried him up to his lodgings; when after sitting some time, the Nawab was pleased to pass very great compliments upon us, commending the place as to what he had hitherto seen of it, and gave us all assurance of his friendship; after which the Governor set by him two cases of rich cordial waters and called for wine, bidding him welcome by firing 21 pieces of Ordnance. Soon after the Governor drank to him the Moghul's health with 31 pieces of Ordnance; and the principal Ministers of State (our friends), as also the Nawab, Dewan, and Buxies, with 21 pieces of Ordnance each, all which healths the Nawab pledged in the cordial waters. So, soon after, the Dinner being ready, which was dressed and managed by a Persian inhabitant, the Governor conducted the Nawab into the Consultation room, which was very handsomely set out in all respects, the dinner consisting of about six hundred dishes, small and great, of which the Nawab, Dewan, and Buxie, and all that came with him, eat very heartily, and very much commended their entertainment. After dinner they were diverted with the dancing wenches. The Nawab was presented with cordial waters, French brandy, and embroidered China quilts, all which he desired. The Dewan, upon his promising us a Perwanna, had a Ruby Ring. The Buxie had one likewise offered him, but refused it, and seemed all day out of humour, occasioned, as

The Dinner.

we are informed, by some words that had passed this day between the Nawab, Dewan, and him before they came hither.

Return to St. Thomé.

"About six in the evening they returned to St. Thomé; the Governor and Council, and gentlemen in town, with the Commanders of the Europe ships, waiting on them without the Gate of the Fort, where they mounted their horses and were attended by Messrs. Marshall and Meverell to the place they received them, and at their going out of St. Thomas's Gate were saluted with 31 pieces of Ordnance.

Nawab proposes going on board the English ships.

"Messrs. Marshall and Meverell returning, acquainted the Governor that the Nawab desired to-morrow morning to go aboard one of the Europe ships, and in order thereto that six Mussoolas [*i. e.*, Mussoola boats] might be sent to Triplicane; which was accordingly done, and the English ships' boats ordered to attend him."

How prevented.

Sunday, 12th July 1701.—"About seven o'clock this morning Messrs. Marshall and Meverell went to Triplicane, in order to wait on the Nawab aboard the English ships, and the Commanders went off to receive him, but the Nawab having been very drunk over night, was not in a condition to go, and deferred it till to-morrow morning.

"The Breakfast we intended aboard ship for the Nawab was sent to St. Thomé, which he accepted very kindly."

Proposed visit to the Company's Garden; also prevented.

Tuesday, 15th July 1701.—"This morning the Nawab sent word to the Governor that he would make him a visit at the Company's Garden; whereupon Narrain was sent to endeavour to divert him from it, which if he could not do, that then to advise the time of his coming. So Narrain about twelve at noon sent to the Governor to acquaint that the Nawab was coming with a great detachment of horse and foot with all his elephants, and what he meant by it he could not imagine. So the Governor ordered immediately to beat up for the Train Bands and the Marine Company, and drew out a detachment of a hundred men under Captain Seaton to attend him and those gentlemen of the Council who went to the Garden to receive the Nawab. But Narrain seeing the Nawab coming in such a manner, told him it would create a jealousy in the Governor, and desired him to halt until he sent the Governor word and received his answer. But before the answer came, the Nawab was got into a Portuguese Chapel very drunk and fell asleep, and as soon as waked, which was about four o'clock in the afternoon, he ordered his Camp to march towards the little Mount, where he pitched his tents, and sent to the Governor to excuse his not coming to the Garden, and desired him to send a dozen bottles of cordial waters, which were sent him."

About this time, the Emperor Aurunzeb took an extraordinary resolution against the different European settlements in India. Both he and his subjects had suffered heavy losses from the depredations of European pirates. Accordingly, he ordered that compensation for these losses should be made by the servants of the different European Companies. Extraordinary demands of Aurungzeb.

In the first instance, these demands were made on Surat and Bombay. Khafi Khan, the Moghul historian, has drawn up a narrative from a Moghul point of view. He, moreover, records his own experiences of the English at Bombay. The narrative may prove an interesting introduction to the story of the proceedings of the Moghuls in the Carnatic, as told in the Madras records :— Moghul ideas of Europeans.

"Every year one of the Emperor's ships went from Surat to the house of God at Mecca. There was no larger ship at Surat. It carried Indian goods to Mocha and Jedda. It brought back to Surat fifty-two lakhs of rupees in gold and silver, or more than half a million sterling. Ibrahim Khan was captain. It carried eighty guns and four hundred muskets, besides other implements of war. Moghul ships.

English pirates. "This royal ship had come within eight or nine days of Surat, when an English ship came in sight, of much smaller size, and nothing a third or fourth of the armament. When it came within gunshot, the royal ship fired a gun at her. By ill luck the gun burst, and three or four men were killed by its fragments. About the same time, a shot from the enemy struck and damaged the mainmast, on which the safety of the vessel depends. The Englishmen perceived this, and being encouraged by it, bore down to attack, and drawing their swords, jumped on board their opponent. The Christians are not bold in the use of the sword, and there were so many weapons on board the royal vessel, that if the captain had made any resistance they must have been defeated. But as soon as the English began to board, Ibrahim Khan ran down into the hold. There were some Turkí girls whom he had bought in Mocha to be his concubines. He put turbans on their heads and swords in their hands, and excited them to fight. These fell into the hands of the enemy, who soon became perfect masters of the ship. They transferred the treasure and many prisoners to their own ship. When they had laden their ship, they brought the royal ship to shore near one of their settlements, and busied themselves for a week searching for plunder, stripping the men and dishonouring the women both old and young. They then left the ship, carrying off the men. Several honourable women threw themselves into the sea to preserve their chastity, and some others killed themselves with knives and daggers.

Moghul threats. "This loss was reported to Aurangzeb, and the news-writers at Surat sent some rupees which the English have coined at Bombay, with a superscription containing the name of their impure King. Aurangzeb then ordered that the English factors who were residing at Surat should be seized. Orders were also given to Itimad Khan, Superintendent of the port at Surat, to make preparations for besieging the fort of Bombay. The evils arising from the English occupation of Bombay were of long standing.

"The English were not at all alarmed at these threatenings. But they were more active than usual in building bastions and walls, and in blocking up the roads, so that in the end they made the place quite impregnable. Itimad Khan saw all these preparations, and came to the conclusion that there was no remedy, and that a struggle with the English would result only in a heavy loss to the customs revenue. He made no serious preparations for carrying the royal order into execution, and was not willing that one rupee should be lost to the revenue. To save appearances, he kept the English factors in confinement, but privately he endeavoured to effect an arrangement. After the confinement of their factors, the English, by way of reprisal, seized upon every Imperial Officer, wherever they found one, on sea or on shore, and kept them all in confinement. So matters went on for a long time. Preparations of the English.

"During these troubles I (Khafi Khan) had the misfortune of seeing the English of Bombay. I had purchased goods at Surat to the value of nearly two lakhs of rupees, and had to convey them along the sea shore through the possessions of the Portuguese and English. On arriving at Bombay, but while I was yet in the Portuguese territory, I waited ten or twelve days for an escort. The merchant for whom I acted had been on friendly terms with an Englishman, *i. e.*, the Governor of Bombay, and he had now written to the Englishman about giving assistance to the convoy. The Englishman sent out his vakeel [*i. e.*, messenger], very kindly inviting me to visit him. The Portuguese captain and my companions were averse to my going there with such valuable property. I, however, put my trust in God, and went to the Englishman. I told the vakeel that if the conversation turned upon the capture of the ship, I might have to say unpleasant things, for I would speak the truth. The vakeel advised me to say freely what I deemed right, and to speak nothing but the truth. Khafi Khan's visit to Bombay.

"When I entered the fortress (*i. e.*, at Bombay) I observed that from the gate there was on each side of the road a Bombay Castle.

line of youths of twelve or fourteen years of age, well-dressed, and having excellent muskets on their shoulders. Every step I advanced, young men with sprouting beards, handsome and well-clothed, with fine muskets in their hands, were visible on every side. As I went onwards, I found Englishmen standing, with long beards, of similar age, and with the same accoutrements and dress. After that I saw musketeers, young men well-dressed and arranged, drawn up in ranks. Further on, I saw Englishmen with white beards, clothed in brocade, with muskets on their shoulders, drawn up in two ranks, and in perfect array. Next I saw some English children, handsome and wearing pearls on the borders of their hats. In the same way, on both sides, as far as the door of the house where he (the Governor) abode, I found drawn up in ranks on both sides nearly seven thousand musketeers, dressed and accoutred as for a review.

Bombay Governor.

"I then went straight up to the place where he was seated on a chair. He wished me 'good day,' his usual form of salutation, then he rose from his chair, embraced me, and signed for me to sit down on a chair in front of him. After a few kind enquiries, he enquired why his factors had been placed in confinement. I gave him to understand that it was on account of the capture of the royal ship. He replied, 'those who have an ill-feeling against me cast upon me the blame for the faults of others; how do you know that this deed was the work of my men?' I told him that 'there were English on board that were in his service.' He said those Englishmen had deserted him and turned Mussulmans, and afterwards had gone away and joined the pirates. I thanked him for his explanation."

---

[1] Khafi Khan translated by Professor Dowson in Elliot's History of India, Volume VII. The Professor has done good service in translating this work. I had formed a poor opinion of Khafi Khan for the undeserved praise he bestowed on Shah Jehan. But other contemporary writers of undoubted integrity, have taken the same favourable view out of pity for the misfortunes of that ill-fated sovereign. Professor Dowson's translation proves that Khafi Khan is at least honest, and not a court scribe. Many of the new facts he has brought to light are confirmed by European authorities.

The proceedings of the Moghuls at Madras were of an equally violent character. The following extracts from a letter, addressed by Governor Pitt to Nawab Dáúd Khan, explains the nature of Aurungzeb's demand from a European point of view :— Demands of the Moghul on Governor Pitt.

"To His Excellency Dáúd Khan.

"This morning our Moollah came to me, who shews me the copy of an order said to be from the great Asad Khan, charging all Europeans with piracy, and that by a writing they are answerable for the same. We have been informed that there was such a writing extorted from the English, French, and Dutch at Surat, which amongst us is of no value, being forced from us; nor will the same be regarded more particularly by us, who have been so great sufferers ourselves; and besides, our King have not been at so little charge as two hundred thousand pagodas to extirpate those villains.

"Your Excellency said to the Moollah that you care not to fight us, but are resolved if possible to starve us by stopping all provisions. We can put no other construction on this, than declaring a war with all Europe nations, and accordingly we shall act. Dated in Fort St. George, 6th February, 1702.

THOMAS PITT."

Next day Madras was in some trepidation. The following extract from the "Consultations" shows the agitation which prevailed amongst the natives :— Commotions at Madras.

Saturday, 7th.—"This day the Nawab's forces plundered our out-towns of some straw and paddy, and drove away the inhabitants; and the poor people that lived in our suburbs and Black-town, being so intimidated by the approach of the Moors army, and the preparations we made for our defence, several thousands deserted us; and the farmers of the tobacco and betel complaining that they could not collect the revenues by reason of these troubles, and more particularly betel being stopped, which would in a few days occasion great clamours amongst the inhabitants; so that for the encouragement of all to steal it in, we have ordered that the farmers cease from collecting these revenues till the troubles are over."

Remonstrance of Governor Pitt.

The following extract is taken from another letter of Governor Pitt to Nawab Dáúd Khan :—

"We have lived in this country nearly one hundred years, and never had any ill designs, nor can Your Excellency, or any one else, charge us with any; and it is very hard that such unreasonable orders should be issued out against us only, when they relate to all Europeans, none excepted as I can perceive; and whether it be for the good of your kingdom to put such orders in execution, Your Excellency is the best judge.

"We are upon the defensive part and so shall continue, remembering the unspeakable damages you have not only done us in our estates, but also in our reputation, which is far more valuable to us, and will be most resented by the King of our nation."

Threats of Nawab Dáúd Khan.

The following extracts tell their own story :—

Thursday, 12th February 1702.—"This day the Governor summoned a General Council to acquaint them with what message the Moollah had brought from the Nawab at St. Thomé, which was such rhodomantade stuff that we could hardly give credit to it. He demanded possession of our Mint; that his people should come into our Town and view our Godowns, and take an account of our estates; and that we should put one hundred men of theirs in possession of the Black town; and that then he would write to the King (Aurungzeb) that we had obeyed his order, and make an attestation in our behalfs, unto which we must wait an answer. Otherwise he would fall in upon us, and make us surrender by force of arms, and cut us all off. He also told the Moollah that if we were merchants, what need had we of such a Fortification and so many Guns; which is an argument which has been much used by the New

Company's servants, since their dropping into this country; and, as we have been informed, the same has been urged to the King and the great men of the Kingdom at the Camp.

"It was agreed that no answer be returned to this message, as not being worth our taking notice of, but tacitly to defy their threats."

Siege of Madras. February to April.

Wednesday, 8th April 1702.—"The Nawab and his army having lain here a considerable time, stopping all trade and provisions, and very much increasing the Company's charges, which has not only been very prejudicial to the Company in their trade and revenues, but likewise to the whole place in general; and finding now that they decline very much in their demands, which we impute to the advice they have that the merchants' demands at Surat are satisfied; we have thought fit, to prevent greater inconveniences, to employ our Selim Beague, an inhabitant of this town, to offer them the sum of 18,000 Rupees; provided they deliver up to our merchants the goods and money they have seized belonging to this place and Fort St. David; which sum of 18,000 Rupees, considering the very long time they have been here, we believe will be no inducement for him to come again, or any of his successors hereafter; and accordingly it is agreed that the President pays the said sum upon the terms aforesaid, and not otherwise."

The English offer terms.

Sunday, 3rd May 1702.—"The Nawab and King's Officers having lain before this place upwards of three months, and interdicted all manner of trade and provisions coming into this place; the latter growing dear make it uneasy to the inhabitants; and there having been some overtures of accommodation from the enemy, which the Governor has been daily importuned by all sorts of people to accept of, occasions his summoning this General Council; whom he acquainted with every particular as entered after this consultation. Which being debated, it was agreed much by the majority that the proposals be accepted of; and that the same be negociated and settled by Chinna Serapa and Narrain, acquainting the Governor from time to time what progress they make therein."

Dáúd Khan raises the siege.

"Whereas by a late order from the King all trading and provisions with the English has been interdicted at Fort St. George and Fort St. David, we the Nawab and Dewan do now reverse the said order, and do grant them free liberty to trade in all places as heretofore they have done, without let or molestation; and to confirm the same to our people, do promise to give them our perwannas directed to all Foujdars. Killadars, Corrodees, Deshais, Destramokys, Poligars, and inhabitants of all places whereto they trade, to be carried by our Chobdars.

"That whatever moneys, etc., have been taken away, either upon the roads or in towns, or in any place whatever, said moneys, etc., shall be returned to the value of a cowry, and our merchants set at liberty.

"That the Villages, and all that has been taken from them, shall be returned, and due satisfaction made for all damages according to account.

"And whereas their trade has been stopped by the King's order, goods and moneys seized, it is requisite that an order from the King be procured to revoke the former, which we oblige ourselves to do; and upon compliance with the aforesaid articles, twenty thousand Rupees is to be paid by the English to the Nawab, and five thousand privately to the Dewan; of which sums half is to be paid upon clearing the Villages, returning the gram they have there seized, taking off the stop on trade and provisions, and sending the Chobdars to the aforesaid officers with perwannas to all parts of the country; whereby to order our trade to be as free as formerly, and to restore all goods which were seized, and now lie in St. Thomé; and when the whole business is completed the English to pay the other half."

Tuesday, 5th May 1702.—"The siege raised!"

Death of William III. Proclamation of Queen Anne.

William the Third died on the 8th March 1702. The news did not reach Madras until the following

September, when Queen Anne was proclaimed with the following ceremonies:—

Thursday, 17th September.—"In pursuance to an order of Consultation, the flag was early this morning hoisted, and at eight o'clock was lowered, when there was two volleys small shot and one hundred cannon discharged by the half minute glass, for the death of our late gracious King William the Third of blessed memory. Then the flag was again hoisted up, when the Mayor and all the Aldermen in their gowns on horseback, with twelve Halberteers and a Company of Grenadiers marching before them, proclaimed our gracious Queen Anne at the Fort Gate, Town Hall, Sea Gate, and Choultry Gate, with many huzzas and great demonstration of joy, with three volleys small shot and one hundred and one pieces of cannon discharged. And in the evening the Governor, attended by all the Gentlemen of the Council, with the Mayor and Aldermen and several other gentlemen in palanquins and horseback, to the Company's Bowling Garden, where there was a handsome treat provided; all Europeans of fashion in the city being invited to the same, where they drank the Queen's health, and prosperity to Old England, with many others."

The same year a terrible disaster befell the Emperor Aurungzeb:— Destruction of a Moghul Army.

Wednesday, 4th November.—"The President is advised from Masulipatam that the Moghul is pitching his Camp near some great mountains, from which of a sudden came so great fall of waters, that it swept away about 150,000 people, with elephants, horses, camels, and baggage, he himself narrowly escaping." [This event is noticed by Elphinstone, who, however, reduces the number of people who perished to 12,000.]

Mr. Pitt was Governor of Madras from 1698 to 1709. During this period the native town was agitated by interminable quarrels between the right Right and left hands.

and left hand castes, about the streets in which they were respectively to live and celebrate their weddings. This antagonism between the two hands is peculiar to Southern India. The details are far too lengthy to be introduced here. It will suffice to say that rules were laid down for the prevention of all such disputes for the future.

Closer relations with Delhi.

The administration of Mr. Pitt is also distinguished by another circumstance. He succeeded in establishing friendly relations with the Moghul Court at Delhi. The circumstances were peculiar. Aurungzeb died in 1707. The event was followed by a terrible war between his sons. The elder gained the victory, but was fearful lest a younger brother should find a refuge in Madras, and make his escape to Persia. Accordingly a friendly letter was sent to Mr. Pitt, by an influential official named Zoudi Khan. The Moghul minister professed great kindness for the English and made a tender of his services to the Madras Governor. Mr. Pitt promptly asked for a firman confirming all the privileges which had been granted by Aurungzeb. The request was acceded to with equal promptitude. Shortly afterwards the prince who had caused all this anxiety was slain in battle.

Curious trade report, 1712.

The new Padishah died in the beginning of 1712. Fresh wars and revolutions broke out, which had a bad effect upon trade. The following extracts from a general letter sent by the Governor and Council at Madras to the Court of Directors in London furnishes some curious particulars respecting the changes in trade. The letter is dated 14th October 1712:—

"In obedience to your commands we shall lay before your Honours the best account we can get concerning the consumption of broad cloth and other manufactures in the Moghul's dominions. The coarse red and green broad cloth is chiefly used among the soldiers and ordinary Moormen for saddles, saddle cloths, sumpture cloth, covers, beds and cushions, for palankeens, carpets to sit upon, mantles to cover them from the rain and sometimes covering for their tents of pleasure. The fine broad cloth as scarlet, aurora, some blue and yellow is used for the inside of tents, for vests or mantles in the rainy season among the great men; covering cloths for the elephants and hackarys; cloth to hang round their drums; for shoulder and waist belts, scabbards to their swords and daggers; for slippers and for covers, beds and pillows, and for palankeens. The embossed cloth is used to hang round the bottom on the inside of the great men's tents three feet high; for spreading to sit upon, and cushions to lean against; and for cloths to cover the elephants and horses. Perpetuanos are only used among the meaner sort of people for caps, coats, and covering cloths to sleep in during the rains. Madras trade in 1712.

"And now we are upon this subject, we must inform your Honours that at least nine-tenths of the woollen manufactures vended in these parts is among the Moors; the Hindus making very little or no use of them. The greatest consumption is in the Moghul's camp, which, when at Lahore or Delhi, is supplied wholly from Surat and Persia; but when at Agra, partly from Surat and partly from Bengal by way of Patna, from which ports the conveyance to the camp is easy and safe. But what is disposed of hereabouts is dispersed among the Nabob's flying armies in the Carnatic country, Bijapore and Golcondah, seldom reaching so far as Aurungabad, because the carriage is very changeable, and the roads are difficult and dangerous to pass. When King Shah

Alum[1] came down to Golcondah with his army in the year 1708 to destroy his brother Kam Bakhsh, we immediately found a quicker vent than ordinary for our broad cloth; and indeed for all other sorts of goods consumed among them. And when Dáúd Khan was formerly Nawab of these parts, he always kept a good body of horse in pay, which obliged the neighbouring Governors to do the same, being always jealous of each other. And among these horsemen by much the greatest quantity of our broad cloth then imported was consumed, the trade from this place to their camps being very considerable. But now our Dewan, who is Subah of all this country, seldom keeps above five hundred horse with him; and the Government in general being grown much weaker than in Aurungzeb's time, none of the great men keep up the number of horse allowed by the King, but apply the money to their own use; and this has brought a considerable damp to our trade in general, but more especially upon the sale of your manufactures. For we have not only lost the camp trade, but the roads are become impassable for want of these horsemen to scour them as usual; so that the merchants are discouraged from coming down with their money and diamonds to buy up and carry away our Europe and other goods as formerly; and we cannot see any likelihood of better times till the Government is well settled and some active man employed on the Government of these parts."

Later records.

The Madras records of a later date contain little matter that will interest general readers. Between the years 1717 and 1720 a Mr. Collet was Governor. At this period the English at Madras possessed slaves in considerable numbers. Many kept slave girls, and two charity schools were built for the

---

[1] This King or Padishah is known in history by the name of Bahadur Shah. He was the son and successor of Aurungzeb.

children of these slaves. There are many allusions to these slaves in the records, but nothing of permanent interest. A good understanding prevailed between the English at Madras and the Nawab of Arcot, and on one occasion Mr. Collet had the honour of entertaining the minister of the Nawab, just as Mr. Pitt had entertained Dáúd Khan.

Mr. Collet's administration is also remarkable for a change in the marriage laws laid down by Mr. Streynsham Masters. The following extracts explain themselves:— Changes in marriage laws.

Thursday, 2nd April 1719.—"The President represents that the Portuguese priests of St. Thomé had very lately taken the liberty to marry some English people belonging to this city without leave; which practice he apprehended to be of dangerous consequence; many of the young Gentlemen in the Company's Service being of good families in England, who would be very much scandalized at such marriages as were like to be contracted here, without the consent of the President; particularly that one Crane, late chief Mate of ship "Falconbridge," was married to a Frenchman's daughter of this place on Sunday last; and in order to it renounced the Protestant religion, which he had professed all his life till within a few days before. The other was one Dutton, an ordinary fellow, who was married a week before at St. Thomé to Ann Ridley, whose father was formerly Governor of the West Coast. Her small fortune being in the hands of the Church, the minister, as one of her guardians, refused his consent; on which they went to St. Thomé, and found a priest to marry them there. The President adds that, to show his resentment of such a practice, he had ordered the Mettos not to suffer any of the Portuguese Padres belonging to St. Thomé to come into the English bounds. He further proposed to the Board to consider of some proper orders to be given for preventing the like practices for the future.

After some consideration, it was agreed that an order be published in the English and Portuguese languages, and put up in writing at the Sea Gate and at the Portuguese Church, that if any Christian inhabitant of Madras shall be married in this city, at St. Thomé, or elsewhere, without leave from the President; that if he be in the Company's service he shall be liable to such penalty as we shall think fit; but if the person so offending shall not be in the Company's service, and only a free merchant or inhabitant of the Town, he shall be expelled the English Government on the Coast of Coromandel. Also any parent consenting to, or promoting, such marriage, without leave as aforesaid, shall be liable to the like penalty of expulsion."

Monday, 6th April.—"The President informs the Board that on a full enquiry into the marriage of the Mate Crane, mentioned in last Consultation, he finds that the said Crane had been bred a Protestant, and continued to profess a Protestant religion till within a few days of his marriage; and then the woman whom he married refused to have the ceremony performed in the English Church, because all Roman Catholics married there are obliged to subscribe a declaration that they will bring up their children in the Protestant religion, by an order of Council dated the 25th of March 1680; and that on her refusal there to comply with that obligation, he had renounced the Protestant religion and declared himself a Roman Catholic in order to marry her. The President therefore proposed to the consideration of the Board, whether that order of Council, dated 25th of March 1680, should be repealed or not; which being freely debated, it was unanimously agreed to repeal the general order, for the following reasons.

"*First*, that the obligation is in its own nature unjust, and a violation of that natural right which all parents have to educate their children in that religion they think most acceptable to God. *Secondly*, that such a promise can be no obligation on the conscience of any person, being unlawful in itself. *Thirdly*, that the requiring such a promise may be attended with ill consequences, as in the instance now before us; the woman refusing to be married in the English Church for that reason only; the consequence of which was, Crane's renouncing the Protestant religion and declaring himself a Roman Catholic.

"Ordered that the Secretary acquaint the Honorable Company's Chaplain of the place in writing with the repeal of the aforesaid order, and that he is not any more to require such subscription."

"The President also acquaints the Board, that the severe methods which he had taken to show his resentment to the Portuguese priests of St. Thomé, for marrying any subject of this Government without his consent, had produced a very good effect; for that the Padre Governor at St. Thomé had sent him a very submissive letter or address, wherein he obliges himself, and those of his fraternity subject to him, not to marry any persons subject to this Government for the future, without asking his previous consent."

In the records of this period there is entered a curious will, which serves to illustrate the ideas of young Englishmen in those days. Charles Davers was the fourth son of Sir Robert Davers, Baronet. He arrived at Madras in 1717, being at that time eighteen years of age; he died in 1720, aged twenty-one. His salary was only five pounds a year, yet it would seem that he had engaged in several trading adventures. His desire to have his name and memory perpetuated is very striking. The will tells its own story:— Curious will, 1720.

Thursday, 22nd September 1720.—"In the name of God, Amen. I, Charles Davers, now of Fort St. George in East India, Merchant, being of sound and perfect mind and memory, do make and ordain this my last will and testament in manner and form following.

"Imprimis, I recommend my soul to God who gave it, hoping through the merits of a crucified Saviour to obtain a joyful resurrection; and my body I commit to the earth to be decently interred; and for all such worldly estates, as these which it has pleased God to bless me with, I give and bequeath as follows; viz.

"Imprimis, I leave unto the Charity School of this place 200 pagodas; and desire the boys belonging to this School may attend me to the place of burial. Item, I leave unto the Master and Mistress of said School 20 pagodas each for mourning. I wish all piety and learning may attend them, and that they may infuse the same into the children, by the help of our Blessed Lord and Saviour Jesus Christ, Amen.

"Item, I leave unto my friend Mr. Thomas Wright 20 pagodas for mourning. I wish all health may attend him in this world and happiness in the next.

"Item, I leave 200 pagodas for a tomb to be erected in the burial place in form as follows. Four large pillars, each to be six covids high, and six covids distance one from the other; the top to be arched, and upon each pillar a cherubim; and on the top of the arch the effigy of Justice. My body to be laid in the middle of the four pillars, with a handsome stone atop of me, raised about four feet; and this inscription in the stone:—'Here lyeth the body of Charles Davers, fourth son of Sir Robert Davers, Bart., who departed this life the———of——Anno Domini——aged—.' The four pillars to be encompassed in with iron rails, which are to go from pillar to pillar; and at every square, steps to be raised with stones, so as people may read the inscription.

"Item, I leave the Honorable Governor, Council, and Secretary of this place, each a gold ring of one pagoda and a half each value, with these words to be engraved in them, 'Charles Davers, obiit,' etc. To whom I wish all tranquillity, health, and prosperity.

"Item, I leave unto Dr. Pitchers, the sum of 30 pagodas in case I die of my present illness, and that I did not pay him before I died.

"Item, I leave unto my friend, Mr. Paul Foxley, 20 pagodas for mourning; to whom I wish all health in this world, and happiness in the next.

"Item, I leave unto the Minister that attend me 20 pagodas for a ring.

"Item, I leave unto my friend Mr. John Maubers 20 pagodas for mourning.

"Lastly, I leave my two trusty and beloved friends Mr. George Sittwel and Mr. Catesby Oadham, my two executors of this my last will and testament, and desire them to see me carried to the place of burial in the manner following, viz.

"My corpse to be carried from the Town Hall at seven o'clock at night. I desire that all the free merchants of my acquaintance to attend me in their palankeens to the place of burial; and as many of the Company's servants as I have had any intimacy within my life-time; that all that attend me may have scarves and hat-bands decent. I desire that Mr. Main, and the Charity boys, may go before my corpse, and sing a hymn; my corpse to be carried by six Englishmen or more if occasion; the minister and the rest of the gentlemen following. I desire of the Honorable Governor that I may have as many great guns fired as I am years old, which is now almost twenty-one. In case it is customary to pay the great guns firing I desire you to do it. I desire the favour of the Captain of the guard to attend me; and that you present him with a gold ring the same as the Governor and Council. And now as to my Estate. I have 1086 ounces of silver, which my father sent me out this year. I am concerned with Mr. Thomas Theobalds in a respondentia bond in the 'George' Brigantine. I have also an adventure with Captain James Hurdis, the prime cost being 72 pagodas and a half. I have at this time in my escritore about 100 pagodas, besides clothes and linen; an account of which I always keep in my escritore. I desire of my two executors to accept of 30 pagodas each for mourning; and each a ring of 15 pagodas value, with my name and time of death engraved upon it.

"After my corpse is buried, which I desire may be done very handsomely, the remainder of my estate I desire may be laid out in rice, and be given to the poor at the burial place, as long as it lasts. This I declare to be my last will and testament.

CHARLES DAVERS."

Captain Hamilton at Madras.

Whilst Mr. Collet was Governor of Madras a certain sea captain, named Alexander Hamilton, paid a visit to Madras. Captain Hamilton was a character in his way. From 1688 to 1723, a period of thirty-five years, he was engaged in trading and travelling by sea and land between the Cape of Good Hope and the Island of Japan. In 1727 he published what he called "A new Account of the East Indies," in two volumes octavo. His account of Madras is an interesting supplement to the information supplied from the Madras records. It is given in his own words:—

Site of Madras.

"Fort St. George or Madras, or, as the Natives call it, China Patam, is a colony and city belonging to the English East India Company, situated in one of the most incommodious places I ever saw. It fronts the sea, which continually rolls impetuously on its shore, more here than in any other place on the coast of Chormondel. The foundation is in sand, with a salt-water river on its back side, which obstructs all springs of fresh-water from coming near the town, so that they have no drinkable water within a mile of them, the sea often threatening destruction on one side, and the river in the rainy season threatening inundations on the other. The sun from April to September is scorching hot; and if the sea-breezes did not moisten and cool the air when they blow, the place could not possibly be inhabited. The reason why a Fort was built in that place is not well accounted for; but tradition says, that the gentleman, who received his orders to build a Fort on that coast, about the beginning of King Charles II's reign after his Restoration, for protecting the Company's trade, chose that place to ruine the Portuguese trade at St. Thomas. Others again alledge, and with more probability, that the gentleman aforesaid, which I take to be Sir William Langhorn, had a mistress at St. Thomas he was so enamoured of, that made him build there, that their interviews might be the more frequent and uninterrupted; but whatever his reasons were, it is very ill situated.[1] The soil about the city is so dry and sandy, that it bears no corn, and what fruits, roots and herbage they have, are brought to maturity by great pains and much trouble. If it be true, that the Company gave him power to settle a colony in any part of that coast that pleased him best, I wonder that he choosed not Cabelon, about six leagues to the southward, where the ground is fertile, and the water good, with the conveniency of a point of rocks to facilitate boats landing; or why he did not go nine leagues farther northerly, and settle at Policat on the banks of a good river, as the Dutch have done since, where the road for shipping is made easy by some sand banks, that reach three leagues off shore, and make the high turbulent billows that come rolling from the sea spend their force on those banks before they can reach the shore. The soil is good, and the river commodious, and convenient in all seasons. Now whether one of those places had not been more eligible, I leave to the ingenious and those concerned to comment on.[2]

Prosperity of Madras during the wars.

"However, the war carried on at Bengal and Bombay, by the English against the Moghul's subjects, from 1685 to 1689,

---

[1] It will have already been seen that this is mere local scandal. The site of the Fort was chosen in 1639 by a Mr. Day.

[2] Hamilton was only acquainted with the local gossip; he knew nothing of authentic history. Cabelon would not have been a fitting site for an English settlement; it was of the utmost importance to choose an island to keep off predatory horsemen. Again, Policat, properly Pulicat, was founded by the Dutch some years before the English founded Madras. At one time the English did settle at Pulicat, but left it on account of the Dutch.

made Fort St. George put on a better dress than he wore before; for the peaceable Indian merchants, who hate contention and war, came flocking thither, because it lay far from those incumberers of trade, and near the diamond mines of Golcondah, where there are, many times, good bargains to be made, and money got by our Governors. The black merchants resorting to our colony, to secure their fortunes, and bring their goods to a safe market, made it populous and rich, notwithstanding its natural inconveniencies. The town is divided into two parts. One where the Europeans dwell is called the White Town. It is walled quite round, and has several bastions and bulwarks to defend its walls, which can only be attacked at its ends, the sea and river fortifying its sides. It is about 400 paces long, and 150 paces broad, divided into streets pretty regular, and Fort St. George stood near its center. There are two Churches in it, one for the English and another for the Romish service. The Governor superintends both, and, in filling up vacancies in the Romish Church, he is the Pope's *Legate a latere* in spiritualities. There is a very good hospital in the town, and the Company's horse-stables are neat; but the old college, where a great many gentlemen factors are obliged to lodge, is ill kept in repair.

Town-hall and Corporation.

"They have a Town-hall, and underneath are prisons for debtors. They are, or were a corporation, and had a Mayor and Aldermen to be chosen by the free Burgers of the town; but that scurvy way is grown obsolete, and the Governor and his Council or party fix the choice. The city had laws and ordinances for its own preservation, and a court kept in form, the Mayor and Aldermen in their gowns, with maces on the table, a clerk to keep a register of transactions and cases, and attornies and solicitors to plead in form, before the Mayor and Aldermen; but, after all, it is but a farce, for, by experience, I found that a few pagodas rightly placed, could turn the scales of justice to which side the Governor pleased, without respect to equity or reputation.

Mayor's Court.

"In smaller matters, where the case, on both sides, is but weakly supported by money, then the Court acts judiciously, according to their consciences and knowledge; but often against law and reason, for the Court is but a Court of conscience, and its decisions are very irregular; and the Governor's dispensing power of annulling all that the Court transacts, puzzles the most celebrated lawyers there to find rules in the statute laws.

"They have no martial law, so they cannot inflict the pains of death any other ways than by whipping or starving; only for piracy they can hang; and some of them have been so fond of that privilege, that Mr. Yale hanged his groom (Cross) for riding two or three days' journey off to take the air; but, in England, he paid pretty well for his arbitrary sentence. And one of a later date, *viz.*, the orthodox Mr. Collet, hanged a youth who was an apprentice to an officer on board of a ship, and his master going a-pirating, carried his servant along with him; but the youth ran from them the first opportunity he met with, on the Island of Junk-Ceylon, and informed the master of a sloop, which lay in a river there, that the pirates had a design on his sloop and cargo, and went armed, in company with the master, to hinder the approach of the pirates, and was the first that fired on them—yet that merciful man was inexorable, and the youth was hanged. **Law at Madras.**

"That power of executing pirates is so strangely stretched that if any private trader is injured by the tricks of a governor, and can find no redress; if the injured person is so bold as to talk of *Lex talionis*, he is infallibly declared a pirate. **Pirates.**

"In the year 1719 I went on a trading voyage to Siam, on the foundation of a treaty of commerce established in the year 1684 between King Charles and the King of Siam's ambassador at London; but, in 1718, Mr. Collet sent one Powney his ambassador to Siam, with full power to annul the old treaty, and to make a new one detrimental to all British subjects, except those employed by Collet himself. It was stipulated, that all British subjects that had not Collet's letter, should be obliged to pay eight per cent. new customs, and measurage for their ship, which come to about five hundred **Hamilton's voyage to Siam.**

pounds sterling for a ship of 300 tuns, to sell their cargoes to whom they pleased, but the money to be paid into the King's cash that he might deliver goods for it at his own prices, whether proper for their homeward markets or no. I coming to Siam, sent my second supercargo up to the city, with orders to try the market, and hire an house for the use of the cargo and ourselves. He could not get a boat to bring him back, before the ship arrived at Bencock (*i. e.*, Bankok), a castle about half-way up, where it is customary for all ships to put their guns ashore. So then being obliged to proceed with the ships to the city, I understood the conditions of the new treaty of commerce, which I would, by no means, adhere to, but desired leave to be gone again. They used many persuasions to make me stay, but to no purpose, unless I might trade on the old and lawful treaty. They kept me from the beginning of August to the latter end of December, before they would let me go, and then I was obliged to pay measurage before they parted with me.

Hamilton's grievance.

"I wrote my grievance to Mr. Collet, complaining of Powney's villanous transactions, not seeming to know that they were done by Collet's order, and let some hints fall of *Lex talionis*, if I met with Powney conveniently, which so vexed Mr. Collet that he formally went to the Town-hall, and declared me a rank pirate, though I and my friends came off with above £3,000 loss.

"I should not have been so particular but that I saw some printed papers at London in 1725, that extolled his piety, charity, and justice in very high encomiums; but it must have been done by some mercenary scribbler that did not know him: but now he is dead, I will say no more of him.

Inhabitants of Black Town.

"The Black Town at Madras is inhabited by Gentoos,[1] Mahometans, and Indian Christians, viz., Armenians and Portuguese, where there are temples and churches for each religion, every one being tolerated, and every one follows his proper employment. It was walled in towards the land when Governor Pitt ruled it. He had some apprehension that the

---

[1] The term Gentoo is applied in Madras to the Tamil-speaking Hindus who occupy the whole of the Carnatic plain in the Eastern Peninsula.

Moghul generals in Golconda might some time or other plunder it, so laying the hazard and danger before the inhabitants, they were either persuaded or obliged to raise subsidies to wall their town, except towards the sea and the White Town.[1]

"The two towns are absolutely governed by the Governor, in whose hands the command of the military is lodged; but all other affairs belonging to the Company are managed by him and his Council, most part of whom are generally his creatures. And I have been and am acquainted with some gentlemen who have been in that post, as well as some private gentlemen who resided at Fort St. George—men of great candour and honour,—but they seldom continued long favourites at court. Governor absolute.

"One of the gates of the White Town at Madras looks towards the sea, and it is for that reason called the Sea-gate. The gate-way being pretty spacious, was formerly the common exchange, where merchants of all nations resorted about eleven o'clock in the forenoon to treat of business in merchandize; but that custom is out of fashion, and the consultation chamber, or the Governor's apartment, serves for that use now, which made one Captain Hard, a very merry man, say, 'that he could never have believed that the Sea-gate could have been carried into the consultation room if he had not seen it.' Sea-gate.

"The Company has their mint here for coining bullion that comes from Europe and other countries, into rupees, which brings them in good revenues. The rupee is stamped with Persian characters, declaring the Moghul's name, year of his reign, and some of his epithets. They also coin gold into pagodas of several denominations and value. There are also schools for the education of children; the English for reading and writing English, the Portuguese for their language and Latin, and the Mahometans, Gentoos, and Armenians for their particular languages. And the English Church is well endowed, and maintains poor gentlewomen in good housewifery, good clothes, and palanquins. Mint, schools, &c.

[1] Here is another instance of Hamilton's ignorance. He was not acquainted with the siege of Madras by Nawab Dáúd Khan.

Diamond mines. "The diamond mines being but a week's journey from Fort St. George, make them pretty plentiful there; but few great stones are now brought to market there, since that great diamond which Governor Pitt sent to England. How he purchased it Mr. Glover, by whose means it was brought to the Governor, could give the best account, for he declared to me that he lost 3000 pagodas by introducing the seller to Mr. Pitt, having left so much money in Arcot as security, that if the stone was not fairly bought at Fort St. George, the owner should have free liberty to carry it where he pleased for a market; but neither the owner nor Mr. Glover was pleased with the Governor's transactions in that affair.

Working of the mines. "Some customs and laws at the mines are, when a person goes thither on that affair, he chooses a piece of ground, and acquaints one of the Moghul's officers, who stay there for that service, that he wants so many covets of ground to dig in; but whether they agree for so much, or if the price be certain, I know not. However, when the money is paid, the space of ground is enclosed, and some sentinels placed round it. The Moghul challenges all stones that are found above a certain weight—I think it is about sixty grains; and if any stones be carried clandestinely away above the stipulated weight, the person guilty of the theft is punished with death. Some are fortunate, and get estates by digging, while others lose both their money and labour.

Decrease of trade. "The current trade of Fort St. George runs gradually slower, the trader meeting with disappointments, and sometimes with oppressions, and sometimes the liberty of buying and selling is denied them; and I have seen, when the Governor's servants have bid for goods at a public sale, some who had a mind to bid more durst not, others who had more courage and durst bid, were brow-beaten and threatened. And I was witness to a bargain of Surat wheat taken out of a gentleman's hands after he had fairly bought it by auction; so that many trading people are removed to other parts, where there is greater liberty and less oppression.

Foreign trade. "The colony at Madras produces very little of its own growth or manufacture for foreign markets. They had formerly a trade to Pegu, where many private traders got pretty good bread by their traffic and industry; but the trade is now removed into the Armenians, Moors, and Gentoo's hands, and the English are employed in building and repairing of shipping. The trade they have to China is divided between them and Surat, for the gold and some copper are for their own markets, and the gross of their cargo, which consists in sugar, sugar candy, alum, China ware, and some drugs, as China root, gallingal, &c., are all for the Surat market.

"Their trade to Persia must first come down the famous Ganges, before it can come into Fort St. George's channels to be conveyed to Persia. They never had any trade to Mocha in the products and manufactures of Coromandel before the year 1713, and Fort St. David supplies the goods for that port, so that Fort St. George is an emblem of Holland in supplying foreign markets with foreign goods.

"The colony is well peopled, for there is computed to be eighty thousand inhabitants in the towns and villages; and there are generally about four or five hundred Europeans residing there, reckoning the gentlemen, merchants, seamen and soldiery. Their rice is brought by sea from Ganjam and Orissa; their wheat from Surat and Bengal; and their firewood from the islands of Diu, a low point of land that lies near Masulipatam, so that any enemy that is superior to them in sea forces may easily distress them." Population.

Captain Hamilton has left the following account of the neighbouring settlement at St. Thomé. It is a curious supplement to the description of the same town by Dr. Fryer:— St. Thomé.

"St. Thomas is next, which lies about three miles to the southward of Fort St. George. The city was built by the Portuguese, and they made the Apostle its godfather; but before that it was called Meliapore. There is a little dry rock on the land within it, called the Little Mount, where the Apostle designed to have hid himself, till the fury of the pagan priests, his persecutors, had blown over. There was a Legend of St. Thomas.

convenient cave in that rock for his purpose, but not one drop of water to drink, so St. Thomas cleft the rock with his hand, and commanded water to come into the clift, which command it readily obeyed; and ever since there is water in that clift, both sweet and clear. When I saw it there were not above three gallons in it. He staid there a few days, but his enemies had an account of his place of refuge, and were resolved to sacrifice him, and in great numbers were approaching the mount. When he saw them coming he left his cave, and came down in order to seek shelter somewhere else and at the foot of the mount, as a testimony that he had been there, he stamped with his bare foot on a very hard stone, and left the print of it, which remains there to this day a witness against those persecuting priests. The print of his foot is about sixteen inches long, and, in proportion, narrower at the heel and broader at the toes than the feet now in use among us. He, fleeing for his life to another larger mount, about two miles from the little one, was overtaken on the top of it before he was sheltered, and there they run him through with a lance and in the same place where he was killed, he lies buried.

Church at St. Thomé.

"When the Portuguese first settled there, they built a church over the cave and well on the Little Mount, and also one over his grave on the Great Mount, where the lance that killed the Apostle is still kept as a relic; but how the Portuguese came by that lance is a question not yet well resolved. In that church there is a stone tinctured with the Apostle's blood that cannot be washed out. I have often been at both mounts, and have seen those wonderful pieces of antiquity.

Company's garden.

"At the foot of the Great Mount the Company has a garden, and so have the gentlemen of figure at Fort St. George, with some summer-houses, where ladies and gentlemen retire in the summer to recreate themselves when the business of the town is over, and to be out of the noise of spungers and impertinent visitants, whom this city is often molested with.

"The city of St. Thomas was formerly the best mart town on the Coromandel coast, but at present has very little trade and the inhabitants, who are but few, are reduced to great poverty. The English settling at Fort St. George were the cause of its ruin, and there is little prospect of its recovery." Decay of St. Thomé.

In 1727, some years after the visit of Captain Hamilton, the Mayor's Court at Madras was re-organised by Royal Charter. It consisted of a Mayor and nine Aldermen, with power to decide all civil cases amongst the English inhabitants; but there was always an appeal to the Governor and Council. The change was carried out with much ceremony. All the gentlemen appeared on horse-back on the parade, and moved in the following procession to the Company's garden-house:— Re-organisation of the Mayor's Court.

"Major John Roach on horseback at the head of a Company of Foot Soldiers, with Kettle drum, Trumpet, and other music. Grotesque procession.

"The Dancing Girls with the Country music.

"The Pedda Naik on horseback at the head of his Peons.

"The Marshall with his staff on horseback.

"The Court Attorneys on horse back.

"The Registrar carrying the old Charter on horseback.

"The Serjeants with their Maces on horseback.

"The old Mayor on the right hand and the new on the left. } Six halberdiers.

"The Aldermen two and two, all on horseback. }

"The Company's Chief Peon on horseback, with his Peons.

"The Sheriff with a White Wand on horseback.

"The Chief Gentry in the Town on horseback."

The further history of Madras shows the rise of political relations between the English and the Native powers. Political relations.

Nawab of Arcot.

Madras was included in the Moghul province of Arcot. The English at Madras paid their yearly rent of twelve hundred pagodas to the Nawab of Arcot. The Nawab was subordinate to the Nizam of the Dekhan, and paid a yearly tribute to the Nizam.[1] The existing state of affairs may be gathered from the following extract from a general letter, dated 1733:—

Hindu and Moghul administration contrasted.

"Before this country was conquered by the Mogul, it was divided into several circles under the government of particular Rajahs, which descended from father to son. Their revenues for the most part were from the produce of the land, and they therefore were always careful to keep up the banks of the tanks, or reservoirs of water, and to cleanse them of the mud; of which they were at the expense themselves, knowing that the land would produce more or less according as they had a quantity of water. But the Moguls who have now the government of the country, and are continued in those governments only during pleasure, do not think themselves under the same obligation to be at that expense for their successors. By which means in process of time the tanks are almost choked up, and great part of the lands lie uncultivated for want of water. This alone would occasion grain to be scarce and of course dear; to which if we add the rapacious disposition of the Moguls, altogether intent upon making the most of their governments while they continue in them, we need not seek far for the reason why, even within these ten years, the lands which are tenanted are let for more than double what they were before."

Breaking up of the Moghul Empire.

In 1738-39, the power of the Moghul King or Padishah received a mortal blow from the Persian

[1] The Nawab of Arcot is sometimes known as the Nawab of the Carnatic. The Nizam of the Dekhan is better known in the present day as the Nizam of Hyderabad.

invasion under Nadir Shah.[1] From that date the Moghul provinces began to grow independent of the Moghul court at Delhi. The Nizam of the Dekhan began to reign as a sovereign prince, and treated the Nawab of Arcot as his feudatory.

Growing independence of the Nizam of Hyderabad.

The Nizam of the Dekhan, better known as the Nizam of Hyderabad, was perhaps the most distinguished man of his time. His real name was Chin Kulich Khan. He is best known by his full title of Nizam-ul-Mulk, or "Regulator of the State." He had served in the armies of Aurungzeb. He had filled important posts in the Court at Delhi. He had been appointed to the government of all the Moghul conquests in the Dekhan. He had engaged in frequent wars against the Mahrattas of Poona to the west, and those of Berar to the northward. He was becoming an independent prince. His dominion extended from the river Godavari southward to the river Kistna. It was bounded on the west by the Mahrattas of Poona; on the north by the Mahrattas of Berar; on the east by the Bay of Bengal.

Dependence of the Nawab of Arcot on the Nizam.

The Nawab of Arcot was a deputy of the Nizam. His province lay to the south of the Nizam's dominions. It extended from the river Kistna southwards to the river Koleroon. It was bounded on the north by the Nizam's territory; on the west by the Mysore country; on the south by the Hindu

[1] The invasion of Nadir Shah was not directly felt at a remote settlement like Madras, excepting that it was followed by Mahratta invasions in the Dekhan and Carnatic. It has an important bearing upon the progress of affairs in Bengal, and will be accordingly noticed hereafter in dealing with that Presidency.

kingdoms of Trichinopoly and Tanjore; on the east by the Bay of Bengal.

Hereditary Nawabs.

The Nawabs were becoming hereditary. The appointment was made by the Nizam. The letters of investiture were received from the Vizier at Delhi. The Nawab paid yearly tribute to the Nizam.

Troubles in the Carnatic.

About 1740, Peninsular India was in a turmoil. Chunda Sahib, a kinsman of the Nawab of Arcot, got possession of the Hindu kingdom of Trichinopoly to the southward. The Nawab was angry because Chunda Sahib would not give up Trichinopoly. The Nizam was angry because the Nawab had withheld all payment of tribute. The Mahrattas of Poona[1] collected chout and plunder in the territories of the Nizam. The Mahrattas of Berar poured into the province of Arcot, and collected chout and plunder in the territories of the Nawab. The Nawab of Arcot was killed in a battle against the Mahrattas.

Mahrattas at Trichinopoly.

There was another complication. Subdar Ali, the son of the dead Nawab, succeeded his father on the throne of Arcot, without any regard to the Nizam. He bribed the Mahrattas to go away by a promise of two millions sterling, and the cession of the kingdom of Trichinopoly. The Mahrattas took Trichinopoly. They carried off Chunda Sahib as a prisoner. Chunda Sahib was kept a prisoner for several years by the Mahrattas, but was ulti-

[1] Strictly speaking, the Poona Mahrattas kept their head-quarters at Satara, and did not return to Poona until some few years afterwards.

mately released, and lived to play a prominent part in history.

Murder of the Nawab.

The Nizam was more angry than ever. The Nawab of Arcot had defied him. He demanded instant payment of arrears of tribute from the Nawab. He threatened to dethrone the Nawab unless the money was paid. The Nawab was already at his wits' end to pay the Mahrattas. He prepared for extremities. He moved into the strong fort at Vellore. He sent his women and treasures to Madras. He levied contributions from every town and fort in the Carnatic. A kinsman named Mortiz Ali refused to pay his quota. The Nawab was peremptory. Suddenly the Nawab was murdered at Vellore at the instigation of Mortiz Ali.

Accession of the Nawab's son.

Next morning Vellore was in a tumult. The Nawab's officers clamoured for revenge. They were quieted for a while by promises of arrears of pay. Mortiz Ali was proclaimed Nawab. He went in great state to Arcot, but public opinion was against him. The Mahrattas at Trichinopoly declared against him. The English at Madras refused to give up the women and treasures of the murdered Nawab. His army demanded instant payment of arrears. He disguised himself as a woman and escaped to Vellore in a covered palanquin. A young son of the late Nawab was proclaimed Nawab. The boy was named Sayyid Muhammad.

Intervention of the Nizam.

In 1743 the Nizam of Hyderabad marched to Arcot with a vast army of eighty thousand horse and two hundred thousand foot. He found the

Carnatic in anarchy. Every governor of a fort, every commander of a district, called himself a Nawab. Eighteen Nawabs paid homage to the Nizam in one day. The Nizam was furious. The next man who dared to call himself Nawab was to be scourged.

Anwar-ud-din.

The Nizam apppointed a general of his own to be Nawab of Arcot. The new Nawab was poisoned. The Nizam appointed another Nawab named Anwar-ud-din. The people of the Carnatic made a clamour. They did not want a new comer. They wanted a Nawab of the old family. New comers neglected the tanks and oppressed the inhabitants. The Nizam was willing to yield. He gave out that Sayyid Muhammad was Nawab; that Anwar-ud-din was only a guardian.

Murder of the young Nawab. Anwar-ud-din becomes Nawab.

In June 1744 there was a wedding at Arcot in the family of the Nawab. A band of Afghans had long been clamouring for arrears of pay. On the day of the wedding they clamoured again; they were turned out of the palace; they feigned great contrition. In the evening the young Nawab was sitting in the hall of the palace with Mortiz Ali and other guests. His guardian was approaching the palace to join in the festivities. The young Nawab went out of the hall into the vestibule to receive his guardian on the steps. He was saluted with feigned respect by the very Afghans who had been so clamourous in the morning; suddenly he was stabbed to the heart by the leader of the Afghans. The murderer was cut to pieces on the spot. Mortiz Ali fled to Vellore. Anwar-ud-din dismissed the multitude. Both the kinsman and the guardian were suspected of being concerned in the murder. The young Nawab was the last of the dynasty. After his death Anwar-ud-din was appointed Nawab by the Nizam.

War between Great Britain and France.

At this crisis war broke out between Great Britain and France. In 1745 an English fleet appeared at Madras. Dupleix was governor of the French settlement at Pondicherry, about a hundred miles to the southward of Madras. There had always been commercial rivalry between the English at Madras and the French at Pondicherry. Dupleix was alarmed at the English fleet. He prevailed on the Nawab to forbid all hostilities between the English and French on the land. The English fleet made a few captures of French ships on the sea and sailed away. In 1746 a French fleet appeared off Madras under La Bourdonnais. The French broke the orders of the Nawab and bombarded Madras. The English surrendered the town of Madras and Fort St. George under promise of ransom. The Nawab was quieted by the assurance that Madras should be made over to him. He was disappointed. He became furious. He attacked the French and was defeated. In 1748 the war was over. Madras was restored to the English by the treaty of Aix-la-Chapelle.

Madras captured and restored.

Peace in Eurpoe: war in India.

In Europe there was peace between Great Britain and France. In Peninsular India there was no peace. The English and French at Madras and

Pondicherry could not quiet down under the treaty of Aix-la-Chapelle. They had both imported soldiers from Europe. There was enmity in their hearts. They only wanted an excuse for fighting. They espoused the cause of rival Nizams and rival Nawabs. They could not fight as hostile nations because of the peace in Europe. They affected to be friends. They only came into collision as supporters of rival princes.

Schemes of Dupleix.

Dupleix had long been planning grand schemes. He wanted to establish French influence in the Carnatic; to found a French empire in India under the shadow of a Native power. He knew that the people hankered after the family of the old Nawabs. He procured the release of Chunda Sahib from the Mahrattas. He set up Chunda Sahib as a rival to Anwar-ud-din. At this moment news came that the Nizam was dead at Hyderabad. He is said to have been more than a hundred years old.

Death of the Nizam: war for the succession.

The Nizam died in 1748. His death was followed by a war for the succession. His eldest son was at Delhi. His second son, Nasir Jung, was in prison for rebellion. This second son escaped from his prison and claimed the throne. A grandson, Muzafir Jung, took up arms against his uncle. Dupleix saw his opportunity. He hoped to place a French Nizam on the throne of Hyderabad and a French Nawab on the throne of Arcot. He supported the grandson against the uncle, just as he was supporting Chunda Sahib against Anwar-ud-din.

Chunda Sahib, the French Nawab: Muhammad Ali, the English Nawab.

Fortune smiled on Dupleix. He gained his object as regards setting up Chunda Sahib as a French Nawab at Arcot. Anwar-ud-din was slain in battle. His troops fled in confusion. His son Muhammad Ali escaped south to Trichinopoly. Henceforth Chunda Sahib, of the old Arcot dynasty, may be distinguished as the French Nawab, in opposition to Muhammad Ali, the son of the new comer, who became known as the English Nawab.

French Nawab set up by Dupleix.

Dupleix achieved a signal triumph. The French marched to Arcot accompanied by their native allies. They enthroned Chunda Sahib as a French Nawab of Arcot. They went to Pondicherry in great glory. Dupleix was presented with eighty-one villages by the new Nawab.

English claimant at Trichinopoly.

Dupleix had made a French Nawab of Arcot. He had yet to make a French Nizam of Hyderabad. Meantime the English had espoused the cause of Muhammad Ali, who was still holding out at Trichinopoly.

Failure of the French claimants to capture Trichinopoly.

Dupleix urged Chunda Sahib to attack Trichinopoly; indeed the immediate capture of Trichinopoly was of paramount importance. It would ruin the English Nawab and fix the French Nawab firmly on the throne. It would enable the confederate forces to march into the Dekhan and place a French Nizam on the throne of Hyderabad. But neither the French Nawab nor the French Nizam had any money. They delayed operations in order to squeeze Hindu Rajas. Suddenly news came that the uncle of the French Nizam had established himself on the throne of Hyderabad, and was marching into the Carnatic at the head of an overwhelming army.

Nazir Jung, the English Nizam.

The news was a crushing blow to Dupleix and his native allies. The new Nizam, Nazir Jung, was joined by all the Rajas and so-called Nawabs in the Carnatic. He was also joined by the English and the English Nawab; consequently he is best distinguished as the English Nizam. He passed Arcot, and marched further south with three hundred thousand horse and foot, eight hundred guns, and thirteen hundred elephants.

Triumph of the English Nizam and English Nawab.

The French took the field with their native allies; but their cause was hopeless. To make matters worse, the officers of the French battalion broke out in mutiny. The French Nizam was forced to surrender. His uncle, the English Nizam, swore on the Koran not to hurt him. He went to pay homage to his uncle, but was thrown into irons. There was thus a complete revolution of affairs. The English Nizam was established at Hyderabad, and the English Nawab was established at Arcot; whilst the French Nizam was a prisoner at Hyderabad and the French Nawab was a fugitive at Pondicherry.

Revolution and transformation.

Dupleix was almost in despair. Suddenly there was a change in the aspect of affairs. It was not a revolution, such as might have occurred in a European court; it was an entire transformation like a new scene in a pantomime.

Murder of the English Nizam; triumph of the French Nizam.

Three turbulent Afghan chieftains raised an uproar in the Nizam's camp; the Nizam gallopped to the spot, and was shot dead. The French Nizam was taken out of his prison and placed upon the throne of Hyderabad.

This unexpected news soon reached Pondicherry. Dupleix and Chunda Sahib were wild with joy. They embraced one another like men escaped from shipwreck. In December 1750 the French Nizam of Hyderabad went to Pondicherry. He entered the city with Dupleix in the same palanquin. He appointed Dupleix to the charge of all the Carnatic country to the south of the Kistna. He appointed Chunda Sahib to be Nawab of Arcot under Dupleix. The French Governor had realised his dream of empire.

Triumph of the French Nawab.

Glory of Dupleix.

In January 1751 the French Nizam returned to the Dekhan. He was accompanied by a French force under Bussy. There was another revolution. The three Afghans were again in discontent. There was another uproar. The French Nizam was pierced through the brain with a javelin. Bussy was not discomfited. There were several state prisoners at Hyderabad. He selected one that seemed likely to suit his purpose, and took him out of the prison, and proclaimed him Nizam of Hyderabad under the name of Salabat Jung.

French at Hyderabad under Bussy.

Revolutions had followed one another with bewildering rapidity. It is difficult to realise the political transformations. Dupleix had displayed genius, energy, tact, and audacity. His success was marvellous. Salabat Jung was a French Nizam in every sense of the word. He not only owed

Salabat Jung, the French Nizam, cedes the Northern Circars to the French.

his throne to the French, but he was only maintained on the throne by Bussy and his French army. He found that not only his throne but his life depended upon the support of a French force. He ceded a territory six hundred miles in length along the eastern coast of the Dekhan, as a permanent provision for the maintenance of a French army. This territory, which rendered the French all-powerful in the Dekhan, was known as the Northern Circars.

English Nawab besieged at Pondicherry.

The fortunes of the French had reached their zenith. The English had lost their footing in the Dekhan; they all but lost their footing in the Peninsula. There was not only a French Nizam of Hyderabad but a French Nawab of Arcot. The English and their Nawab were still holding out at Trichinopoly; but the place was closely besieged by the French and their Nawab. The fall of Trichinopoly was a mere question of time; it would have been followed by the ruin of the English and the destruction of their Nawab. Such was the crisis of the war; the moment when Robert Clive gained name and fame.

Clive relieves Trichinopoly by the capture and defence of Arcot.

Robert Clive was born in 1725; he came to India in 1744. He was a writer in the Company's service at Madras. Subsequently he served as a volunteer in the war, and obtained a commission. In August 1751 he was a young Captain of twenty-six. He saw, with the instinct of a soldier, that nothing but the relief of Trichinopoly could save the English and their Nawab from destruction;

that the only way to relieve Trichinopoly was to draw the enemy elsewhere. He proposed to capture Arcot, the old capital of the Nawabs. He led a small force from Madras to Arcot. He marched without concern through a terrible storm of rain and lightning. The garrison at Arcot was in alarm, and fled at his approach. He entered Arcot and occupied the fort. The enemy did exactly what Clive wanted them to do; they sent an army of ten thousand men from Trichinopoly to recover Arcot. Clive had only a hundred and twenty Europeans and two hundred sepoys. He held out at Arcot for fifty days. He resisted every assault. He filled up every breach as soon as it was made. He sallied forth at night and harassed the besiegers. He kept the enemy in constant alarm. His prowess spread far and wide. The Mahrattas were struck with admiration; and marched to his help. The commander of the besieging army was more alarmed than ever; he threatened, he offered bribes; he tried to carry Arcot by storm. All was in vain. He was compelled to break up his camp, and leave Arcot in the possession of Clive.

Glory of Clive.

The story of the defence of Arcot is famous in history. The name of Captain Clive was on every tongue. He was praised by William Pitt, the great war minister of England. Pitt declared that Clive was a "heaven-born general."

English Nawab at Arcot: French Nizam at Hyderabad.

The defence of Arcot changed the fortunes of the war. The French were still all-powerful in the Dekhan. Their Nizam, Salabat Jung, was still reigning at Hyderabad. But their cause was lost in the Peninsula. They were compelled to raise the siege of Trichinopoly. Their Nawab surrendered to a Hindu Raja and was put to death. The English Nawab, Muhammad Ali, was placed on the throne of Arcot. In the end Dupleix was ruined. Chunda Sahib perished. In 1754 peace was made between the English and French in India; it was agreed that the existing status should be maintained—a French Nizam at Hyderabad, and an English Nawab at Arcot. Meanwhile Dupleix returned to France a broken-hearted man.

CHAPTER VI.

ENGLISH IN BENGAL.

1640—1750.

THE English found it far more difficult to settle in Bengal than in Madras. At Madras they purchased a site for a settlement from a Hindu Raja; they had built a factory and a strong fort fifty years before the Moghuls invaded Peninsular India. In Bengal the English found the Moghuls already in possession; consequently they had great difficulty in establishing a trade; at last they were allowed to establish factories, but were strictly prohibited from building fortifications of any kind. Moghul obstructiveness.

The Moghuls were always jealous of Europeans. Shah Jehan, the father of Aurungzeb, became Emperor in 1628. He had special reasons for hating the Portuguese. They had established a settlement at Hughli, on the river of the same name, about a hundred and twenty miles from the Bay of Bengal. They had refused to help him when he rebelled against his father, and he never forgot the affront. Old hatred of the Portuguese.

Muhammadans had other complaints against the Portuguese. They are thus set forth by Khafi Khan in a fair and impartial spirit:— Mussulman complaints against the Portuguese.

"The officers of the King of Portugal occupied several ports, and had built forts in strong positions. They founded villages and acted very kindly towards the people, and did not vex them with oppressive taxes. They allotted a separate quarter for the Mussulmans who dwelt with them, and appointed a Kazi over them to settle all matters of taxes and marriage. But the Muhammadan call to prayer and public devotion were not permitted in their settlements: If a poor Mussulman traveller had to pass through their possessions, he would meet with no other trouble; but he would not be able to say his prayers at his ease. On the sea the Portuguese are not like the English; they do not attack other ships, provided the ships can show a pass from some Portuguese commandant. If no such pass can be produced they will attack the ship. They will also attack the ships of Arabia and Muskat, with which two countries they have a long-standing enmity. If a ship from a distant port is wrecked and falls into their hands, they look upon it as their prize. But their greatest act of tyranny is this. If a subject of these misbelievers dies leaving young children and no grown-up son, the children are considered wards of the State. They take them to their places of worship, their churches, which they have built in many places; and the Padres, that is to say the priests, instruct the children in the Christian religion, and bring them up in their own faith, whether the child be a Mussulman or a Hindu. They will also make them serve as slaves."[1]

Revenge of Shah Jehan on Hughli, 1633.

When Shah Jehan became Padishah he received bitter complaints against the Portuguese from the Nawab of Bengal. They had fortified Hughli; planted great guns on their walls and bastions; carried on a traffic in slaves; and set the Nawab and his officers at defiance. Shah Jehan was exceedingly angry; he remembered his old wrongs, and exacted a terrible revenge. Hughli was surrounded by a Moghul army; a bastion was blown

[1] See Professor Dowson's translation of Khafi Khan in Elliot's History of India, volume vii.

up by a mine; the shipping was set on fire and a large number of prisoners was sent to Agra. Sons and daughters of the Portuguese were placed in the imperial harem, or distributed amongst the grandees. Many parents were forced by threats of a cruel death to abandon Christianity and accept the Koran.[1]

English at Piply, 1633.

These horrors took place in 1632; one year afterwards the English obtained permission to trade in Bengal. The destruction of Hughli had not frightened them; on the contrary, they hoped to get the Portuguese trade into their own hands. But the Moghuls were resolved that no Europeans whatever should defy them for the future. No English ships were allowed to enter the Hughli river; none were allowed to go beyond the port of Piply.

English trade duty free, 1640.

In 1640 the English obtained further privileges from the Moghul. One of the daughters of Shah Jehan had been severely burned by her clothes catching fire. The factors at Surat were requested to send a surgeon to Court. A certain Dr. Gabriel Boughton attended on the princess, and effected a perfect cure. Shah Jehan was overjoyed, and told Dr. Boughton to name his own reward. The patriotic surgeon requested that the English Company might be allowed to trade in Bengal without payment of any duty.

---

[1] According to Moghul story, Shah Jehan was worked upon by a favourite wife, who was a zealous or fanatical votary of Islam. Shah Jehan was himself as lax and indifferent on religious matters as any of his predecessors. The facts stated in the text are taken from Stewart's History of Bengal; occasoinally other authorities are quoted.

English factory at Hughli.

The boon was granted; Boughton obtained the firman, and proceeded overland to Bengal. He reached Piply, and saved an English ship from the payment of duties. At that time Shah Shuja, the second son of Shah Jehan, was Viceroy of Bengal. Dr. Boughton paid his respects to the Viceroy. He cured one of the ladies of the prince of some sickness. The English were then permitted to build a factory at Hughli, but without fortifications. Henceforth Dr. Boughton was the hero of the Company's service, and obtained a lasting name in the early annals of British India.

Saltpetre factory at Patna.

The English made large profits by their trade in Bengal. They built factories in other places besides Hughli, and sent home cargoes of silks, cottons, and other commodities. Especially they built a factory amongst the saltpetre grounds near Patna. Saltpetre was in great demand in those days, for civil war was beginning between Charles the First and his Parliament, and saltpetre was required for the manufacture of gunpowder.

Absence of records at Calcutta.

None of the early records have been preserved at Calcutta. They were all destroyed in 1756, when Calcutta was captured by the ruling Nawab. Duplicates have doubtless been preserved in the India Office, but have never been rendered available. It is, however, possible to glean a few facts from the histories of Stewart, Holwell, and others.

War between the sons of Shah Jehan, 1656.

In 1656 there was a fratricidal war between the four sons of Shah Jehan for the possession of the imperial throne. Shah Shuja, Viceroy of Bengal, took a part in the war, but was utterly defeated. The fate of this prince throws some light upon the existing state of affairs. He bribed some Portuguese pirates to carry him with all his family and treasures from Dacca to Arakan. The King of Arakan was a half-barbarous pagan. At first he treated the imperial prince with hospitality and respect. After a while he began to hanker after the prince's jewels. Then he wanted to take one of Shah Shuja's daughters as a wife. The blood of the Moghul fired up at this insulting demand. It is needless to dwell on a sad story. The prince was despoiled of all his treasures, and he and all his household were brutally murdered.

Moghul wars for the succession.

These wars for the succession broke out at the death of every Moghul sovereign, and often whilst the sovereign was still alive. They were always attended with bloodshed, and productive of much misery. The country was laid waste and plundered. The people were at the mercy of every band of horsemen, whether marching to victory or flying for their lives. Rajas withheld their tribute; Zemindars kept back the rents. There was no one to keep the peace or protect the inhabitants. Lawlessness and rapine reigned supreme.

Invasion of Bengal by the King of Arakan.

Bengal did not escape the general anarchy. The King of Arakan, seeing that no attempt was made to avenge the murdered prince, invaded Bengal with an army of Mughs. There were many Portuguese pirates in his service; they were the scum of Goa and Malacca. In former times they had supplied the slave market at Hughli; they still carried on the work of kidnapping and plunder in every creek and channel of the Sunderbunds. Sometimes their galleys penetrated to Dacca, and they became the terror of Lower Bengal.

Ravages of the Rajas of Assam and Cooch Behar.

Other destroying agents were at work, which can scarcely be realised in the present day. The Raja of Assam was plundering Bengal to the northward of Dacca. The Raja of Cooch Behar was engaged in other directions. All the Moghul soldiers of the province were far away to the westward; they were engaged in the terrible struggle which was convulsing Hindustan.

Amir Jumla, Viceroy of Bengal, 1658.

In 1658 the fratricidal war was over. Aurungzeb ascended the throne of the Moghuls the same year that saw the death of Oliver Cromwell. The celebrated Amir Jumla, the friend and adherent of Aurungzeb, was appointed Viceroy of Bengal. He laboured hard to restore order in Bengal. He invaded Assam as far as the Chinese frontier, but lost the greater part of his army. He perished of the disease which attacked him during that ill-fated expedition.[1]

Shaista Khan, Viceroy, 1664.

Meanwhile, Aurungzeb was anxious about Bengal. In time of peace the province yielded a yearly revenue of half a million sterling to the imperial treasury, after payment of all salaries and expenses. In 1664 a kinsman of Aurungzeb, named

---

[1] The story of the Moghul invasion of Assam belongs to general history. It will be told in Vol. IV, Part 2, of the author's History of India.

Shaista Khan, was appointed Viceroy of Bengal.[1] This Muhammadan grandee has been praised to the skies as a pattern of excellence by courtly scribes. In reality he was an oppressor of the Moghul type, crafty and unscrupulous to the last degree.

Punishment of the King of Arakan.

Suppression of Portuguese pirates.

Shaista Khan punished the King of Arakan, and suppressed the Portuguese pirates, but he effected his purpose by clever perfidy rather than by force of arms. He tempted the pirates to join him with their galleys by the promise of double pay. He employed them in destroying the fleet of Arakan. Having thus got them in his toils, he dismissed them from his service, and left them to starve and die.

Complaints of the English.

The English at Hughli bitterly complained of the oppressions and exactions of Shaista Khan. Indeed, during the reign of Aurungzeb, the Nawabs of Bengal were very extortionate. That sovereign kept a very sharp eye on the revenue. The Nawab was not allowed to collect the revenue, and only drew his regular salary; consequently he was greedy of presents and bribes. The collection and disbursement of the revenues was the duty of an officer appointed direct by the Padishah and known as the King's Dewan. Every Dewan knew that his place and promotion depended on the amount of surplus revenue which he yearly remitted to the imperial treasury. Any collusion with the Nawab under the searching eye of Aurungzeb was liable to be followed by ruin and confiscation.

---

[1] Shaista Khan was uncle to Aurungzeb. He is the same man that had such a narrow escape from Sivaji, the Mahratta. See *ante*, page 15.

Commutation of duties.

Shaista Khan ignored the grant of freedom from duty which the English obtained from Shah Jehan. This was according to Moghul custom; no sovereign or governor was liable for the engagements of his predecessor. Shaista Khan insisted on the payment of the duties. The English at Hughli found it expedient to commute the payment by a yearly present of three thousand rupees to the Nawab.

Tavernier's journey from Agra to Dacca and Hughli, 1665-66.

Some idea of the contemporary state of Hindustan and Bengal may be gathered from Tavernier's Travels. Tavernier was a French jeweller; he went from Agra to Dacca in 1665-66, and there had an adventure with the Nawab Shaista Khan. From Dacca he went to Hughli, where he made acquaintance with the English and Dutch factories. The following extracts from the itinerary of the journey will speak for themselves[1]:—

Agra.

25th November 1665.—"I departed from Agra towards Bengal."

Bengal Revenue.

1st December.—"I met a hundred and ten waggons, every waggon drawn by six oxen, and in every waggon fifty thousand rupees. This is the revenue of the province of Bengal, with all charges defrayed, and the Governor's purse well filled, comes to fifty-five lakhs of rupees."

Rhinoceros.

2nd December.—"Crossing a field of millet, I saw a rhinoceros feeding upon millet canes, which a little boy of nine or ten years old gave him to eat. When I came near the boy, he gave me some millet to give the rhinoceros; who immediately came to me, opening his chops three or four times; I put the millet into his mouth, and when he had swallowed it, he still opened his mouth for more.

---

[1] Tavernier's Travels in India, Book I, Chap. 8.

5th December.—" I arrived at Aurungabad.[1] Formerly this village had another name; but being the place where Aurungzeb gave battle to his brother Sultan Shuja, who was Governor of all the province of Bengal, Aurungzeb, in memory of the victory he had won, gave it his own name, and built there a very fair house, with a garden, and a little mosque." Aurungabad.

6th December.—" I saw the river Ganges. Monsieur Bernier, the King's physician, and another person whose name was Rachepot, with whom I travelled, were amazed to see that a river that had made such a noise in the world was no broader than the river Seine before the Louvre, believing before that it had been as wide as the Danube above Belgrade. There is also so little water in it from March to June or July, when the rains fall, that it will not bear a small boat. When we came to Ganges, we drank every one of us a glass of wine, mixing some of the river water with it, which caused a griping. But our servants that drank it alone were worse tormented than we. The Hollanders, who have a house upon the bank of the Ganges, never drink the water of this river until they have boiled it. But for the natural inhabitants of the country, they are so accustomed to it from their youth that the King and the Court drink no other. You shall see a vast number of camels every day whose business only it is to fetch water from the Ganges." River Ganges.

7th December.—" I arrived at Allahabad. It is a great city, built upon a point of land where the Ganges and Jumna meet. There is a fair castle of hewn stone, with a double moat, where the Governor resides. He is one of the greatest lords in India; and being very sickly, he has always about him ten Persian physicians. He had also in his service Claudius Malle of Bourges, who practises surgery and physic both together. This was he that advised us not to drink of Ganges water, but rather to drink well water. The chief of these Persian physicians, whom this Governor hires with Allahabad.

[1] This village must not be confounded with the city of Aurungabad in the Dekhan, the head-quarters of the Viceroy of the Moghul Dekhan.

his money, one day threw his wife from the top of a battlement to the ground, prompted to that act of cruelty by some jealousies he had entertained. He thought the fall had killed her, but she had only a rib or two bruised; whereupon the kindred of the woman came and demanded justice, at the feet of the Governor. The Governor sending for the physician, commanded him to be gone, resolving to retain him no longer in his service. The physician obeyed, and putting his maimed wife in a palanquin, he set forward upon the road with all his family. But he was not gone above three or four days' journey from the city, when the Governor finding himself worse than he was wont to be, sent to recall him; which the physician perceiving, stabbed his wife, his four children and thirteen female slaves, and returned again to the Governor, who said not a word to him, but entertained him again into his service."

Crossing a river. *8th December.*—"I crossed the river in a large boat, having stayed from morning till noon upon the bank side expecting Monsieur Maille to bring me a passport from the Governor. For there stands a daroga upon each side of the river, who will not suffer any person to pass without leave, and he takes notice what sort of goods are transported, there being due from every waggon four rupees, and from every coach one, not accounting the charge of the boat, which you must pay beside."

Benares. *11th December.*—"I reached Benares. It is a large city, and handsomely built, the most part of the houses being either of brick or stone, and higher than in any other cities of India; but the inconveniency is, that the streets are very narrow. There are many inns in the town; among the rest one very large, and very handsomely built. In the middle of the court are two galleries, where are to be sold calicuts, silks, and other sorts of merchandise. The greatest part of the sellers are the workmen themselves, so that the merchants buy at the first hand. These workmen, before they expose anything to sale, must go to him that has the stamp, to have the King's seal set upon their linen and silks, otherwise they would be fined and lambasted with a good cudgel. This city is situated upon the north side of Ganges that runs by the walls, and into which there falls also another river, some two leagues upward towards the west. In Benares stands one of the idolators' principal pagodas."

21st December.—"I arrived at Patna. It is one of the greatest cities of India, upon the bank of Ganges, toward the west, not being less than two leagues in length. But the houses are no fairer than in the greatest part of the other cities of India, being covered with bamboo or straw. The Holland Company have a house there, by reason of their trade in saltpetre, which they refine at a great town called Choupar, which is also situated upon Ganges, ten leagues above Patna. Patna.

"Coming to Patna, we met the Hollanders in the street returning from Choupar, who stopped our coaches to salute us. We did not part till we had emptied two bottles of Shiras wine in the open street, which is not taken notice of in that country where people meet with an entire freedom without any ceremony.

"I stayed eight days at Patna."

4th January 1666.—"I came to Rajmahal. It is a city upon the right hand of Ganges; and if you go by land, you shall find the highway, for a league or two, paved with brick to the town. Formerly the Governors of Bengal resided here, it being an excellent country for hunting, besides that it was a place of great trade. But now the river having taken another course, above a good half league from the city, as well for that reason as to keep in awe the King of Arakan, and several Portuguese banditti, who are retired to the mouths of Ganges, and made excursions even as far as Dacca itself; both the Governor and the merchants have removed themselves to Dacca, which is at present a large city and a town of great trade." Rajmahal.

6th January.—"Six leagues from Rajmahal, I parted from Monsieur Bernier, who was going to Cossimbazar and thence to Hughli by land." Parting from Bernier.

7th January.—"I saw such a vast number of crocodiles, that I had a great desire to shoot at one, to try whether the Crocodiles.

vulgar report were true, that a musket shot would not pierce their skin. The bullet hit him in the jaw, and made the blood gush out; however he would not stay in the place, but plunged into the river."

8th January.—" I saw again a great number lying upon the bank of the river, and made two shots at two with three bullets at a time. As soon as they were wounded, they turned themselves upon their backs, opening their throats, and died upon the spot."

Dacca.

13th January.—" I came to Dacca. It is a great town, that extends itself only in length, every one coveting to have a house by the Ganges side. The length of this town is above two leagues. And indeed from the last brick bridge to Dacca, there is but one continued row of houses separated one from the other, inhabited for the most part by carpenters, that build galleys and other small vessels. These houses are properly no more than paltry huts built up with bamboos, and daubed over with fat earth. Those of Dacca are not much better built. The Governor's palace is a place enclosed with high walls, in the midst whereof is a pitiful house built only of wood. He generally lodges in tents, which he causes to be set up in a great court of that enclosure. The Hollanders finding that their goods were not safe in the ordinary houses of Dacca, have built them a very fair house; and the English have another, which is reasonably handsome. The church of the Austin Friars is all of brick, and is a very comely pile.

" When I travelled last to Dacca, the Nawab Shaista Khan, who was then Governor of Bengal, was at war with the King of Arakan, whose naval force consists generally of 200 galeasses, attended by several other smaller vessels. These galeasses run though the Gulf of Bengal, and enter into the mouth of Ganges, the sea flowing up higher than Dacca. Shaista Khan, uncle to Aurungzeb, the present Moghul, and the best head-piece that ever was in all his territories, found out a way to corrupt several of the King of Arakan's captains, so that of a sudden forty galeasses, commanded by Portuguese, came and joined themselves with him. To engage more firmly all the new multitude to his service, he gave a larger pay to all the Portuguese officers, and to the soldiers proportionably. But those of the country had no more than their ordinary pay doubled. It is an incredible thing to see how swiftly these galeasses cut their way in the water. Some are so long that they carry fifty oars of a side, but they have but two men to an oar: There are some very curiously painted, and upon which there is no cost of gold and azure spared. The Hollanders have some of their own to transport their goods; and sometimes they are forced to hire others, whereby many people get a good livelihood."

14th January.—"Being the next day after my arrival at Dacca, I went to wait upon the Nawab, and presented him with a garment of cloth of gold, laced with a gold needlework lace of point of Spain, with a scarf of gold and silver of the same point, and a very fair emerald jewel. Towards evening, being returned to the Hollander's house where I lodged, the Nawab sent me pomegranates, China oranges, two Persian melons, and three sorts of pears." Visits the Nawab.

15th January.—"I showed my goods to the Nawab, and presented him with a watch in a gold enamelled case, with a pair of little pistols inlaid with silver, and a very fair prospective glass. What I gave to the father and the son, a young lord about ten years old, stood me in about five thousand livres."

16th January.—"I treated with the Nawab about the prices of my goods: and at length I went to his steward to take my letter of exchange to be paid at Cossimbazar. Not but that he would have paid me my money at Dacca; but the Hollanders, who understood things better than I did, told me it was very dangerous to carry money to Cossimbazar, whither there was no going but over the Ganges by water, the way by land being full of bogs and fens. And to go by water is no less dangerous, by reason that the boats which they use are very apt to tip over upon the least storm, and when the mariners perceive that you carry money along with you it is an easy thing for them to overset the boat, and afterwards to come and take up the money that lies at the bottom of the river."

20th January.—"I took leave of the Nawab, who desired me to come and see him again, and caused a pass to be delivered me, wherein he gave me the title of one of the gentlemen of his house, which he had done before, when he was Governor of Ahmedabad, when I went to him, to the army, in the province of Deccan, into which the Raja Sevaji was entered. By virtue of these passes I could travel over all the countries of the Great Moghul, as being one of his household."

Hospitalities. *21st January.*—"The Hollanders made a great feast for my sake, to which they invited the English and some Portuguese, together with the Austin Friars of the same nation."

22nd January.—"I made a visit to the English. The President of the English factory at Dacca was Mr. Prat."

29th January.—"I left Dacca in the evening. The Hollanders bore me company for two leagues with their little barques armed, nor did we spare the Spanish wine all that time."

Hughli. *20th February.*—"I arrived at Hughli, where I stayed till the 2nd of March, during which time the Hollanders bid me very welcome, and made it their business to shew me all the divertisements which the country was capable to afford. We went several times in pleasure-boats upon the river, and we had a banquet of all the delicacies that the gardens of Europe could have afforded us; salads of all sorts, colewarts, asparagus, pease; but our chiefest dish was Japan beans, the Hollanders being very curious to have all sorts of pulse and herbs in their gardens, though they could never get artichokes to grow in that country."

Tavernier's grievances. Tavernier had a grievance against Nawab Shaista Khan. The bill of exchange was stopped, and payment was refused until he deducted twenty thousand rupees from the sum total. Tavernier had also grievances against the Emperor Aurungzeb, and some of the grandees at Delhi. The fact is only worth mentioning as an instance of the oppressive conduct of the Nawab, and the difficulties in the way of trading in India in the seventeenth century.

Persecution of Hindus, 1680.

About 1680 Aurungzeb began to persecute the Hindus. He was determined to make them Muhammadans. He carried on persecuting wars, and turned Hindu temples into Mussulman mosques. He collected the hateful tax known as the Jezya; this was a capitation tax levied from all who refused to become Muhammadans; it had been abolished in India by the celebrated Akbar.

Jezya demanded from Europeans.

Shaista Khan was ordered to carry out this work of persecution in Bengal. He levied the Jezya upon Hindus, and demanded it from Europeans. The English and Dutch refused to pay Jezya. Shaista Khan let them off on the condition that they brought him a yearly present of Persian horses.

The English oppressed.

Hitherto the English settlements in Bengal were superintended by the Governor of Madras. In 1677 Governor Masters wrote to Shaista Khan from Madras, that if he continued his oppressions, the English would certainly withdraw from Bengal. In 1681 the Directors withdrew Bengal from the supervision of Madras, and appointed the Agent at Hughli to be Governor of all the factories in Bengal.

Mr. Job Channock.

Mr. Job Channock was the most noted of the English Governors of Hughli. He was cruelly treated by Shaista Khan; on one occasion he was scourged. At last, as already told in the Madras records, he left Bengal with all the Company's servants and effects and went away to Madras.[1]

Ibrahim Khan Nawab, 1689. Foundation of Calcutta.

Shortly afterwards Shaista Khan left Bengal. Ibrahim Khan was appointed Nawab in his room; he was the same man who is glorified in the Madras records as "the famously just and good Nawab Ibrahim Khan."[2] He invited the English to return to Bengal. Mr. Channock returned, but not to Hughli. He was resolved to keep away from Hughli. He built a factory in the village of Chutanuttee, about twenty miles nearer the sea. This was the germ which was afterwards to grow into the City of Palaces.

Loss of the saltpetre trade.

The religious zeal of Aurungzeb seems to have reached the ears of the Sultan of Turkey. Both were Sunnís. The Sultan wrote to Aurungzeb begging him to forbid his subjects from selling saltpetre to Christians, as it was often burnt for the destruction of good Muhammadans. Aurungzeb issued the necessary prohibition, and the English lost for a while their saltpetre trade at Patna.

Hindu rebellion in Bengal, 1696.

The "famously just and good Nawab Ibrahim" turned out to be a very weak ruler in Bengal. In 1696 the Hindu Rajas westward of the Hughli broke into open rebellion. The Raja of Burdwan was at the head of the rebels. The Nawab did nothing to stop the outbreak. He said that a civil

---

[1] See *ante*, page 90.

[2] *Ibid.*

war was a dreadful evil; that many people were always slaughtered; and that if the rebels were let alone, they would soon disperse themselves.

Azim-u-shan Viceroy, 1696.

The rebellion was not a formidable affair. The so-called army of the Raja of Burdwan was routed by fifty English soldiers in front of the factory at Chutanuttee. But Aurungzeb was very angry at the Hindu rebellion. He recalled the Nawab, and appointed one of his own grandsons to be Viceroy of the three united provinces—Bengal, Behar, and Orissa. The name of the grandson was Azim-u-shan.

Fortification of Calcutta.

The Hindu rebellion was lucky for the Europeans. The Nawab had told them to defend themselves, and they had run up walls and bastions round their respective factories. This was the origin of the three European forts or towns, namely, the English at Calcutta, the French at Chandernagore, and the Dutch at Chinsura. Both Chandernagore and Chinsura were in the immediate neighbourhood of Hughli; accordingly both were about twenty miles from Calcutta.

English hold the rank of Zemindar.

Azim-u-shan, the new Viceroy of Bengal, was like the run of Moghul princes. He was idle, fond of pleasure, and ready to grant anything for money. By a suitable present the English obtained a grant of the three villages of Chutanuttee, Govindpore, and Kalicotta. The importance of this grant is liable to be overlooked. It raised the English to the condition of a Zemindar, similar to the position which they already filled at Madras. They paid a yearly rent of Rs. 1,195 for the three villages; this amount had been paid to the King's Dewan by the Zemindars who had previously held the villages. They administered justice amongst the natives of the three villages after the manner of Zemindars. In other words, they fined, whipped, and imprisoned at will, in the same way that the Justices at Madras punished offenders in Black Town.

Objections overruled.

The Moghul Governor at Hughli did not like to see the English acting as Zemindars. He wanted to send a Kazi to Calcutta to administer justice in accordance with Muhammadan law. But the English made another present to the Viceroy, and the Governor of Hughli was told to leave the English alone.

Murshed Kuli Khan Nawab, 1707.

Aurungzeb died in 1707. Azim-u-shan, the young Viceroy, went away from Bengal to take a part in the war for the succession. He left a deputy behind to serve both as Nawab and as King's Dewan. The new Nawab is best known by his title of Murshed Kuli Khan. The city of Murshedabad is named after him to this day.

Zemindars oppressed.

The main object of the new Nawab was to collect revenue and remit a large surplus to Delhi. He hoped by so doing to gain favour with the Moghul court. His proceedings are thus described by Stewart:—

"Murshed Kuli Khan began to put in practice a system of the greatest oppression upon the Zemindars or Hindu landholders; which, although it much augmented the revenue of the State, rendered his name dreaded and detested throughout the provinces.

"In order to make a full investigation of the value of the lands, he placed the principal Zemindars in close confinement, and gave the collection into the hands of expert Aumils, or collectors, who received the assessments from the farmers and paid the amount into the public treasury. He also ordered the whole of the lands to be re-measured; and having ascertained the quantity of fallow and waste ground belonging to every village, he caused a considerable proportion of it to be brought into cultivation; for which purpose the collectors were authorised to make advances of money to the lower order of husbandmen, to purchase stock, and to reimburse themselves by a certain portion of the produce.

Employment of new collectors. Remeasurement of lands.

"When he had thus entirely dispossessed the Zemindars of all interference in the collection, he assigned to them an allowance, either in land or money, for the subsistence of their families, called *nankar;* to which was added the privilege of hunting, of cutting wood in the forests, and of fishing in the lakes and rivers: these immunities are called *bunkar* and *julkar.*[1]

Subsistence allowances to Zemindars.

"The only persons who were exempted from these despotic regulations were the Zemindars of Bhirbhum and Kishnaghur. The first was a popular and virtuous character, named Assud Allah, an Afghan chief, who, with his followers, undertook to defend this territory against the wild Hindu mountaineers of Jeharcund. This person dedicated half his income to charitable purposes, either in supporting the religious and learned, or in relieving the distresses of the poor and needy: he was besides attentive to all the duties of his religion, and deviated not from the ordinances of the law. To have attacked such a character would have exposed the Nawab to great opprobrium, and would have incited against him the popular clamour, and possibly would have injured him in the esteem of every devout Mussulman.

Zemindars of Bhirbhum and Kishnaghur, exempted.

"The other Zemindar owed his security to the nature of his country, which was full of woods, and adjoining to the

[1] The literal meaning of these three words is, the business of bread, wood, and water.

mountains of Jeharcund, whither, upon any invasion of the district, he retired to places inaccessible to his pursuers, and annoyed them severely in their retreat: the country was besides unproductive; and the expenses of collection, and of maintaining it, would have exceeded the amount of the revenue.

"These two Zemindars, therefore, having refused the summons to attend at the court of Murshedabad, were permitted to remain on their own estates, on condition of regularly remitting their assessment through an agent stationed at Murshedabad.

Submission of Tipperah, Cooch Behar, and Assam.

"The Rajas of Tipperah, Cooch Behar, and Assam, whose countries, although they had been overrun by the Muhammadan arms, had never been perfectly subdued, and who therefore continued to spread the umbrella of independence and to stamp the coin in their own names, were so impressed with the idea of the power and abilities of Murshed Kuli Khan, that they forwarded to him valuable presents, consisting of elephants, wrought and unwrought ivory, musk, amber and various other articles, in token of their submission: in return for which, the Nawab sent them dresses of honour, known as khilluts, by the receipt and putting on of which they acknowledged his superiority. This interchange of presents and compliments became an annual custom during the whole time of his government, without either party attempting to recede from, or advance beyond, the implied line of conduct.

Administration of justice.

"Murshed Kuli Khan devoted two days in the week to the administration of justice, presiding in person in court: and so impartial was he in his decisions, and so rigid in the execution of the sentence of the law, that he put his own son to death for an infraction of its regulations; and his decisions thereby became celebrated throughout Hindustan. This, however, must be considered as respecting Muhammadans; for in the collection of the revenues he allowed his officers to be guilty of great cruelty and oppression; and wherever any person opposed his will, he marked him as the victim of his revenge.

"Murshed Kuli Khan continued to make the collections through his Aumils by displacing the Zemindars, with a few exceptions, where he found the latter worthy of trust and confidence. He admitted no charges for troops, but those paid and mustered by himself. Two thousand cavalry and four thousand infantry, under the command of Nazir Ahmad, who had been originally a private soldier, were found sufficient to enforce the payment of all the revenues of Bengal: for so severe were his regulations, and such the dread of his power and resolution, that his commands were implicitly obeyed; and it was sufficient for him to send a single messenger to sequester a Zemindari, or to seize on a culprit at the greatest distance. Despotic powers.

"Such were the respect and dignity kept up by the Nawab at his court, that, in his presence, no person was allowed to salute or speak to another; nor were any of his officers or Rajas allowed to sit before him. Rajas refused seats.

"He prohibited the Zemindars, and other Hindus of opulence, from riding in palanquins; obliging them to make use of an inferior kind of conveyance, called a dooly, or chowpaleh. Whoever deviated, in the smallest degree, from his general regulations was certain to experience the effects of his resentment. Zemindars prohibited palanquins.

"In the affairs of government he showed favour to no one; and always rewarded merit wherever he found it. He employed none but Bengalli Hindus in the collection of the revenues, because they were most easily compelled by threats or punishment to disclose their malpractices and their confederates; and their pusillanimity secured him from any insurrection or combination against the State. In the few instances in which he found that they had defrauded him, or had made away with the revenue and were unable to make good the deficiency, he compelled the offender, with his wife and children, to become Muhammadans. Reasons for employing only Bengallis.

"Raja Oudy Narain, whose family had long enjoyed the Zemindari of the district of Rajeshahi, was so distinguished by his abilities and application, that the Nawab entrusted Story of Raja Oudy Narain.

him with the superintendence of the greater portion of the collections, and placed under his orders Gholam Muhammad Jemadar, with two hundred horse, who in a short time became a great favourite of his principal; but in consequence of his pay having been kept back for many months, the Jemadar's people mutinied, and the Nawab, without inquiring minutely into the matter, ordered a chosen detachment to quell the disturbance. A conflict ensued in the vicinity of the Raja's house, in which the Jemadar was killed and many of his people put to death. This circumstance so hurt and terrified Oudy Narain, that he put an end to his own existence.

Zemindari of Rajeshahi.

"The Zemindari of Rajeshahi was in consequence taken away from the family, and conferred on Ramjewun and Kanoo Kenoor, two Zemindars who resided on the eastern side of the river, in consideration of their having been more punctual in the payment of their rents than the other Zemindars of Bengal.

Daily audit of accounts.

"The Nawab, however, never placed confidence in any man; he himself examined the accounts of the exchequer every day; and, if he discovered any of the Zemindars or others remiss in their payment, he placed either the principal or his agent in arrest, with a guard over him, to prevent his either eating or drinking till the business was settled: and in order to prevent the guards from being bribed or negligent in their duty, he placed spies over them, who informed him of the smallest deviation from his orders.

Torture of Zemindars.

"A principal instrument of the Nawab's severity was Nazir Ahmad, to whom, when a district was in arrear, he used to deliver over the captive Zemindar to be tormented by every species of cruelty, as hanging up by the feet, bastinadoing, setting them in the sun in summer; and by stripping them naked, and sprinkling them frequently with cold water in winter.

Cruelties of the Deputy Dewan.

"But all these acts of severity were but trifles compared with the wanton and cruel conduct of Sayyid Reza Khan, who was married to Nuffisah Begum, the grand-daughter of the

Nawab, and who had been appointed Deputy Dewan of the province. In order to enforce the payment of the revenues, he ordered a pond to be dug, which was filled with everything disgusting, and the stench of which was so offensive as nearly to suffocate whoever approached it: to this shocking place, in contempt of the Hindus, he gave the name of Bikoont, which, in their language, means Paradise; and after the Zemindars had undergone the usual punishments, if their rent was not forthcoming, he caused them to be drawn, by a rope tied under the arms, through this infernal pond. He is also stated to have compelled them to put on loose trowsers, into which were introduced live cats. By such cruel and horrid methods he extorted from the unhappy Zemindars everything they possessed, and made them weary of their lives."

The proceedings of Murshed Kuli Khan as regards the English are also described by Stewart. The following extracts are interesting:—

Demands of Murshed Kuli Khan upon the English.

"Murshed Kuli Khan was sensible that Bengal owed much of its wealth to its external commerce: he therefore gave every encouragement to foreign merchants, especially to the Moghuls and Arabians, from whom he only exacted the prescribed duties of 2 per cent., and did not permit the custom house officers to take more than their regulated fees; but he was too keen a politician not to observe with jealousy the fortified factories of the Europeans, and the great advantages which the English had over the merchants, in consequence of the firmān and nishāns, which they had obtained (he said) by means of bribery and corruption, and which permitted them to trade, either duty free, or for the paltry consideration of 3,000 rupees per annum.[1]

The Governor sets aside the privileges of the English. 1713.

"When, therefore, Murshed Kuli Khan felt himself perfectly secure in his government, he set at nought the orders of the prince Shuja, and of the emperor Aurungzeb; and demanded from the English, either the same duties

[1] See *ante*, page 154.

that were paid by Hindu subjects, or a constant renewal of presents, both to himself and to all inferior departments. Such conduct, of course, irritated the English agents, who wrote a detail of their grievances to the Directors of the Company in England, and solicited permission to send an embassy to Dehli, to complain to the emperor Farrukh Siyar of the Nawab's conduct. Their suggestion was approved of by the Company; and orders were sent to the governors of Madras and Bombay to unite their grievances in the same petition with those of Bengal.

English embassy to Delhi, 1715.

"The nomination of the ambassadors was left to Mr. Hedges, the governor of Calcutta, who selected, for this purpose, Mr. John Surman and Edward Stephenson, two of the ablest factors in the Bengal service, joining to them an Armenian named Khoja Serhaud, who understood both the English and Persian languages, and who had been for many years the principal merchant in Calcutta. Mr. William Hamilton also accompanied the embassy as surgeon.

Delhi unknown to the English at Calcutta.

"At that period the government of Calcutta were very ignorant of the politics and intrigues of the court of Dehli; and the ambassadors had no other lights to direct their proceedings, than such as they obtained from the Armenian, who, although he had never been at Dehli, had procured a certain degree of information from some of his countrymen, whose extensive commercial concerns led them over every part of India; and who was very solicitous to be admitted into this honourable commission in hopes of acquiring a large profit by the goods he should carry, free of charges and duties, in the train of the embassy. The presents designed for the emperor and his officers consisted of curious glass-ware, clock-work, brocades and the finest manufactures of woollen-cloths and silks, valued, altogether, at 30,000*l.*, which Khoja Serhaud, in his letters to Dehli, magnified to 100,000*l.*, and gave such a description of the varieties which were coming, that Farrukh Siyar ordered the embassy to be escorted by the governors of the provinces through whose territories it might pass. The train proceeded on the Ganges from Calcutta to

Patna, and thence by land to Dehli, where they arrived on the 8th of July, 1715, after a march of three months."

Copies of all the letters received by the Governor of Calcutta from the envoys at Delhi have been preserved at Madras. Before selecting extracts, it may be as well to offer a few explanations. Records of the embassy preserved at Madras.

Farrukh Siyar was reigning as Padishah, or emperor at Delhi. He was fretting under the domination of two brothers, his Vizier and Chief Amir, who had placed him on the throne. Their names were Abdulla and Husain, but they are best known as the two Sayyids. Farrukh Siyar, made emperor by the two Sayyids.

A powerful grandee, named Khan Dauran, was hostile to the two brothers, and was consequently intriguing against them. Khan Dauran hostile to the two Sayyids.

The first extract from the letters describes the reception of the envoys at Delhi, and their being presented with certain nondescript vestments and ornaments, called seerpaws, culgees, and congers. It will be seen from what follows that they courted both the Vizier Abdulla and Khan Dauran:— Extracts from the Madras records.

"*Delhi, 8th July 1715.*—We passed the country of the Jauts with success, not meeting with much trouble, except that once in the night rogues came on our camp, but, being repulsed three times, they left us. We arrived at Furrukabad the 3rd instant (July), where we were met by Padre Stephanus, bringing two seerpaws, which were received with the usual ceremony by John Surman and Khoja Serhaud. The 4th, we arrived at Baorapoola, three coss from the city, sending the Padre before to prepare our reception, that, if possible, we might visit the King the first day, even before we went to the house which was got for us. Accordingly the 7th, in the morning, we made our entry with very good order; there Reception of the English embassy at Delhi.

being sent a Munsubdar of two thousand, with about 200 horse and peons, to meet us; bringing likewise two elephants and flags. About the middle of the city, we were met by the Sallabut Khan Bahadur, and were by him conducted to the palace, where we waited till about twelve o'clock till the King came out. Before which time we met with Khan Dauran Bahadur, who received us very civilly, assuring us of his protection and good services. We prepared for our first present, *viz.*, 1,001 gold mohurs, the table clock set with precious stones, the unicorn's horn, the gold escritoire, the large piece of ambergreese, the astoa and chelumgie Manilla work, and the map of the world. These, with the Honorable the Governor's letter, were presented, every one holding something in his hand as usual. John Surman received a vest and culgee set with precious stones; and Serhaud a vest and cunger set with precious stones likewise, amid the great pomp and state of the Kings of Hindoostan. We were very well received; and on our arrival at our house, we were entertained by Sallabut Khan (Khan Douran's deputy) with dinner sufficient both for us and our people. In the evening he visited us again and stayed about two hours. The great favour Khan Dauran is in with the King gives us hopes of success in this undertaking. He assures us of his protection, and says the King has promised us very great favours. We have received orders first to visit Khan Dauran as our patron; after which we shall be ordered to visit the Grand Vizier and other grandees. We would have avoided this, if we could, fearing to disoblige the Vizier; but finding it not feasable, rather than disoblige one who has been so serviceable, and by whose means we expect to obtain our desires, we comply with it."

Embassy advised by Zoudi Khan.

From the next extract it will be seen that the envoys were acting under the advice of a certain Zoudi Khan. This was the very grandee who wrote to Governor Pitt at Madras[1] :—

" *Delhi, 17th July* :—We have lately sent to Your Honor the good news of our safe arrival here, the visit of the King, and

[1] See *ante*, page 116.

the civil treatment we met with, all which will, without doubt, be very welcome news. We have since visited several grandees as the Vizier (Abdulla Khan) and Khan Dauran; where we were received with all the respect that could be expected, and gives me some hopes that all will end well; but what gives me the most encouragement (for I am well acquainted with these nobles: as long as they are expecting to get anything they are always complaisant), is that the method we are at present taking is consistent and with the advice and counsel of Zoudi Khan. We visited that gentleman the 11th current, and met with the same treatment he has always given to Englishmen, with the highest acknowledgments of the favours he has received from them, that as yet he had never been able to retaliate any of them, but hoped he had now an opportunity of doing something. He pressingly advised us to do nothing without the advice, counsel, and order of Khan Dauran (and the main instrument of our affairs) Sallabut Khan; that the turn of affairs at the Durbar obliged us to it. This, which he told us by word of mouth, he wrote me when I sent Your Honor's letter to him. We are convinced he advises like a friend, and were intent on the method, but at the same time very cautious how we any ways disoblige the Vizier; we being very sure that Zoudi Khan was very intimate there, sent and advised him when we intended to visit, that he would use his interest for our better reception, intending to manage the Durbar by his means. He assured us that we might be satisfied as to the important Durbar. The good prospect we have of our affairs makes Khoja Serhaud very good-humoured, and at present tractable, in hopes he shall obtain his promised reward and considered that everything is come to its crisis. I take particular care that he remains so, and as much as possible persuade every one with me to do the like; which I fear gains me but little good will. But as passion must now be curbed, except we expect to be laughed at, we must be very circumspect in our actions and counsels."

Breach between the Emperor and the two Sayyids.

The next extract shows something of the progress of the breach between the King, or Emperor, and the two Sayyid brothers :—

"*Delhi, 4th August.*—Three days after our arrival here the King left the city, under pretence of visiting a sacred place, about six coss from thence. But the true reason (we are of opinion) was to clear himself of a kind of confinement, which he thought he suffered whilst in the Fort. Afterwards on the petition of his grandees to return to the city, the time of the rains being improper for travelling, he showed himself resolved to proceed either to Lahore or Ajmeer. Neither could all the arguments used avert his intended journey. This startled us, and considering with how great trouble and risk we had brought the present thus far, and how to carry it on at this time of the year, we were something at a stand. At last we concluded to give the gross of our present in, notwithstanding the King was abroad. But in delivering some of the fine clocks, they were ordered to be returned and kept in good order till he came back to the city, he having now determined only to visit a sacred place about forty coss from Delhi; after which he would return. This stopped our presenting the remainder of our goods, but we concluded that it was necessary to attend his Majesty in this tour. We now continue in the camp, leaving Mr. Stephenson and Mr. Phillips to take care of what goods remain in the city; and in case that the King should proceed further, that they may concert measures to bring the goods after us. We are in this interval preparing petitions to be delivered to his Majesty, hoping we shall do something for our Honourable Masters that has not been yet obtained. The patronage and management of this negotiation is in the hands of the greatest favourite at Court, Khan Dauran, and under him Sayyid Sallabut Khan. Withall, we being no ways unmindful of an old friend Zoudi Khan, without whose advice, we enter upon nothing. But he being at present in so low a station is not able to obtain the King's ear. However we are satisfied that in whatever lies in his power, he does and will assist us, but particularly in the Vizier's Durbar.

"Husain Ali Khan is lately gone into the Dekhan country, having the entire command of all that part of his kingdom. Your Honors have undoubtedly heard how great he has made himself even to vie with the command of his imperial Majesty, as lately appeared in the disputes between himself and Amír Jumla[1] whilst at Court, when he obliged his antagonist, contrary to the King's desires, to remove from Court to Patna, whereby, through the interest of Husain, and his own mismanagement, he is quite ruined. Wherefore we humbly recommend a very good correspondence with Husain. Otherwise, whatever we shall be able to do here will be of very little service before him."

Husain sent to be Viceroy of the Dekhan.

New intrigues came to light. Dâúd Khan, the same man who besieged Madras in Governor Pitt's time, had been appointed Nawab of Guzerat. He received secret orders from the Emperor to cut off Husain. It will be seen from the following extracts that the English envoys at Delhi had some inkling of what was going on :—

Dâúd Khan ordered to cut off Husain.

"*Delhi, 31st August.*—We have advices here that Husain Ali Khan and Dâúd Khan[2] are come to a rupture in Burhanpur, so that it is likely a battle will ensue, the latter having engaged many of the Dekhan country to his party. It is whispered at this Court that this is a design laid to involve Husain Ali Khan in trouble, and retrench his grandeur, which of late has not been very pleasing.

Expected rupture.

[1] This Amír Jumla was one of the Emperor's favourites. He is distinct from the Amír Jumla who was Viceroy of Bengal under Aurungzeb.

[2] The name of Dâúd is spelt in various ways in the old records,—Dawood, Daoud, Daood, &c. For the sake of uniformity it has been spelt throughout the present volume in the modern mode. It seems to be equivalent to the David of the Jews.

Return of the Emperor to Delhi.

"The King, proceeding no further than Paniput,[1] returned to the city on the 15th, but, being a little disordered in his health, has not made any public appearance. So that we have not had an opportunity to deliver the remaining part of our present, or commence our negotiation, which shall be done by the 1st proximo."

Sickness of Farrukh Siyar.

"*Delhi, 6th October.*—We designed to have presented our petition on the first good opportunity; but His Majesty's indisposition continuing, and Mr. Hamilton having undertaken to cure him, it has been thought advisable by our friends, as well as by ourselves, to defer delivering it till such time as it shall please God that His Majesty in some measure returns to his former state of health. Which advice, we intend to follow, considering that, whilst he is in so much pain, it can be but a very indifferent opportunity to beg favours of him. The first distemper the Doctor took him in hand for, was swellings in his groin, which, thanks be to God, he is in a fair way of curing; but within these few days last past he has been taken with a violent pain, which is likely to come to a fistula; it hinders His Majesty from coming out, so naturally puts a stop to all manner of business, wherefore we must have patience perforce.

Death of Dâúd Khan.

"Your Honors will have heard of the death of Dâúd Khan in the Dekhan, slain in a battle with Husain Ali. (This was a desperate conflict, in which a matchlock ball struck Dâúd Khan at the moment when victory had declared on his side.) This has given a great deal of uneasiness to this Court, it being quite otherwise laid by the King and his favourites; and that which was designed for Husain Ali's ruin, has proved a great addition to his former glories. The King at first seemed to resent it to his brother Abdulla, who not taking it so patiently as he expected, he has altered his resolution to sending Husain Ali Khan a seerpaw and other marks of favour. We have advised in our letters to the

[1] The shrine of a Muhammadan saint of great repute, and famous in history as the scene of two of the greatest battles ever fought in India; *viz.*, that which overturned the Afghan dynasty and established the Moghul emperors in 1525; and that which nearly crushed the Mahrattas in 1761.

Governor and Council of Madras to have particular regard to the friendship of that great Amîr; otherwise whatever we shall be able to do here for that coast will be of little service, unless backed with his favour."

After this a marriage was arranged between the King and the daughter of the Raja of Marwar, or Jodhpur. It was somewhat delayed by the illness of the King. Dr. Hamilton, the surgeon to the envoys, succeeded in effecting a cure. The following extract tells part of the story:— **Marriage of Farrukh Siyar to the daughter of the Jodhpur Raja.**

"*Delhi, 7th December.*—We write Your Honors the welcome news of the King's recovery. As a clear demonstration to the world, he washed himself the 23rd ultimo, and accordingly received the congratulations of the whole Court. As a reward for Mr. Hamilton's care and success, the King was pleased on the 30th to give him in public, *viz.*, a vest, a culgee set with precious stones, two diamond rings, an elephant, horse, and 5,000 rupees; besides ordering at the same time all his small instruments to be made in gold, with gold buttons for his coat and waistcoat, and brushes set with jewels. The same day Khoja Serhaud received an elephant and vest as a reward for his attendance on this occasion. **English surgeon rewarded.**

"We have esteemed this as a particular happiness, and hope it will prove ominous to the success of our affairs, it being the only thing that detained us hitherto from delivering our general petition. So, pursuant to the orders we received from Khan Dauran, the King's recovery was succeeded by the giving in the remainder of our present (reserving a small part only till the ceremony of his marriage should be over); and then delivered our petition to Khan Dauran, by his means to be introduced to his Majesty. Sallabat Khan, who has all along managed our affairs under Khan Dauran, being at that instant, and some time before, much indisposed, we were obliged to carry it ourselves; not without taking care to have his recommendation annexed. Since the delivery, Khoja Serhaud has been frequently with Khan **Business of the embassy delayed by the marriage.**

Dauran, to remind him of introducing it to His Majesty; but has always been informed, no business can go forward till the solemnization of the King's wedding is over, when he has promised a speedy dispatch. All offices have been shut up for some days, and all business in the kingdom must naturally subside to this approaching ceremony, so that we cannot repine at the delay.

"The Rajputs are likely to receive great honor by this wedding; the King having consented to all their desires in respect to the ceremonials; and this evening goes on his throne attended by his whole nobility on foot, to receive his spouse. All the Fort and street through which he passes will be made resplendent with innumerable lights; and in fine all will appear as glorious as the riches of Hindoostan and two months indefatigable labour can provide."

Slow progress.

The following extracts show the disturbed state of public affairs:—

"*Delhi, 8th January 1716.*—As to the course of our negotiations, we can give but a very slender account of their progress; for, although our affairs are fallen into the patronage of one of the most able men in this Court to dispatch them, if he pleases, yet his dilatory methods of proceeding are such as must make us pursue our designs with patience for the present. Our petition is returned, after having passed the examination of the books; the next that follows will be the King's signing; after which we shall take care to give Your Honors a particular account of it.

"We have lately been surprized with the King's designs of departing from this place, but, God be thanked, he is delayed for some days at least. We shall make the best use we can of the delay, if possible, to effect our business before his departure, but which we cannot rely on.

"Two nights ago Amír Jumla arrived in this place from Behar, attended by about eight or ten horsemen, much to the surprise of this city; for it is but at best supposed that he has made an elopement from his own camp for fear of his soldiers who mutinied for pay. The particulars of all which we are not yet acquainted with, nor what reception he is like to meet with from his Majesty."

Mutiny of the Moghul army at Delhi.

"*Delhi, 10th March.*—Your Honors will doubtless have heard by flying reports the troubles that have possessed this place for the past month, occasioned by the coming of Amír Jumla and all his forces, as it is said without the King's order. All the Tartars mutinously joined to demand their pay, which they gave out they would force either from the Vizier or Khan Dauran. This was certainly the grounds of gathering forces on all sides, the Vizier himself having not less than 20,000 horse, all which continually filled the streets and attended him when he went to the King. Khan Dauran and the rest of the Amírs, or grandees, with their forces and all the King's household troops, kept guard round the Fort for about twenty days. The Vizier was obstinately bent not to pay the Tartars anything, without very particular examination and accounts to be made up for the plundering the town of Patna; which conditions the Tartars did not think to comply with till such time as they found the Vizier was not to be bullied; when they seemed to be willing to come to a composition, which was effected by breaking their party, and the King's orders for Amír Jumla's procedure for Lahore. The King ordered Chín Kulich Khan[1] to go and see Amír Jumla out of the city; divesting him of all his posts at Court, as also of his titles, Jaghir, etc., with his glorious additional titles, which are ordered for the future never to be used. It is the general observation of this city that this has only been a scheme laid, if possible, to entrap the Vizier, and take away his life; but he has been so continually on his guard that nothing could be effected. So once more all is calmed, much to his (the Vizier's) honour, and the entire disgrace of all Tartars in general; they being almost all turned out of service, a few great ones excepted. Amír Jumla is now twenty coss off this place on his way to Lahore, at present without any command post. But it is reported he will enjoy the former

---

1 This was the man who afterwards became famous as Subahdar, or Viceroy, of the Dekhan, under the name of "Nizam-ul-Mulkh."

by the King's favour. These troubles occasioned the shutting up all the cutcherries for this month, so that no business could possibly go on; in which ours met the same fate with the rest, being just in the same state as a month ago. Khan Dauran very frequently promises that he will make an end with all possible expedient; but he is such a strange dilatory man, and withal inaccessible, that we have occasion to summon the utmost of our patience. There is no help for it, for, with all this dilatoriness, he is the only reigning man in the King's Durbar, so that we hope he will at last consider, and for his own honour, see us handsomely despatched with all full grant to all our petitions.

Arrest and massacre of the Sikhs at Delhi.

"The great rebel Guru (Bandu, the Sikh) who has been for these twenty years so troublesome in the province of Lahore, is at length taken with all his family and attendance by the Subahdar, or Viceroy, of that province. Some days ago they entered the city laden with fetters, his whole attendants which were left alive being about 780, all severally mounted on camels, which were sent out of the city for that purpose, besides about 2,000 heads stuck upon poles, being those who died by the sword in battle. He was carried into the presence of the King, and from thence to a close prison. He at present has his life prolonged with most of his officers, in hopes to get an account of his treasure in several parts of his kingdom, and of those that assisted him, when afterwards he will be executed for the rest. There are one hundred each day beheaded. It is not a little remarkable with what patience they undergo their fate, and to the last it has not been found that one has apostatised from the new formed religion.''

Strange procrastination and forgetfulness of Khan Dauran.

"*Delhi, 21st March.*—We have frequently complained to Your Honors of the strange dilatoriness of our patron Khan Dauran. He is never known to sit out in public, and return answers to any manner of business; so that what can be said to him in the way from his apartment to his palankeen, is

---

[1] This religion was a sort of compound of Hinduism and Muhammadanism, in which the leading doctrines of both were reconciled by a strange kind of compromise.

all that can be got; which is so very little for a man of a great business, that many days pass before an opportunity can be had even for the least answer; and that his own servant, Sayyid Sallabut Khan, who has the management of our affairs under him, and is as intimate as any one with him, can do as little that way as other people. Wherefore the main part of all our business has been managed by notes. This has been a great occasion of the dilatoriness of our affairs; all which we were obliged to bear with abundance of patience; still having very fair promises that our business should be done to our satisfaction. Nay, Khan Dauran himself very often, both by word of mouth, and in several notes, promised to do it. A few days ago when Serhaud went to pay his respects as usual to Khan Dauran, and put him in mind of our petition, he was very surprisingly asked what petition? 'Have not I done all your business?' To which Khoja Serhaud answered; but the time and place not allowing of a further explanation, he got into his palankeen and went away. This strange forgetfulness made us, in very pathetic terms, enquire of Sallabut Khan what we might expect after so many promises of having our business effected to our satisfaction. When we had so long and patiently waited, and been at so great an expence, to be thus answered was very surprizing, and what we did not nor could not expect in the least. We were answered that daily experience might convince us of the strange carriages and forgetfulness of that great man. Still bidding us not to despond, but that everything would go very well after so many fair promises as we before had received. This gave us but small satisfaction and the rather made us the more inquisitive, which gave us this further light, *viz.*, that Khan Dauran had been advised by his own officers that it was not his business to persuade the King to sign our petition, but that it was better to get the Vizier to advise the King what things were proper to be granted us. We were in hope that in case we would have got those petitions granted us by the means of Khan Dauran, that afterwards the Vizier would not gainsay it, as at least by a little bribery it might have passed. There have been several endeavours made to get an opportunity to speak with Khan Dauran, so as to convince him; but none has been procurable. We fear the petition in this interim may be gone in, and will come out signed by the Vizier as before mentioned.

More delays. "Yesterday the King, contrary to the advice of the Vizier, and purely on his own will, went out a hunting and all the grandees to their tents. The place at present mentioned is about eighteen coss off; but God knows what may be the designs of it, or where he will march to. This obliges us to follow him to-morrow or next day, leaving Mr. Edward Stephenson and Phillips behind to take care of the Honourable Company's effects here. Should the petition come out signed as above mentioned, we shall be obliged to make a new address to the Vizier; which will not only protract this negotiation, but must lay us open to a denial, and at the best very expensive. We shall advise Your Honors as soon as we have any hopes of success, which God send, or what we shall be obliged to recede from."

Fighting at the Moghul Court. "*Delhi, 20th April.*—Whilst the King was encamped fourteen coss from Delhi in order to hunt, there happened a quarrel between the people of Khan Dauran and Mahmud Amil Khan, as they came from the Durbar; which, after their masters got into their tents, ended in a downright fight, wherein they fired with small arms, bombs and great guns for about two hours, notwithstanding the King's repeated command to forbear, yet was it at last made up after about a hundred men were killed and wounded. The King was highly displeased with the liberty they took, and resented it to both of them. But at present all is made up, and His Majesty again reconciled to them."

Alarm of the Moghul. The story of the further delays that ensued may be passed over in silence. Suddenly the news reached Delhi, that the English at Surat had removed to Bombay, in order to escape from the oppression of the Nawab of Surat. The Court at Delhi was alarmed lest the English should again make war on the Moghul ships. Every demand was granted. A firman was made out and signed. The following extract describes the farewell audience:—

"*Delhi, 7th June 1717.*—The 23rd ultimo, John Surman received from his Majesty a horse and cunger, as was pre-appointed; and the 30th ultimo we were sent for by Khan Dauran to receive our dispatches, which we had accordingly; a serpaw and culgee being given to John Surman, and serpaws to Serhaud and Edward Stephenson, as likewise to the rest of our companions. We were ordered to pass, one by one, to our obeisance; then to move from the Dewan. We did so. But when it came to Mr. Hamilton's turn, he was told the King had granted him a vest as a mark of his favour, but not for his dispatch. So he was ordered up to his standing again. Whilst he was performing this, the King got up. We were highly surprised at this unexpected motion, not having the least notice of it till that minute, either from our patron or any of authority; it being near a twelvemonth since Mr. Hamilton had been in private with His Majesty, and in all this time not the least notice taken. We were very much concerned at his detainment, and the more because we were assured of his firm aversion to accepting the service, even with all its charms of vast pay, honour, &c.; that if the King did detain him by force, if he outlived the trouble of his esteeming imprisonment, he might be endeavouring at an escape, which every way had its ill consequences. **Farewell audience.**

"To free our Honorable Masters from any damages that might accrue to them from the passionate temper of the King, our patron Khan Dauran was applied to for leave, twice or thrice; but he positively denied to speak or even have a hand in this business, till our friend Sayyid Sallabut Khan had an opportunity to lay the case open to him, when he ordered us to speak to the Vizier, and, if by any means we could gain him to intercede, that he would back it. **Troubles of the English doctor.**

"We made a visit to the Vizier the 6th instant, and laid the case open to him in a petition from Mr. Hamilton, of how little service he could be without any physic, language or experience in the country medicines, or their names; besides which the heart-breaking distractions of being parted for ever from his wife and children would be insupportable, and entirely take away his qualifications for the King's service; that under the favour of His Majesty's clemency, with the utmost submission, he desired that he might have leave to depart with us. From ourselves we informed the Vizier that we should have esteemed this a very great honour, but finding the Doctor under these troubles not to be persuaded, we were obliged to lay the case before His Majesty, and we humbly desired he would use his intercessions to the King, that His Majesty might be prevailed upon to dispatch him. The good Vizier readily offered to use his utmost endeavours; and since the case was so, the business was to gain the Doctor's dispatch without displeasing the King; and he ordered a petition to be drawn up to His Majesty in the same form as that given to himself. It was sent him, and the Vizier was as good as his word; writing a very pathetic address to His Majesty, enforcing Mr. Hamilton's reasons and backing them with his own opinion, that it was better to let him go. The King returned an answer, which came out the 6th, as follows: 'Since he is privy to my disease, and perfectly understands his business, I would very fain have kept him, and given him whatsoever he should have asked. But seeing he cannot be brought on any terms to be content I agree to it; and on condition that after he has gone to Europe and procured such medicines as are not to be got here and seen his wife and children, he return to visit the Court once more, let him go.' We hope in God the troublesome business is now blown over."

Death of Hamilton: inscription on his tomb.

The English mission to Delhi, and story of Dr. Hamilton's success in curing the great Moghul, were long remembered at Calcutta. Hamilton died soon after his return to Bengal. The news of his death was sent to Delhi, but the Emperor, Farrukh Siyar, would not believe it. He sent an officer of rank to make enquiries at Calcutta. The tombstone of the dead surgeon is still to be seen. It bears an English epitaph, together with a Persian inscription, which has been thus translated :—

> "William Hamilton, Physician in the service of the English Company, who had accompanied the English ambassadors to the enlightened presence, and having made his own name famous in the four quarters of the earth by the cure of the Emperor, the asylum of the world, Muhammad Farrukh Siyar, the victorious; and, with a thousand difficulties, having obtained permission from the Court which is the refuge of the universe, to return to his country; by the Divine decree, on the fourth of December 1717, died in Calcutta, and is buried here."

Within two or three years of the departure of the English mission from Delhi, the reign of Farrukh Siyar was brought to a troubled close. The two brothers found it impossible to trust the sovereign whom they had placed on the throne. They surrounded the palace with their armies. During the night the wildest rumours were spreading through Delhi. Husain had brought up an army of Mahrattas from the Dekhan; it was said that the Mahrattas were plundering the city. The Muhammadans turned out in a panic and massacred hundreds of Mahrattas. At early morning the tumult was over. *Bloody quarrels at Delhi.*

All that night a tragedy had been going on in the palace. Farrukh Siyar refused to leave the harem. It was no time for respecting the harem. Abdulla Khan ordered a band of Afghans to force *Murder of the Emperor Farrukh Siyar.*

the doors. Farrukh Siyar was half dead with fear. The women filled the air with shrieks and screams; they tried in vain to screen him. He was dragged from their arms and thrust into a dungeon. A hot iron was drawn across his eyes; henceforth he was unfit to reign. A child was taken out of the state prison and placed upon the throne. The kettle-drums were sounded at the palace gate. The cannon boomed through the morning air. All men knew that Farrukh Siyar had ceased to reign; that another Emperor was reigning in his stead. Delhi was tranquil. Two months afterwards, Farrukh Siyar was murdered in his dungeon. His remains were buried in the famous tomb of Humayun.[1]

English settlements in Bengal, 1720.

The state of Calcutta at this period is best gathered from the narrative of Captain Hamilton, the same man who has described Madras and Fort Saint George in 1720, or thereabouts. Captain Hamilton furnishes not only a curious account of Calcutta, but notices all the English settlements in Bengal, beginning with Piply. The following extracts appear authentic:—

Ruin of Piply by the removal to Hugli and Calcutta.

"Piply lies on the banks of a river supposed to be a branch of the Ganges, about five leagues from that of Ballasore; formerly it was a place of trade, and was honoured with English and Dutch factories. The country produces the same commodities that Ballasore does; at present it is reduced to beggary by the removal of the English factory to Hughly and Calcutta, the merchants being all gone. It is now inhabited by fishers, as are also Ingellie, and Kidgerie, two neighbouring islands on the west side of the mouth of Ganges. These

[1] Scott's History of the Successors of Aurungzeb.

islands abound also in tame swine, where they are sold very cheap, for I have bought one-and-twenty good hogs, between 50 and 80 pound weight each, for seventeen rupees, or forty-five shillings sterling. Those islands send forth dangerous sand banks, that are both numerous and large, and make the navigation out and in to Hughly River both troublesome and dangerous; and after we pass those islands, in going up the river the channel for shipping is on the east side, and several creeks run from the channel among a great number of islands, formed by different channels of Ganges, two of which are more remarkable than the rest, viz., Coxe's and Sagor Islands, where great ships were obliged to anchor to take in part of their cargoes, because several places in the river are too shallow for great ships to pass over, when their whole cargoes are aboard.

"There are no inhabitants on those islands, for they are so pestered with tigers that there could be no security for human creatures to dwell on them; nay, it is even dangerous to land on them, or for boats to anchor near them, for in the night they have swimmed to boats at anchor, and carried men out of them; yet among the Pagans, the Island Sagor is accounted holy, and great numbers of Jougies go yearly thither in the months of November and December, to worship and wash in salt-water, though many of them fall sacrifices to the hungry tigers. Coxe's and Sagor Islands.

"The first safe anchoring place in the river, is off the mouth of a river about twelve leagues above Sagor, commonly known by the name of Rogue's River, which had that appellation from some banditti Portuguese, who were followers of Sultan Shuja, when Amír Jumla, Aurungzeb's general, drove that unfortunate prince out of his province of Bengal; for those Portuguese, having no way to subsist, after their master's flight to the kingdom of Arakan, betook themselves to piracy among the islands at the mouth of the Ganges; and that river having communication with all the channels from Chittagong to the westward, from this river they used to sally out, and commit depredations on those that traded in the river of Hughly. Anchorage at Rogue's River.

Danish house.

"About five leagues farther up, on the west side of the river of Hughly, is another branch of the Ganges, called Ganga. It is broader than that of Hughly, but much shallower, and more incumbered with sand banks; a little below the mouth of it the Danes have a thatched house, but for what reasons they kept a house there, I never could learn.

Calculta, Juanpardoa, and Radnagur.

"Along the river of Hughly there are many small villages and farms, intersperst in those large plains, but the first of any note on the river's side is Calculta, a market town for corn, coarse cloth, butter, and oil, with other productions of the country. Above it is the Dutch Bankshall, a place where their ships ride when they cannot get farther up for the too swift currents of the river. Calculta has a large deep river that runs to the eastward, and so has Juanpardoa; and on the west side there is a river that runs by the back of Hughly Island, which leads up to Radnagur, famous for manufacturing cotton cloth, and silk romaals, or handkerchiefs. Buffundri and Trefindi, or Gorgat and Cottrong, are on that river, which produce the greatest quantities of the best sugars in Bengal.

Ponjelly.

"A little higher up on the east side of Hughly River, is Ponjelly, a village where a corn mart is kept once or twice in a week; it exports more rice than any place on this river; and

Tanna Fort.

five leagues farther up on the other side, is Tanna Fort, built to protect the trade of the river, at a place convenient enough, where it is not above half a mile from shore to shore; but it never was of much use, for in the year 1686, when the English Company quarrelled with the Moghul, the Company had several great ships at Hughly, and this Fort was manned in order to hinder their passage down the river. One 60-gun ship approaching pretty near the Fort, saluted it with a broadside, which so frightened the Governor and his myrmidons, that they all deserted their post, and left their castle to be plundered by the English seamen. About a

Governapore.

league farther up on the other side of the river, is Governapore, where there is a little pyramid built for a landmark, to confine the Company's Colony of Calcutta, or Fort

William. On that side, and about a league farther up, stands Fort William.

Settlement at Calcutta by Job Channock, 1690.

"The English settled at Calcutta about the year 1690, after the Moghul had pardoned all the robberies and murders committed on his subjects. Mr. Job Channock being then the Company's Agent in Bengal, he had liberty to settle an emporium in any part on the river's side below Hughly; and for the sake of a large shady tree chose that place, though he could not have chosen a more unhealthful place on all the river; for three miles to the north-eastward, is a salt water lake that overflows in September and October, and then prodigious numbers of fish resort thither; but in November and December when the floods are dissipated, those fishes are left dry, and with their putrefaction affect the air with thick stinking vapours, which the north-east winds bring with them to Fort William, that they cause a yearly mortality. One year I was there, and there were reckoned in August about twelve hundred English, some military, some servants to the Company, some private merchants residing in the town, and some seamen belonging to shipping lying at the town; and before the beginning of January there were four hundred and sixty burials registered in the clerk's book of mortality.

Despotic power of Mr. Channock.

"Mr. Channock choosing the ground of the colony, where it now is, reigned more absolute than a Raja, only he wanted much of their humanity, for when any poor ignorant native transgressed his laws, they were sure to undergo a severe whipping for a penalty, and the execution was generally done when he was at dinner, so near his dining-room that the groans and cries of the poor delinquent served him for music.

Story of Mr. Channock's Native wife.

"The country about being overspread with Paganism, the custom of wives burning with their deceased husbands, is also practised here. Before the Moghul's war, Mr. Channock went one time with his ordinary guard of soldiers, to see a young widow act that tragical catastrophe; but he was so smitten with the widow's beauty, that he sent his guards to

[1] This name is somtimes spelt Charnock.

take her by force from her executioners, and conducted her to his own lodgings. They lived lovingly many years, and had several children. At length she died, after he had settled in Calcutta; but instead of converting her to Christianity she made him a proselyte to Paganism; and the only part of Christianity that was remarkable in him, was burying her decently. He built a tomb over her, where all his life after her death, he kept the anniversary day of her death by sacrificing a cock on her tomb, after the Pagan manner; this was and is the common report, and I have been credibly informed, both by Christians and Pagans, who lived at Calcutta under his Agency, that the story was really true matter of fact.

Fort William and English houses.

"Fort William was built an irregular tetragon, of brick and mortar, called puckah, which is a composition of brick-dust, lime, molasses, and cut hemp; and when it comes to be dry, is as hard and tougher than firm stone or brick. The town was built without order, as the builders thought most convenient for their own affairs; every one taking in what ground best pleased them for gardening, so that in most houses you must pass through a garden into the house; the English building near the river's side, and the natives within-land.

Story of Sir Edward Littleton.

"The Agency continued till the year 1705. Then the old and new Companies united, and then it became a split Government, the old and new Companies' servants governing a week about, which made it more anarchical than regular. Sir Edward Littleton was Agent and Consul for the new Company at Hughly when this union of the Companies was made; and then he was ordered to remove his factory to Calcutta, and, being of an indolent disposition, had left his accounts with the Company run behind. He was suspended, but lived at Calcutta till 1707, when he died there. He was the only President or precedent in the Company's service that lost an estate of seven hundred pounds per annum in so profitable a post in their service.

Mr. Weldon.

"This double-headed Government continued in Calcutta till January 1707. Then Mr. Weldon arrived with the Company's commission to settle it at Bombay and Fort St. George, which were under the management of a Governor and Council, which those of the direction in England took to be a better way to promote their own creatures, as well as their own interest. His term of governing was very short, and he took as short a way to be enriched by it, by harassing the people to fill his coffers.

"Yet he was very shy in taking bribes, referring those honest folks, who trafficked that way, to the discretion of his wife and daughter, to make the best bargain they could about the sum to be paid, and to pay the money into their hands. I could give many instances of the force of bribery, both here and elsewhere in India, but am loth to ruffle the skin of old sores.

Scandals about bribes.

"About fifty yards from Fort William stands the church built by the pious charity of merchants residing there, and the Christian benevolence of sea-faring men, whose affairs call them to trade there; but Ministers of the Gospel being subject to mortality, very often young merchants are obliged to officiate, and have a salary of 50*l.* per annum added to what the Company allows them, for their pains in reading prayers and sermons on Sundays.

Divine Service.

"The Governor's house in the Fort, is the best and most regular piece of architecture that I ever saw in India. And there are many convenient lodgings, for factors and writers, within the Fort, and some store-houses for the Company's goods, and the magazines for their ammunition.

Governor's house.

"The Company has a pretty good hospital at Calcutta, where many go in to undergo the penance of physick, but few come out to give account of its operation. The Company has also a pretty good garden that furnishes the Governor's table with herbage and fruits; and some fish-ponds to serve his kitchen with good carp, calkops, and mullet.

Hospital, garden, and fish-ponds.

"Most of the inhabitants of Calcutta that make any tolerable figure have the same advantages; and all sorts of provisions, both wild and tame, being plentiful, good and cheap, as well as clothing, make the country very agreeable, notwithstanding the above-mentioned inconveniencies that attend it.

Docks on the opposite bank.

"On the other side of the river are docks made for repairing and fitting their ships' bottoms, and a pretty good garden belonging to the Armenians, that had been a better place to have built their Fort and Town in for many reasons. One is, that, where it now stands, the afternoon's sun is full in the fronts of the houses, and shines hot on the streets, that are both above and below the Fort; the sun would have sent its hot rays on the back of the houses, and the fronts had been a good shade for the streets.

Social life of the English in Bengal.

"Most gentlemen and ladies in Bengal live both splendidly and pleasantly, the forenoons being dedicated to business, and after dinner to rest, and in the evening to recreate themselves in chaises or palankins in the fields, or to gardens, or by water in their budgeroes, which is a convenient boat that goes swiftly with the force of oars. On the river sometimes there is the diversion of fishing or fowling, or both; and before night they make friendly visits to one another when pride or contention do not spoil society, which too often they do among the ladies, as discord and faction do among the men. And although the 'Conscript Fathers' of the colony disagree in many points among themselves, yet they all agree in oppressing strangers who are consigned to them, not suffering them to buy or sell their goods at the most advantageous market, but of the Governor and his Council, who fix their own prices, high or low, as seemeth best to their wisdom and discretion: and it is a crime hardly pardonable for a private merchant to go to Hughly, to inform himself of the current prices of goods, although the liberty of buying and selling is entirely taken from him before.

English soldiers.

"The garrison of Fort William generally consists of two or three hundred soldiers, more for to convey their fleet from Patna, with the Company's saltpetre, and piece goods, raw silk and some opium belonging to other merchants, than for the defence of the Fort; for, as the Company holds their colony in feetail of the Moghul, they need not be afraid of any enemies coming to dispossess them. And if they should, at any time, quarrel again with the Moghul, his prohibiting his subjects to trade with the Company would soon end the quarrel.

Transit duties levied by petty Rajas.

"There are some impertinent troublesome Rajas, whose territories lie on the banks of the Ganges, between Patna and Cossimbazaar, who pretend to lay a tax on all goods and merchandize that pass by, or through their dominions on the river, and often raise forces to compel payment; but some forces from Fort William in boats generally clear the passage, though I have known some of our men killed in the skirmishes.

Different religions.

"In Calcutta all religions are freely tolerated but the Presbyterian, and that they brow-beat. The Pagans carry their idols in procession through the town. The Roman Catholicks have their Church to lodge their idols in, and the Mahometan is not discountenanced; but there are no polemics, except what are between our High-church men and our Low, or between the Governor's party and other private merchants on points of trade.

Injustice of the English Governors.

"The colony has very little manufactory of its own, for the Government, being pretty arbitrary, discourages ingenuity and industry in the populace; for, by the weight of the Company's authority, if a native chances to disoblige one of the upper-house, he is liable to arbitrary punishment, either by fine, imprisonment or corporal sufferings. I will give one instance, out of many that I knew, of the injustice of a Governor of the double-headed Government in the year 1706.

Story of Captain Perrin and Governor Sheldon.

"There was one Captain Perrin, master of a ship, who took up about five hundred pounds on respondentia from Mr. Ralph Sheldon, one of the Governors, on a voyage to Persia, payable at his return to Bengal. Perrin, having dispatched his affairs in Persia sooner than he expected, called at Goa on his way home, and bought a Surat-built ship very cheap, and carried her to Calicut and took in a quantity of pepper for the Bengal market; and having brought in his other ship good store of Persian wines, called at Fort St. George to dispose of what he could there, but, finding no encouragement from that market, carried it to Bengal. On his arrival he complimented Mr. Sheldon with the offer of his pepper and wine, but he declined meddling with that bargain farther than with as much of the pepper, at the current price, as would balance his account of principal and respondentia. Accordingly Perrin delivered so much pepper, and, on the delivery, required his bond up, but the Governor told him, that he being a fellow troubled with the spirit of interloping in buying goods, and taking freights where he could best get them, he would keep that bond as a curb on him, that he should not spoil his markets for the future. Poor Perrin used all his rhetoric to get his bond up, but to no purpose; and the Governor, moreover, gave his wine a bad name, so that he could not dispose of that either; and all this oppression was in order to strain him, that he might be obliged to sell his new purchased ship, at a low price, to him and his associates; which, at last, he was obliged to do, holding a quarter part in his own hands, to secure the command of her to himself, which after all he could hardly do. Perrin made his complaint to me, but I was in no condition to assist him, because I, having three or four large ships at Bengal, was reckoned a criminal guilty of that unpardonable sin of interloping. However I advised Perrin to comply with his inexorable master, on any terms of agreement whatsoever; which he endeavoured to do, that he might at least keep the command of his ship, where he was so much concerned, and had hardly done it but by accident. One day, meeting me on the green near the Fort, he stopt me to relate his griveances, and begged that, if he was turned out of his own ship, he might have an employ in one of mine, which I promised he should.

Hamilton's interference.

"Sheldon espied us, out of a window, holding a long confabulation, and being impatient to know about what, sent a servant to call Perrin; and he, obeying the summons, was interrogated about what our discourse was; and he told the promise I had made him. Sheldon told him that he was as capable to employ him as I could be. Perrin answered that he knew that, but wished that he would be as willing too; so Sheldon promised that he should command his own ship to Persia.

Story of the Persian wine.

"But the wine still lay unsold, though it was scarce then in Bengal; but the name that it got, first at Fort St. George, and afterwards in Fort William, stuck so fast to it, that none of it would go off at any price; so I advised him to carry it off in the night, in my boats, on board of one of my ships, and I would try if I could serve him in selling it; which accordingly he did, and two gentlemen of the Council, being that season bound for England, coming one day to dine with me, I treated them, and the rest of my company, with that Persian wine, which they all praised, and asked me where I got it. I told them that, knowing that good wines would be scarce at Bengal that year, I had provided a good quantity at Surat, from whence I had come that season. Every one begged that I would spare them some chests, which I condescended to do as a favour; and next day sent them what they wanted, at double the price the owner demanded for it, while he had it; and so got off above a hundred and twenty chests, which enabled Mr. Perrin to satisfy most of his creditors.[1]

Territory and population of the Company's settlement.

"The Company's colony is limited by a land-mark at Governapore, and another near Barnagul, about six miles distant; and the salt-water lake bounds it on the land side. It may contain, in all, about ten or twelve thousand souls; and the Company's revenues are pretty good, and well paid. They rise from ground-rents and consulage on all goods imported by British subjects; but all nations besides are free from taxes.

Barnagul.

"Barnagul is the next village on the river's side, above Calcutta, where the Dutch have the house and garden.

Danish colony.

"There are several other villages on the river sides, in the way to Hughly, which lies twenty miles above Barnagul, but none remarkable, till we come to the Danes' factory, which

---

[1] It must be borne in mind that Captain Hamilton was an interloper, and therefore a natural enemy of the Company, and very prone to believe anything evil concerning them.

stands about four miles below Hughly; but the poverty of the Danes has made them desert it, after having robbed the Moghul's subjects of some of their shipping, to keep themselves from starving.

Danish and French Companies.

"Almost opposite to the Dane's factory is Bankebanksal,[1] a place where the Ostend Company settled a factory, but, in the year 1723, they quarrelled with the Fouzdar or Governor of Hughly, and he forced the offenders to quit their factory, and seek protection from the French at Chandernagore, where their factory is, but, for want of money, are not in a capacity to trade. They have a few private families dwelling near the factory, and a pretty little church to hear Mass in, which is the chief business of the French in Bengal.

Dutch factory at Chinsura.

"About half a league farther up is Chinsura, where the Dutch emporium stands. It is a large factory, walled high with brick. And the factors have a great many good houses standing pleasantly on the river's side; and all of them have pretty gardens to their houses. The settlement at Chinsura is wholly under the Dutch Company's Government. It is about a mile long, and about the same breadth, well inhabited by Armenians and the natives. It is contiguous to Hughly, and affords sanctuary for many poor natives, when they are in danger of being oppressed by the Moghul's Governor, or his harpies.

Hughly.

"Hughly is a town of a large extent, but ill built. It reaches about two miles along the river's side, from Chinsura before mentioned to Bandel, a colony formerly settled by the Portuguese, but the Moghul's Fouzdaar governs both at present. This town of Hughly drives a great trade, because all foreign goods are brought thither for import, and all goods of the product of Bengal are brought hither for exportation. And the Moghul's custom-house is at this place. It affords rich cargoes for fifty or sixty ships yearly,

---

[1] The term "Banksoll" has always been a puzzle to the English in India It is borrowed from the Dutch. The "Soll" is the Dutch or Danish "Zoll," the English "Toll." The Banksoll was thus the place on the "bank" where all tolls or duties were levied on landing goods.

besides what is carried to neighbouring countries in small vessels; and there are vessels that bring saltpetre from Patna, above fifty yards long, and five broad, and two and a half deep, and can carry above two hundred tons. They come down in the month of October, before the stream of the river, but are obliged to track them up again, with strength of hand, about a thousand miles. To mention all the particular species of goods that this rich country produces is far beyond my skill; but, in our East India Company's sales, all the sorts, that are sent hence to Europe, may be found; but opium, long pepper and ginger are commodities that the trading shipping in India deals in, besides tobacco, and many sorts of piece goods that are not merchantable in Europe.

"Now this being my farthest travels up the famous Ganges, Cossimbazaar.
I must advance farther on the report of others, and so I begin with Cossimbazaar, about hundred miles north of Hughly, where the English and Dutch have their respective factories, and, by their Companies' orders, the seconds of Council ought to be chiefs of those factories. The town is large, and much frequented by merchants, which never fails of making a place rich. The country about it is very healthful and fruitful, and produces industrious people, who cultivate many valuable manufactories.

"Murshedabad is but twelve miles from it, a place of much Murshedabad.
greater antiquity, and the Moghul has a mint there. It was, in former times, the greatest place of trade and commerce on the Ganges, but now its trade and grandeur adorns Cossimbazaar.

"About forty or fifty miles to the eastward of Murshedabad, Malda.
on another channel of the Ganges, is Malda, a large town, well inhabited and frequented by merchants; the English and Dutch had factories there, but whether they are continued still, I know not.

"Patna is the next town frequented by Europeans, where Patna.
the English and Dutch have factories for saltpetre and raw silk. It produces also so much opium that it serves all the countries in India with that commodity. It is the place of

residence of the Viceroy of Bengal, who is always of the blood royal. The town is large, but the houses built at some distance from one another. The country is pleasant and fruitful; and the town lies in 26 degrees of latitude to the northward of the equator.

Benares. "Benares lies about a hundred miles farther up the river, celebrated for its sanctity by all persons over India, where paganism prevails. Here are seminaries and universities for the education of youth, and to initiate them into the mysteries of their religion. Aurungzeb restrained the priests from showing the madness of their zeal, for they found out some weak dotards, who, for ostentation, would go to the top of a high tower, and leap down where divers pointed weapons were placed in the spot they were to fall on, and among them they ended their silly lives. It is still in so much veneration that I have known young and old Banyans go from Surat thither over land, out of devotion, which is computed to be a distance of four hundred miles. The priests fill brass and copper pots, made in the shape of short-necked bottles, with Ganges water, which they consecrate and seal up, and send those bottles, which contain about four English gallons, all over India, to their benefactors, who make them good returns, for whoever is washed with that water just before they expire, are washed as clean from their sins as a new-born babe.

Dacca. "I have ventured so far into this *tenra-incognita* on the Ganges, that I dare venture no farther, but must visit Dacca, which lies under the tropic of Cancer, on the broadest and eastermost branch of Ganges. The city is the largest in Bengal, and it manufactures cotton and silk the best and cheapest. The plenty and cheapness of provisions are incredible, and the country is full of inhabitants, but it breeds none of tolerable courage, for five or six armed men will chase a thousand. Yet, about two centuries ago, Dacca had its own Kings, but when Jehangir, the Emperor of the Moghuls, over-ran Bengal with a victorious army, a detachment of twenty thousand men was sent down to Dacca, on whose approach the poor Bengal King surrendered his kingdom, without once drawing his sword in its defence, and so it easily became annexed to the Moghul's dominions.

"That branch of the Ganges disembogues into the sea at Chittagong, or, as the Portuguese call it, Xatigam, about fifty leagues below Dacca; and this place confines the Moghul's dominions to the eastwards. The distance between Sagor, the westernmost channel of the Ganges, and Chittagong easternmost, is about a hundred leagues, the maritime coast being divided into many small islands made by the currents of the Ganges, but very few are inhabited, because they are so pestered with tigers that there is little safety for other inhabitants; and there are also many rhinoceroses on those islands, but they are not so dangerous neighbours as the tigers, yet, when provoked, they will assault any living thing. Nature has endued him with two particular rarities out of her stores. One is a large horn placed on his nose. The second is a coat of mail to defend him from the teeth or claws of other fierce animals. His tongue is also somewhat of a rarity, for, if he can but get any of his antagonists down, he will lick them so clean that he leaves neither skin nor flesh to cover their bones; but he is seldom known to be an aggressor, except when he meets with an elephant; then he sharpens his horn and assaults, though he is much inferior to the elephant in bulk and strength, being no bigger than a very large ox, yet he often overcomes in spite of the elephant's teeth. Chittagong.

"Sundiva is an island four leagues distant from the rest, and so far it lies in the sea; it is about twenty leagues in circumference, and has three fathoms water within a mile of the shore, and it may serve to shelter small ships from the raging seas, and winds of the south-west monsoons. I was credibly informed by one that wintered there, that he bought 580 pounds weight of rice for a rupee, or half a crown, eight geese for the same money, and sixty good tame poultry for the same, and cloth is also incredibly cheap. It is but thinly inhabited, but the people simple and honest. Sundiva.

"The religion of Bengal by law established, is Mahometan; yet for one Mahometan there are above a hundred Pagans, A hundred pagans to one Mussulman.

and the public offices and posts of trust are filled promiscuously with men of both persuasions.

Lightness of Moghul taxation.

"The Hindus are better contented to live under the Moghul's laws than under pagan Princes, for the Moghul taxes them gently, and every one knows what he must pay, but the pagan Kings or Princes tax at discretion, making their own avarice the standard of equity; besides there were formerly many small Rajas, that used, upon frivolous occasions, to pick quarrels with one another, and before they could be made friends again, their subjects were forced to open both their veins and purses to gratify ambition or folly."

Hamilton's imperfect information.

Such were the European settlements in Bengal as they appeared to a ship captain in the early years of the eighteenth century. Of the Moghul government of the Nawab, Hamilton knew nothing. He says that a prince imperial resided at Patna as Viceroy of Bengal. But there had been no Viceroy of Bengal resident in the province since the death of Aurungzeb in 1707. At the time of Hamilton's voyages up the River Hughli, Murshed Kuli Khan, or one of his successors, must have been Nawab of Bengal, residing at Murshedabad.

Death of Murshed Kuli Khan.

Murshed Kuli Khan died in 1724. He was succeeded in turn by a son-in-law and grandson. Neither of these two Nawabs were men of any character. In 1742 the grandson was overthrown by a rebel, named Aliverdi Khan. This man is a type of the adventurers who were abroad in those days.

Rise of Aliverdi Khan.

Aliverdi Khan is said to have been originally a hookah-bearer to the Nawab. He was ultimately made deputy governor of Behar. At this period he conquered most of the Hindu Rajas in Behar, either by force or treachery. One story will serve as an illustration of his administration.

Raja of the Chukwars.

There was a once famous Raja in Behar, known as the Raja of the Chukwars. He had a town, named Samba over against Monghyr. The English knew him well, for he levied duties on all goods going up or down the river between Calcutta and Patna, and there had been many a fight between the English escort and the Raja and his followers. He was, in fact, one of those petty Rajas who collected, or tried to collect, arbitrary imposts on all goods passing through their neighbourhood. No doubt these imposts were a kind of black mail.

Independence of the old Raja: submission of the young Raja.

This Raja of the Chukwars had always set the Moghuls at defiance; he would pay neither tribute nor homage to Aliverdi Khan. He died about 1730; his son succeeded to the Raj. The son submitted to Aliverdi Khan and paid a yearly tribute. Both sides feared treachery. Accordingly it was agreed that when the Raja paid his yearly tribute, he should be accompanied by thirty followers and no more. In like manner it was agreed that the officer who received the tribute should also have only thirty followers. This rule was strictly observed for four years in succession.

Treachery of Aliverdi Khan.

On the fifth year, when the tribute was about to be paid, the Company's servants at Calcutta were sending goods and treasure to Patna under the charge of an escort of soldiers. The goods were in charge of a young merchant named Holwell. Holwell and the Major commanding the escort saw a boat passing by, and called on it to stop as they wanted some fish. The boat came up with six baskets on board. Instead of fish, they contained the bleeding heads of the Raja and his thirty followers. All had been murdered by the treachery of the officer of Aliverdi Khan. It turned out that an ambuscade had been set by the order of Aliverdi Khan; that the Raja and his thirty followers had all been treacherously attacked, murdered, and beheaded; that the heads had been sent away to Patna to satisfy Aliverdi Khan. That same night the Raja's town of Samba was sacked and burnt by the forces of Aliverdi Khan.[1]

Persian invasion under Nadir Shah, 1738-39.

Meanwhile the force of the Moghul empire was fast wasting away. Farrukh Siyar was little better than a pageant. His successors fooled away their time with concubines and buffoons, and left the administration in the hands of corrupt and unscrupulous ministers. The empire of Akbar and Aurungzeb was only held together under their feeble successors by the force of old routine and the prestige of a name. In 1738-39, the empire received a mortal blow. Nadir Shah of Persia advanced with a large army upon Delhi. The story of the invasion of Nadir Shah reveals the fact, that the Moghul empire was rotten to the core. It furnishes such a terrible picture of the defenceless state of Hindustan, and is so often referred to in

[1] Holwell's Tracts. Mr. Holwell states that he himself was an eye-witness, having been with the English boats at the time.

the later records, that it cannot be passed over in silence.

The Persian empire was founded by the Sufi dynasty in the beginning of the sixteenth century, on the ruins of the great Tartar empire created in the fourteenth century by Timur. The Sufi dynasty lingered on for two centuries, and was then overthrown by an Afghan invasion shortly after the death of Aurungzeb in the beginning of the eighteenth century. The Afghan conquest of Persia is one of the most horrible stories of rapine and outrage in the annals of the world. Amidst the general anarchy, a freebooter assumed the sovereignty of Persia, under the name of Nadir Shah. He founded a new Persian empire which threatened to rival that of Darius. He conquered all the region to the eastward,—Bokhara, Kabul, and Kandahar.

Afghan conquest of Persia; rise of Nadir Shah.

It was natural that Nadir Shah should have overrun Kabul and Kandahar. He scarcely wanted to invade India; he was drawn into it by the senseless conduct of the Moghul and his ministers. He sent ambassadors to Delhi; he received no congratulations, and no replies. His ambassadors were not even dismissed; they were kept waiting on at Court. He was surprised; he grew exasperated. The way was open before him; the passes had ceased to be guarded. In former times, a yearly subsidy of twelve lakhs of rupees had served to block up the passes. Part of the money was distributed to the hill tribes; the remainder was spent

Causes of the Persian invasion of India.

on garrisons. The worthless Vizier at Delhi kept back the money for his own use. The posts were abandoned. The army of Nadir Shah moved on unchecked towards Delhi. Meanwhile no reports of the threatened danger reached the doomed capital; or if any warnings were received, they were wholly disregarded until there was no possibility of repelling the invasion.

Incapacity, corruption, and treachery.

At last the news arrived at the Moghul Court that Nadir Shah was coming. A vast mob of Hindustanis was gathered together to resist the Persian invaders. Nadir Shah gained an easy victory. There was no real opposition. The two leading Moghul grandees were quarrelling for the post of Amír-ul-Umra, literally Amir of Amirs, otherwise the chief of all the grandees. One bribed Nadir Shah to return to Persia by a payment of two millions sterling; and was rewarded for his success by being appointed to the coveted post. The disappointed rival was so exasperated that in sheer revenge he opened up a communication with Nadir Shah; told him that the two millions sterling was a mere drop in the ocean when compared with the vast riches which were accumulated in the city and palace at Delhi. In this manner, out of the meanest spite and malice against the Emperor and his ministers, he prevailed on Nadir Shah to advance and plunder Delhi.[1]

[1] This is the story told by the Mussulman author of the Siyar-ul-Mutakherin. Chín Kulich Khan, the Nizam of the Dekhan, is said to have been the man who purchased the return of Nadir Shah; whilst Sádut Khan, the Nawab of Oude, is said to have been the traitor.

The story of what followed is horrible. Nadir Shah went to Delhi. He took up his quarters in the palace. His Persian troops were scattered over the city. Suddenly it was noised abroad that Nadir Shah was killed. The Hindustanis rose up and began to murder the Persians. Hundreds were slaughtered in the panic. The news reached Nadir Shah. He called together his forces. He ordered a general massacre. The mosque is still pointed out in the principal street of Delhi, known as the Chandni Chouk, where Nadir Shah took his seat whilst the massacre was going on. The murders and outrages that were perpetrated in Delhi, under the eye of the conqueror, are beyond description. Whenever the Persians found a dead comrade, they desolated the whole neighbourhood, butchered the people, and committed unspeakable atrocities. In the evening Nadir Shah proclaimed a general pardon. The dead bodies were thrown up in vast heaps with the beams and rafters of the ruined houses, and the whole was set on fire. There was no distinction between Mussulman and Hindu. The spoil was beyond all computation. Besides the general plunder, the hoarded wealth of generations was carried off from the imperial palace at Delhi. The peacock throne vanished for ever.

Massacre, outrage, and spoliation.

The capture and sack of Delhi by Nadir Shah heralded the downfall of the Moghul empire. The governors of provinces asserted their independence of the Moghul Emperor, and ceased to remit revenue to Delhi. The Mahrattas had long ceased to

Breaking up of the Moghul Empire.

fear the Moghul power; they had established dominions in Malwa and Berar. But hitherto they had been kept tolerably quiet, as far as Delhi was concerned, by the yearly payment of stipulated shares of the imperial revenue, under the name of *chout*. After the sack of Delhi by the Persians, there was no *chout* forthcoming to keep the Mahrattas quiet, and they soon began to help themselves. They began to plunder the Dekhan and the Carnatic, and they soon began to plunder Behar, Bengal, and Orissa.

State of Bengal.

When Nadir Shah invaded Hindustan, the grandson of Murshed Kuli Khan was Nawab of Bengal, Behar, and Orissa. The court of Murshedabad was a sink of iniquity and centre of oppression. There was no hope of redress from Delhi; the court and capital of the Moghul were so prostrate that no heed was paid to Bengal. At last a conspiracy was formed against the Nawab at Murshedabad; and the conspirators opened up a secret communication with Aliverdi Khan, the deputy Nawab of Behar, who was residing at Patna.

The Seits, or Hindu bankers.

It would be difficult for any European pen to describe the open and avowed depravity of Murshedabad during the generation which preceded the rise of British power. One incident is told, which was said to have driven the conspirators into rebellion; but it fails to convey an idea of the open and flagrant debauchery of the Nawab. The Seits or Setts were Hindu bankers settled at Murshedabad. They were the Rothschilds of India.

Their enormous wealth gave them unbounded influence. If there was one man more than another who might hope to escape from the oppression of the Nawab, it was Jugget Seit, the head of the family.

A son or grandson of Juggut Seit was married in great state at Murshedabad. There were rumours about the beauty of the bride; and the Nawab demanded that she should be sent to the palace and her face unveiled in his presence. The old Hindu banker prayed to be spared this terrible indignity. The Nawab was deaf to all his prayers; threatened to surround his house with horsemen and carry off the bride by force. The banker submitted to the shame; he revenged the affront by promoting the conspiracy in favour of Aliverdi Khan. Lawlessness of the Nawab.

It would be useless to dwell on the progress of the intrigue between Murshedabad and Patna. It was reported at the time that the Nawab had sent his submission to Nadir Shah; that the conspiracy was undertaken under a show of punishing the Nawab for his want of fidelity to the Moghul; and it is very probable that the return of Nadir Shah to Persia, and utter prostration of Delhi, encouraged Aliverdi Khan to make an attempt on the government of Bengal. Conspiracy.

In 1741-42, Aliverdi Khan marched an army from Patna to Murshedabad. The Nawab came out to meet the rebel, but his generals were traitors. His artillery would have sufficed to crush the rebellion; but the guns were only loaded with Rebellion an usurpation of Aliverdi Khan, 1741-42.

powder. Under such circumstances the Nawab was soon killed, and then all the generals and grandees went over to Aliverdi Khan.

Usurpation of Aliverdi Khan, 1742.

In this fashion, Aliverdi Khan usurped the throne of Bengal. The Moghul Court at Delhi had been paralysed by the invasion of Nadir Shah, and had neither the power nor the will to interfere. Before that invasion the Moghul court had been compelled to make disgraceful treaties with the Mahrattas. After the invasion it was confidently asserted that the court at Delhi got rid of the Mahrattas by telling them to go and collect *chout* in Bengal.

Mahrattas invade Bengal, 1742-50.

It is impossible to unravel the intrigues of this period. One thing is certain, that before Aliverdi Khan was fairly established upon the throne at Murshedabad, the Mahrattas began to invade the provinces of Behar and Orissa. These Mahratta invasions were repeated almost every year from 1742 to 1750. It is needless to dwell on the murder, plunder, and outrage that ensued. The people fled from their houses, and crossed the Ganges in shoals, in order to escape to the jungles. The markets were deserted; the lands were untilled; and the whole country was a ruin. In 1750 there was peace. Orissa was abandoned to the Mahrattas, and the Nawab agreed to pay a yearly tribute, or *chout*, for Bengal and Behar.

War between England and France, 1744.

The great European event at this period was the war between England and France. News of the breaking out of the war reached Calcutta in 1744. The English at Calcutta and the French at Chandernagore were compelled to live in peace. The Nawab strictly prohibited all hostilities between the two nations within his territories; and he was strong enough to be implicitly obeyed.

But whilst there was peace in Bengal there was war in Madras. In Southern India, as already seen, the English and French had gone to war with a will. In 1748, the war had been brought to a close in Europe by the peace of Aix la Chapelle. But not even the peace in Europe could stop the war between the English and French in Southern India. Rival Nizams were fighting for the throne at Hyderabad. Rival Nawabs were fighting for the throne of the Carnatic. English and French fought on opposite sides. At last, as already stated, peace was concluded in 1754 between the English at Madras and the French at Pondicherry. The French had established their own Nizam at Hyderabad. The English had established their own Nawab in Carnatic territory.[1]

Peace between English and French in India, 1754.

[1] The principal authorities for the sketch of Bengal are Stewart's History of Bengal, Orme's Hindustan, Holwell's Tracts, and the Siyar-ul-Mutakherin.

Synchronistical Table of

DELHI.	
Sack and massacre at Delhi by Nadir Shah	1738-39
Assassination of Nadir Shah in Persia	1747
Ahmad Shah Abdali founds an Afghan Empire	"
First Afghan invasion of Hindustan under Ahmad Shah Abdali	"
Death of Muhammad Shah, Emperor of Delhi	1748
AHMAD SHAH, son of Muhammad Shah, succeeds	"
Growing influence of the Mahrattas: intrigues at Delhi for the post of Vizier	"
Ghazi-u-din, Vizier at Delhi, exercises great influence, deposes and blinds AHMAD SHAH	1754
ALAMGHIR II succeeds to the throne at Delhi, aged sixty-six .	"
Second Afghan invasion under Ahmad Shah Abdali, who enters Delhi, plunders Mathura, and makes Nujib-u-daula, the Rohilla Afghan, guardian of Alamghir II	1757
Ghazi-u-din returns to Delhi, supported by the Mahrattas .	1758
Shahzada, eldest son of Alamghir II, flies from Delhi to Bengal to escape from the Vizier	"
Alamghir II murdered by Ghazi-u-din for intriguing with the Afghans	1759
Shahzada in Bengal proclaims himself Emperor under the title of Shah Alam	"
Ghazi-u-din places a puppet prince on the throne at Delhi .	"
Third Afghan invasion: Ahmad Shah Abdali places Jewan Bakht, eldest son of Shah Alam, on the throne at Delhi under the guardianship of Najib-u-daula, the Rohilla Afghan	"
Wars between the Afghans and Mahrattas	1760
Total defeat of the Mahrattas by the Afghans at Paniput .	1761

British Indian History.

Bengal.	
Aliverdi Khan usurps the Nawabship of Bengal, Behar, and Orissa	1742
Mahrattas begin yearly invasions	,,
Grant of chout to the Mahrattas	1750
Native contractors of the Company, like Omichund, replaced by Native agents or gomastas	1753
Death of Aliverdi Khan: succession of his grandson Suraj-u-daula as Nawab . . . . *April*	1756
Capture of Calcutta by Suraj-u-daula . . . . *June*	,,
Clive and Watson recover Calcutta . . . *January*	1757
Chandernagore captured . . . . *March*	,,
Battle of Plassey . . . . *May*	,,
Meer Jaffier set up as Nawab by the English	,,
Colonel Forde sent to the Dekhan	1758
Defeat of the Dutch	1759
Appearance and flight of the Shahzada	,,
Shazada proclaimed Emperor under the title of Shah Alam .	,,
Clive returns to England	1760
Defeat of Shah Alam and the Nawab Vizier of Oude . .	,,
Shah Alam at Patna	1761
Meer Jaffier deposed	,,
Meer Cossim Ali Khan Nawab	,,
Breach between the Nawab and the English	1762
Massacre at Patna	1763
Meer Jaffier Nawab	,,
Battle of Buxar; defeat of Shah Alam and the Nawab Vizier of Oude	1764
Lord Clive accepts the Dewani of Bengal, Behar, and Orissa from the Emperor Shah Alam	1765

CHAPTER VII.

CALCUTTA AND ITS CAPTURE.

1750—56.

State of Calcutta, 1750-56.

ALL this while the English settlement at Calcutta was like an oasis of European civilisation in a desert of Hinduism and Islam. The English factory, with its warehouses, workshops, offices, and outlying houses, covered about a hundred acres on the bank of the Hughli. The native town consisted of three or four large villages, more or less remote from the English factory, and from each other. Some houses may have been built of brick and chunam; some were made of clay and whitewashed; the bulk were hovels of mud and straw. There were pagodas, mosques, tanks, and two or three churches. But Calcutta was not a metropolis. The English factory was only an emporium of the English trade in Bengal. Native villages near the factory were growing into a city under the stimulus of manufacture and trade.

Mahratta ditch.

The English at Calcutta were never attacked by the Mahrattas. As far back as 1742, the native inhabitants had been in great alarm, and obtained permission to dig a ditch at their own expense round the Company's bounds, *viz.*, from the northern part of Chutanuttee to the southern part of Govindpore.

It was known as the Mahratta ditch, and would have sufficed to protect the settlement against the flying parties of light Mahratta horse. It ran along the ground now occupied by the Circular Road. If completed, it would have described a semicircle of seven miles. But the Mahrattas never came, and after six months the work was abandoned. The Mahratta ditch only extended three miles; but, as far as it went, it served as a boundary of the English settlement at Calcutta on the land side.

The population of Calcutta in the middle of the eighteenth century is involved in some mystery. In 1752, it was estimated at four hundred thousand souls; probably it was little more than half that number.[1] The European element did not number more than two or three hundred souls. As compared with the native element, it was probably little more than one in a thousand. Population.

Between 1752 and 1876, the European element has increased from two or three hundred to nine thousand souls. It has converted the group of native villages into a city of palaces. The roads, the streets, the squares, and the markets, are all European. The villages of mud and straw have grown into a metropolis of brick and stone. The outlying village of Chowringhee, with the surrounding marshes and Calcutta of 1752 and 1876 compared.

[1] Mr. Holwell, who filled the post of English Zemindar of Calcutta in 1752, calculated that there were fifty thousand houses within the Company's bounds, each containing on the average about eight inmates. Mr. Beverley, in his Report on the Census of 1876, points out that this estimate is empirical. The fifty thousand huts and hovels were not likely to contain on an average more than four or five inmates each.

rice-fields, has become the aristocratic quarter of the European population. The swamp and jungle which separated Chowringhee from the river, has been formed into the large grassy plain known as the Maidan. The old city has passed away; the landmarks have disappeared. Yet it is still possible to picture Calcutta as it was in 1750;—when the British empire was about to dawn; when Robert Clive was making a name in the Madras Presidency; when Warren Hastings was landing in Bengal for the first time.

European element at Calcutta.

The European element in Calcutta was strictly commercial. All rank, excepting that of soldiers and officers in the garrison, was expressed in business terms. The Company's servants were divided into the four grades of writers, factors, junior merchants, and senior merchants.[1] The Governor was originally known as the Agent of the Court of Directors. This commercial term of "Agent" has outlived the growth of empire; to this day it is applied to the representatives of the Viceroy at the courts of Native Princes. The Governor presided over a Council of ten or twelve members. Some were absent from Calcutta; they served as Chiefs of inland factories at Dacca, Cossimbazar, and Patna; those who remained at Calcutta formed a Board with the Governor as President. Salaries were absurdly low; they were only fractions of the real income. The Company's servants traded

---

[1] The writers were originally termed "apprentices," but the latter name had fallen into disuse.

on their own account in the eastern seas. They derived large perquisites, such as commissions and presents, from native merchants and contractors. They began to live in a liberal style. The Directors in England grew angry and suspicious. They sent out strict orders against extravagance. Nothing was really done to check the growing evil.

The outward life of the English at Calcutta was all of the business type. They bought, they sold, they overlooked, they kept accounts, they wrote letters, they regulated establishments and expenditure. Large ships from Europe brought woollen goods, cutlery, iron, copper, and quicksilver. The same ships carried away cotton piece-goods, fine muslins, silks, indigo, spices, and Indian rarities. Smaller ships, chartered by the Company's servants, were sent to different ports in the eastern seas as private adventures. Public auctions or outcries were held for the sale of goods; and buying and selling at outcry was one of the excitements of Calcutta life. European commodities were despatched to remote factories. Native manufactures were received in return. But the sale of European commodities was never on a very extensive scale; and during the decline of the Moghul empire there was a great falling off in the trade. On the other hand, the export business of providing Indian commodities and manufactures for the home markets was greater than ever. There was a general demand for Indian cottons and muslins throughout the British Isles. It was not until a later period in the

Trade at Calcutta.

century that Manchester began to appear as a formidable rival to Bengal.[1]

Social life. Social life, whether at Calcutta or at the factories up country, was much the same in character. The Company's servants lived together in the factory; they boarded together like members of one family or firm. This practice was falling into disuse at Calcutta; marriages with English women had broken up the establishment into households. It was still kept up at the subordinate factories, where the English lived in greater isolation. The mornings were devoted to business. Then followed the mid-day dinner and the afternoon siesta. In the cool of the evening they took the air in palanquins, or sailed on the river in budgerows. They angled for mango fish, or shot snipe and teal. The evening wound up with supper. There were quarrels, scandals, and controversies. Possibly there were some excesses. There was always the show of religion and decorum which characterised the early half of the eighteenth century. The Chaplain read prayers every morning, and preached on Sundays. There were intervals

---

[1] The old trade rivalries between English and India manufacturers are now forgotten. Between 1780 and 1790 the Court of Directors were thrown into alarm at the superiority of the muslins manufactured by Manchester. About the same time the calico printers in England were taking alarm at the improvements in the printing of Indian calicoes imported into England by the East India Company. They were petitioning Parliament to prevent the emigration of artists to India; to prohibit the exportation of plates, blocks, and materials for the printing business; and also to lay such additional duty upon goods printed in India as would be sufficient to put the white piece-goods printed in England on an equal footing with Indian goods at foreign markets.

of excitement apart from the daily business. Ships brought news from Europe; from the outer presidencies; from the far-off settlements in China, Sumatra, Pegu, and other remote quarters. Above all, every ship that came from Madras brought tidings of the war between the French and English in Southern India—the victories of Clive and gradual defeat of all the schemes of Dupleix.

Native life, Hindu and Muhammadan.

The native population at Calcutta lived in the same isolated fashion as in the present day. The Hindus were not so well off, but their Hinduism was more rampant, for as yet they had not profited by European education or yielded to the influences of civilisation. They worshipped their household gods. They made their pujas before the idols in the pagodas. They sacrificed goats at Kali Ghat. They celebrated their festivals with flags, flowers, sweetmeats, and sacred readings. They dragged about their idol cars with shouts of praise and victory. They bathed in the Ganges with rites and invocations. They feasted crowds of Brahmans. They performed their usual ceremonies at births, deaths, and marriages. They perpetrated horrors in the name of religion, which have passed away under the pressure of British rule. The sick and aged are no longer launched upon the Ganges to perish in the sacred waters. The living widow has ceased to mount the pile with her dead husband, and perish in the flames within sight of the English settlement. Men no longer swing themselves on iron hooks to appease avenging deities. Parents no longer sacrifice a child to the alligators at Saugor. The Mussulmans were the same then as they are now. They went to prayers in the mosque, celebrated the Muharram, fasted at the Ramadhan, and rejoiced at the Eed. They have lost their political ascendancy, but their religion is unchanged.

English supreme within the Company's bounds.

Within the limits of the Mahratta ditch the English Governor and Council reigned supreme. At one time, the Moghul authorities outside would have liked to interfere in matters of revenue; they never cared much about the administration of justice. As far as natives were concerned, the English were free to exercise the powers of life and death. They had nothing to fear from Hughli, Murshedabad, or Delhi; and the time had not come for them to have anything to fear from Westminster Hall.

Administration of justice amongst the English.

The administration of justice, wherever Englishmen are concerned, has always been a matter of paramount importance. Wherever there is an English element, there is a development of English courts of justice and forms of law. In the earlier history of the English settlements in India, the Governor exercised a paternal authority as the agent of the Court of Directors—the local head of the Company's establishment. In course of time the authority of the Governor proved insufficient. The servants of the Company were engaged in private trade; they quarrelled amongst themselves; they had causes against natives; they wanted to settle their disputes in a court of law. Accordingly a Mayor's Court was formed at each of the three English Presidencies, consisting of a Mayor and nine Aldermen. It decided all civil cases, subject to an appeal to the Governor and Council. It held courts of quarter sessions for the trial of all criminal cases. It might pass a capital sentence; it could not inflict a capital punishment without a royal warrant from England.

Administration of justice amongst the natives.

The administration of justice amongst the Hindu population was a very different affair. It followed Moghul forms. Under Moghul rule, the Zemindars administered justice as well as collected the revenue. Under the English rule at Calcutta, a servant of the Company was appointed Zemindar; he performed the same conflicting duties, revenue and judicial, as those which were performed under the Moghul government. The English Zemindar administered justice after the manner of native Zemindars. He sentenced offenders to be whipped, fined, or imprisoned at his own will and pleasure; and the punishment was carried out without further parley. In cases of murder he did not condemn the murderer to be hanged. Possibly a public hanging, without judge or jury, might have raised an outcry amongst the enemies of the Company in England. Accordingly the Zemindar ordered the murderer to be whipped; and this sentence was carried out so severely as to cause the death of the murderer. But the sentence was never carried out until it had been confirmed by the

President.[1] With the exception of capital cases, the power of the Zemindar was unlimited. He condemned thieves and other culprits to work in chains on the roads. It might be for life; it might be for a fixed period. There was no appeal. In civil cases concerning property, there was an appeal to the Governor and Council. Muhammadans do not appear to have sought redress at the court of the English Zemindar. Probably they had a Kazi of their own.

Revenue of the English at Calcutta.

The English Zemindar also collected the revenues from the native inhabitants dwelling within the Company's bounds. A quit-rent of three rupees was raised from every beega of land belonging to the Company which was occupied by native householders. Duties were levied on all goods that were carried into Calcutta from the

---

[1] That a murderer should have been whipped to death under any circumstances, by the order of any Englishman, appears incredible. I append the exact words in Mr. Holwell's letter to the proprietors of East India stock, and the public:—"The Zemindar acts in a double capacity, distinct, and independent of each other (with very few exceptions); the one as Superintendent and Collector of your revenues; the other as Judge of the Court of Cutcherry, a tribunal constituted for the hearing, trying, and determining all matters and things, both civil and criminal, wherein the natives only, subjects of the Moghul, are concerned. He tried in a summary way, had the power of the lash, fine, and imprisonment; he determined all matters of *meum* and *tuum*; and in all criminal cases proceeded to sentence and punishment immediately after hearing, except where the crime (as murder) requires the lash to be inflicted until death, in which case he suspends execution of the sentence until the facts and evidence are laid before the President, and his confirmation of the sentence is obtained. He has also the power to condemn thieves and other culprits to work in chains upon the roads, during any determinate space of time, or for life. In all causes of property, an appeal lay to the President and Council against his decrees."—See Holwell's India Tracts, page 120. It should be added that Mr. Holwell filled the post of Zemindar of Calcutta from 1752 until 1756, when Calcutta was captured by Suraj-u-daula.

interior, or out of Calcutta into the interior. Other taxes were farmed out to natives for yearly block sums. Some farmers bought the privilege of collecting taxes at certain fixed rates on every article exposed for sale in the several bazars. Other farmers bought the monopoly of some trade, such as glass-making, vermillion manufacture, ship-caulking, chest-making, and the manufacture of fireworks; and no one could work at any of these callings without buying the license of the farmer. Others, again, bought the sole right of selling certain commodities, such as tobacco, bang, old iron, dammer, and oakum; and no one else could deal in these goods without a license from the farmer. Offenders against any of these monopolies were punished by fine or imprisonment. One farmer bought the right to levy a yearly tax of six annas on every beast of burden. Another bought a similar right to levy fees on ferry boats;—sixteen cowries on every passenger; forty cowries for every parcel of greens; eighty cowries for every cow, calf, or horse. The fines levied in the Zemindar's Court formed another source of revenue. There were also various fees which were paid to the Zemindar. There was a commission of five per cent. on all sums recovered by the decree of the Zemindar; on the sale of all houses, boats, and sloops; and on all mortgage bonds registered by the Zemindar. There was a fee on every new sloop, varying from fifty rupees to a hundred, according to the burden; a fee of four rupees and four annas on every slave registered by the purchaser; a fee of three rupees from each party on every marriage; and similar fees, varying in amount, on arbitration bonds, on re-measurements of lands in settlement of disputes between householders, and other miscellaneous matters.[1]

Total revenue. The total amount of revenue collected at Calcutta in the middle of the last century was ridiculously small, when compared with the collection in the present day. In 1876, the municipal taxation in Calcutta amounts to twenty-six lakhs of rupees per annum, or about two hundred and sixty thousand pounds sterling. In 1755, the year before the capture of Calcutta by Suraj-u-daula, the whole revenue collected by the English Zemindar scarcely exceeded a single lakh of rupees, or about ten or twelve thousand pounds sterling. The proceeds under each head were often absurdly small. The rent-paying lands extended over two thousand acres, or nearly five thousand five hundred beegas; the yearly quit-rent thus amounted to about sixteen thousand rupees, or less than two thousand pounds. The bazar duties produced about twelve thousand rupees per annum; the glass-making farm about five hundred rupees; the vermillion farm about two hundred rupees; the ship-caulking farm about five hundred rupees; the tobacco farm about one hundred and twenty rupees; the bang farm

[1] See Holwell's despatch, dated 15th December 1752, on the office of the Zemindary and state of the Company's revenues. Reprinted in Holwell's Tracts. Most of the information given hereafter as regards Calcutta is taken either from Holwell or from the records in the Home Office.

about seventeen hundred rupees; the chest-maker's farm about seventy-five rupees; the dammer and oakum farm about seven hundred rupees; the beasts of burden farm about two hundred rupees; the ferry-boat farm about one hundred and fifty rupees.

The poverty of the people of Calcutta, and of Bengal generally, may be inferred from the fact that many of the duties were collected in cowries, whilst many bazar transactions were in cowries. A rupee, generally valued at two shillings sterling, is equal to sixteen annas; an anna is about equal to three half-pence, and one anna is also equal to about three hundred cowries. In the present day two or three onions may be bought for ten cowries in the Calcutta bazars; so may a teaspoonful of salt, or three or four chillies, or a piece of saffron, or a few herbs. A small handful of rice may be bought for twenty or thirty cowries. General use of cowries.

The police of Calcutta consisted of a native force under a Kotwal. The duties of the Kotwal have been compared to those of a Mayor in England in the olden time. They might be better described as those of an ordinary superintendent of police, combined with certain magisterial powers; but the working of this branch of the administration is somewhat obscure. The Kotwal patrolled the town at night, and maintained peace and order at all times. The office of Kotwal was a Mussulman institution.[1] The Kotwal, or head of police.

[1] Madras, as already seen, was originally rented from a Hindu Rajah. Accordingly, the police duties were performed by a Hindu official, known as the Pedda Naik.

Subordinate factories.

From 1750 up to 1756 the English at Calcutta lived in peaceful security. Calcutta continued to be the head factory and seaport. There were three or four other factories in the interior, which were subordinate to Calcutta. On the north-east there was a factory for the muslin manufactures at Dacca. On the north-west there was a factory at Cossimbazar in the neighbourhood of Murshedabad, the capital of the three provinces. Beyond Cossimbazar there was another factory at Patna, the capital of Behar. The water communication ran from Calcutta up the river Hughli past Cossimbazar and Monghyr to the city of Patna. Beyond Patna were the cities of Allahabad, Agra, and Delhi; but they were little known to the English. News-letters brought intelligence from time to time of the revolutions which were transpiring at the court of Delhi, or the intrigues and assassinations that were carried on at Murshedabad during the declining years of Aliverdi Khan. But these were only matters of interest so far as they were likely to interfere with the ordinary course of trade in Bengal and Behar.

Changes in the transaction of business: abolition of contractors like Omichund.

About this period, the Company ordered a change to be made in the mode of carrying on business in India. Prior to 1753, it had been the custom for the Company's servants to procure piece-goods and other native manufactures through native merchants by regular contracts. Amongst all the Calcutta merchants, the most wealthy and influential was a Hindu named Omichund. This man had devoted himself during forty years to the accumulation of riches. His fortune was estimated at four millions of rupees, or more than four hundred thousand pounds sterling. His house was divided into various departments like a palace. His retinue of armed men resembled that of a prince rather than that of a merchant. He traded all over Bengal and Behar. He established so great an influence at the court of Murshedabad by presents and services, that he proved a useful mediator to the English President and Council at Calcutta in all times of difficulty. The consequence was, that Omichund was largely employed by the English at Calcutta. He provided more of the Company's investments than any other contractor; but he took advantage of his position to increase his profits. For years, the manufactures he supplied deteriorated in quality and increased in price. Accordingly, in 1753, the Company abandoned the system of dealing with native merchants. They sent Gomastas, or native agents, to provide investments at the different cloth markets in the provinces, which were known by the name of Aurungs. The result was, that Omichund lost a lucrative branch of his business, and was vexed beyond measure. Subsequently, he was suspected of being mixed up with the misfortunes that ultimately befel Calcutta; but the nature and extent of his intrigues have never been fully ascertained.

In April 1756 Aliverdi died, and was succeeded by a grandson, the notorious Suraj-u-daula. The young Nawab is described by European and native

Suraj-u-daula, Nawab, 1756.

authorities as everything that is bad. Above all, he hated the English with all the virulence of a young prince invested with despotic power, and utterly ignorant of European nations. The story of his proceedings has become nearly obsolete. It will suffice to say that his wrath against the English was stirred up by a variety of causes. Another war was expected between Great Britain and France; and he was told that the English at Calcutta were strengthening those fortifications in order to fight the French at Chandernagore. He had reason to be offended with some people at his court; and they had gone to Calcutta, and thence escaped his vengeance. But rapacity seems to have been his ruling motive. He had formed exaggerated notions of the wealth of Calcutta; and no doubt tales were told of the riches of the English, as extravagant as the thousand and one stories of the Arabian Nights, and as unreal as the fabled treasures of ancient Maharajas.

Capture of the English factory at Cossimbazar.

In the first instance the young Nawab vented his wrath on the English factory at Cossimbazar, in the immediate neighbourhood of his capital at Murshedabad. He surrounded the English factory at Cossimbazar with his soldiers, plundered it of all its money and goods, and threw the English traders into prison. In June 1756, he marched against Calcutta with an army of fifty thousand men, and a train of artillery.

Capture of Calcutta.

The English at Calcutta were a mere handful of men; there were scarcely five hundred men, including mixed races, in all the settlement; of these, only a hundred and seventy were European soldiers, and scarcely ten of these soldiers had seen any service beyond parade. The fighting began on Wednesday, the fifteenth of June. On Saturday, the women were carried to the ships, and many of the English escaped at the same time, including Mr. Drake, the Governor. The remainder surrendered to the Nawab on Sunday afternoon.

Holwell's narrative of the tragedy of the Black Hole.

The story of what followed aroused the horror of Europe. The prisoners, to the number of a hundred and forty-six, were assembled in a verandah, which had been built in the front of the barracks for the convenience of the European soldiers. At one end of the barracks was the common dungeon of the garrison, known as the Black Hole. The story of what followed is best told by Mr. Holwell, one of the English prisoners who survived the night. In the absence of Mr. Drake, Mr. Holwell had been treated as the Acting Governor. This narrative tells his own personal experiences as well as what he saw of the sufferings of others. It was written as a letter to a friend, and is given almost word for word[1]:—

Difficulty in writing the narrative.

"The confusion which the late capture of the East India Company's settlements in Bengal must necessarily excite in the city of London, will, I fear, be not a little heightened by the miserable deaths of the greatest part of those gentlemen, who were reduced to the sad necessity of surrendering themselves prisoners at discretion in Fort William.

[1] "Letter from J. L. Holwell, Esq., to William Davis, Esq., from on board the *Syren* sloop, the 28th of February 1757."—Printed in Holwell's Tracts.

Importance of Holwell's narrative.

"By narratives made public, you will only know that of one hundred and forty-six prisoners, one hundred and twenty-three were smothered in the Black Hole prison, in the night of the 20th of June, 1756. Few survived capable of giving any detail of the manner in which it happened; and of these I believe none have attempted it. For my own part, I have often sat down with this resolution, and as often relinquished the melancholy task, not only from the disturbance and affliction it raised afresh in my remembrance, but from the consideration of the impossibility of finding language capable of raising an adequate idea of the horrors of the scene I essayed to draw. But as I believe the annals of the world cannot produce an incident like it in any degree or proportion to all the dismal circumstances attending it, and as my own health of body and peace of mind are once again, in a great measure, recovered from the injuries they suffered from that fatal night, I cannot allow it to be buried in oblivion; though still conscious that, however high the colouring my retentive memory may supply, it will fall infinitely short of the horrors accompanying this scene. These defects must, and I doubt not will, be assisted by your own humane and benevolent imagination; in the exercise of which I never knew you deficient where unmerited distress was the object.

Tranquillity of mind on the voyage to England.

"The sea-air has already had that salutary effect on my constitution I expected; and my mind enjoys a calm it has been many months a stranger to, strengthened by a clear cheerful sky and atmosphere, joined to an unusual pleasant gale, with which we are passing the equinoctial. I can now, therefore, look back with less agitation on the dreadful night I am going to describe; and with a grateful heart sincerely acknowledge, and deeply revere, that Providence which alone could have preserved me through that and all my succeeding sufferings and hazards.

State of the prisoners on the evening of the capture.

"Before I conduct you into the Black Hole, it is necessary you should be acquainted with a few introductory circumstances. The Nawab and his troops were in possession of the Fort before six in the evening. I had in all three interviews with him: the last in Durbar[1] before seven, when he repeated his assurances to me, *on the word of a soldier,* that no harm should come to us; and indeed I believe his orders were only general. That we should for that night be secured; and that what followed was the result of revenge and resentment in the breasts of the lower Jemadars,[2] to whose custody we were delivered, for the number of their order killed during the siege. Be this as it may, as soon as it was dark, we were all, without distinction, directed by the guard over us, to collect ourselves into one body, and sit down quietly under the arched veranda or piazza, to the west of the Black Hole prison, and the barracks to the left of the court of guard; and just over against the windows of the governor's easterly apartments. Besides the guard over us, another was placed at the foot of the stairs at the south end of this veranda, leading up to the south-east bastion, to prevent any of us escaping that way. On the parade (where you will remember the two twenty-four pounders stood) were also drawn up about four or five hundred gun-men with lighted matches.

"At this time the factory was in flames to the right and left of us; to the right the armory and laboratory; to the left the carpenter's yard: though at this time we imagined it was the Company's cloth warehouses. Various were our conjectures on this appearance; the fire advanced with rapidity on both sides; and it was the prevailing opinion that they intended suffocating us between the two fires: and this notion was confirmed by the appearance, about half an hour past seven, of some officers and people with lighted torches in their hands, who went into all the apartments under the easterly curtain to the right of us; to which we apprehended they were setting fire, to expedite their scheme of burning us. On this we presently came to a resolution of rushing on the guard, seizing their scimitars, and attacking the troops upon the parade, rather than be thus tamely roasted to death. But to be satisfied of their intentions, I advanced, at the

Factory in flames.

---

[1] The Durbar was the Assembly of the chief men at Court.

[2] An officer of the rank of Sergeant.

request of Messrs. Baillie, Jenks and Revely, to see if they were really setting fire to the apartments, and found the contrary; for in fact, as it appeared afterwards, they were only searching for a place to confine us in; the last they examined being the barracks of the court of guard behind us.

Bravery of Mr. Leech.

"Here I must detain you a little, to do honour to the memory of a man to whom I had in many instances been a friend, and who, on this occasion, demonstrated his sensibility of it in a degree worthy of a much higher rank. His name was Leech, the Company's smith, as well as clerk of the parish; this man had made his escape when the Moghuls entered the Fort, and returned just as it was dark, to tell me he had provided a boat, and would ensure my escape, if I would follow him through a passage few were acquainted with, and by which he had then entered. (This might easily have been accomplished, as the guard put over us took but very slight notice of us.) I thanked him in the best terms I was able; but told him it was a step I could not prevail on myself to take, as I should thereby very ill repay the attachment the gentlemen and the garrison had shewn to me; and that I was resolved to share their fate, be it what it would: but pressed him to secure his own escape without loss of time; to which he gallantly replied that "then he was resolved to share mine, and would not leave me."

Prisoners driven through the Barracks into the Black Hole.

"To myself and the world I should surely have stood excused in embracing the overture above-mentioned, could I have conceived what immediately followed; for I had scarce time to make him an answer, before we observed part of the guard drawn up on the parade, advance to us with the officers who had been viewing the rooms. They ordered us all to rise and go into the barracks to the left of the court of guard. The barracks, you may remember, have a large wooden platform for the soldiers to sleep on, and are open to the west by arches and a small parapet-wall, corresponding to the arches of the veranda without. In we went most readily, and were pleasing ourselves with the prospect of passing a comfortable night on the platform, little dreaming of the infernal apartment in reserve for us. For we were no sooner all within the barracks, than the guard advanced to the inner arches and parapet-wall; and, with their muskets presented, ordered us to go into the room at the southernmost end of the barracks, commonly called the Black Hole prison; whilst others from the Court of Guard, with clubs and drawn scimitars, pressed upon those of us next to them. This stroke was so sudden, so unexpected, and the throng and pressure so great upon us next the door of the Black Hole prison, there was no resisting it; but like one agitated wave impelling another, we were obliged to give way and enter; the rest followed like a torrent, few amongst us, the soldiers excepted, having the least idea of the dimensions or nature of a place we had never seen: for if we had, we should at all events have rushed upon the guard, and been, as the lesser evil, by our own choice cut to pieces.

"Amongst the first that entered were myself, Messrs. **Eight o'clock.**
Baillie, Jenks, Cooke, T. Coles, Ensign Scot, Revely, Law, Buchanan, and others. I got possession of the window nearest the door, and took Messrs. Coles and Scot into the window with me, they being both wounded (the first I believe mortally). The rest of the above-mentioned gentlemen were close round me. It was now about eight o'clock.

"Figure to yourself, my friend, if possible, the situation of **The situation.**
a hundred and forty-six wretches, exhausted by continual fatigue and action, thus crammed together in a cube of about eighteen feet, in a close sultry night, in Bengal, shut up to the eastward and southward (the only quarters from whence air could reach us) by dead walls, and by a wall and door to the north, open only to the westward by two windows, strongly barred with iron, from which we could receive scarce any the least circulation of fresh air.

"What must ensue appeared to me in lively and dreadful **Despair.**
colours, the instant I cast my eyes round, and saw the size and situation of the room. Many unsuccessful attempts were made to force the door; for having nothing but our hands to work with, and the door opening inward, all endeavours were vain and fruitless.

Necessity for tranquillity.

"Observing every one giving way to the violence of passions, which I foresaw must be fatal to them, I requested silence might be preserved, whilst I spoke to them, and in the most pathetic and moving terms which occurred I begged and intreated that as they had paid a ready obedience to me in the day, they would now for their own sakes, and the sakes of those who were dear to them and were interested in the preservation of their lives, regard the advice I had to give them. I assured them the return of day would give us air and liberty; urged to them that the only chance we had left for sustaining this misfortune and surviving the night was the preserving a calm mind and quiet resignation to our fate; intreating them to curb, as much as possible, every agitation of mind and body, as raving and giving a loose to their passions could answer no purpose, but that of hastening their destruction.

Fearful prospect.

"This remonstrance produced a short interval of peace, and gave me a few minutes for reflection: though even this pause was not a little disturbed by the cries and groans of the many wounded, and more particularly of my two companions in the window. Death, attended with the most cruel train of circumstances, I plainly perceived must prove our inevitable destiny. I had seen this common migration in too many shapes, and accustomed myself to think on the subject with too much propriety to be alarmed at the prospect, and indeed felt much more for my wretched companions than myself.

Bribing the Jemadar: the Nawab asleep.

"Amongst the guards posted at the windows, I observed an old Jemadar near me, who seemed to carry some compassion for us in his countenance; and indeed he was the only one of the many in his station who discovered the least trace of humanity. I called him to me, and in the most persuasive terms I was capable, urged him to commiserate the sufferings he was a witness to, and pressed him to endeavour to get us separated, half in one place, and half in another; and that he should in the morning receive a thousand rupees for this act of tenderness. He promised he would attempt it, and withdrew; but in a few minutes returned, and told me it was impossible. I then thought I had been deficient in my offer, and promised him two thousand. He withdrew a second time, but returned soon, and (with, I believe, much real pity and concern) told me it was not practicable; that it could not be done but by the Nawab's order, and that no one dared awake him.

"During this interval, though their passions were less violent, their uneasiness increased. We had been but few minutes confined before every one fell into a perspiration so profuse you can form no idea of it. This consequently brought on a raging thirst, which still increased, in proportion as the body was drained of its moisture. Perspiration.

"Various expedients were thought of to give more room and air. To obtain the former, it was moved to put off their clothes. This was approved as a happy motion, and in a few minutes I believe every man was stripped (myself, Mr. Court, and the two wounded young gentlemen by me excepted). For a little time they flattered themselves with having gained a mighty advantage; every hat was put in motion to produce a circulation of air; and Mr. Baillie proposed that every man should sit down on his hams. As they were truly in the situation of drowning wretches, no wonder they caught at every thing that bore a flattering appearance of saving them. This expedient was several times put in practice, and at each time many of the poor creatures, whose natural strength was less than others, or had been more exhausted, and could not immediately recover their legs, as others did, when the word was given to rise, fell to rise no more; for they were instantly trod to death, or suffocated. When the whole body sat down, they were so closely wedged together that they were obliged to use many efforts before they could put themselves in motion to get up again. Expedients for relief.

"Before nine o'clock every man's thirst grew intolerable, and respiration difficult. Our situation was much more wretched than that of so many miserable animals in an exhausted receiver; no circulation of fresh air sufficient to continue life, nor yet enough divested of its vivifying particles to put a speedy period to it. Nine o'clock.

Effluvia. "Efforts were again made to force the door, but in vain. Many insults were used to the guard, to provoke them to fire in upon us (which, as I learned afterwards, were carried to much greater lengths, when I was no more sensible of what was transacted). For my own part, I hitherto felt little pain or uneasiness, but what resulted from my anxiety for the sufferings of those within. By keeping my face between two of the bars, I obtained air enough to give my lungs easy play, though my perspiration was excessive, and thirst commencing. At this period, so strong a volatile effluvia came from the prison that I was not able to turn my head that way for more than a few seconds of time.

Water. "Now every body, excepting those situated in and near the window, began to grow outrageous, and many delirious; WATER, WATER, became the general cry. And the old Jemadar, before mentioned, taking pity on us, ordered the people to bring some skins of water, little dreaming, I believe, of its fatal effects. This was what I dreaded. I foresaw it would prove the ruin of the small chance left us, and essayed many times to speak to him privately to forbid its being brought; but the clamour was so loud it became impossible. The water appeared. Words cannot paint to you the universal agitation and raving the sight of it threw us into. I had flattered myself that some, by preserving an equal temper of mind, might outlive the night; but now the reflection which gave me the greatest pain, was, that I saw no possibility of one escaping to tell the dismal tale.

Sad results. "Until the water came, I had myself not suffered much from thirst, which instantly grew excessive. We had no means of conveying it into the prison, but by hats forced through the bars; and thus myself, and Messrs. Coles and Scot (notwithstanding the pains they suffered from their wounds) supplied them as fast as possible. But those who have experienced intense thirst, or are acquainted with the cause and nature of this appetite, will be sufficiently sensible it could receive no more than a momentary alleviation; the cause still subsisted. Though we brought full hats within the bars, there ensued such violent struggles, and frequent contests, to get at it, that before it reached the lips of any one, there would be scarcely a small tea-cup full left in them. These supplies, like sprinkling water on fire, only served to feed and raise the flame.

"Oh! my dear Sir, how shall I give you a conception of what I felt at the cries and ravings of those in the remoter parts of the prison, who could not entertain a probable hope of obtaining a drop, yet could not divest themselves of expectation, however unavailing! And others calling on me by the tender considerations of friendship and affection, and who knew they were really dear to me. Think, if possible, what my heart must have suffered at seeing and hearing their distress, without having it in my power to relieve them; for the confusion now became general and horrid. Several quitted the other window (the only chance they had for life) to force their way to the water, and the throng and press upon the window was beyond bearing; many forcing their passage from the further part of the room, pressed down those in their way, who had less strength, and trampled them to death. Ravings.

"Can it gain belief, that this scene of misery proved entertainment to the brutal wretches without? But so it was; and they took care to keep us supplied with water, that they might have the satisfaction of seeing us fight for it, as they phrased it, and held up lights to the bars, that they might lose no part of the inhuman diversion. Diversion of the guards.

"From about nine to near eleven, I sustained this cruel scene and painful situation, still supplying them with water, though my legs were almost broke with the weight against them. By this time I myself was very near pressed to death, and my two companions, with Mr. William Parker (who had forced himself into the window), were really so. Eleven o'clock.

"For a great while they preserved a respect and regard to me, more than indeed I could well expect, our circumstances considered; but now all distinction was lost. My friend Baillie, Messrs. Jenks, Revely, Law, Buchanan, Simson, and several others, for whom I had a real esteem and affection, Rank and distinction forgotten.

had for some time been dead at my feet, and were now trampled upon by every corporal or common soldier, who, by the help of more robust constitutions, had forced their way to the window, and held fast by the bars over me, till at last I became so pressed and wedged up, I was deprived of all motion.

Centre of the Black Hole.

"Determined now to give every thing up, I called to them, and begged, as the last instance of their regard, they would remove the pressure upon me, and permit me to retire out of the window to die in quiet. They gave way; and with much difficulty I forced a passage into the centre of the prison, where the throng was less by the many dead (then I believe amounting to one-third) and the numbers who flocked to the windows; for by this time they had water also at the other window.

The platform.

"In the Black Hole there is a platform[1] corresponding with that in the barracks: I travelled over the dead, and repaired to the further end of it, just opposite the other window, and seated myself on the platform between Mr. Dumbleton and Capt. Stevenson, the former just then expiring. I was still happy in the same calmness of mind I had preserved the whole time; death I expected as unavoidable, and only lamented its slow approach, though the moment I quitted the window, my breathing grew short and painful.

Death of Mr. Eyre.

"Here my poor friend Mr. Edward Eyre came staggering over the dead to me, and with his usual coolness and good-nature, asked me how I did! but fell and expired before I had time to make him a reply. I laid myself down on some of the dead behind me, on the platform; and recommending myself to heaven, had the comfort of thinking my sufferings could have no long duration.

Insupportable thirst.

"My thirst grew now insupportable, and difficulty of breathing much increased; and I had not remained in this situation, I believe, ten minutes, when I was seized with a

[1] This platform was raised between three and four feet from the floor, open underneath: it extended the whole length of the east side of the prison, and was above six feet wide.

pain in my breast, and palpitation of my heart, both to the most exquisite degree. These roused and obliged me to get up again; but still the palpitation, thirst, and difficulty of breathing increased. I retained my senses notwithstanding, and had the grief to see death not so near me as I hoped; but could no longer bear the pains I suffered without attempting a relief, which I knew fresh air would and could only give me. I instantly determined to push for the window opposite to me; and by an effort of double the strength I ever before possessed, gained the third rank at it, with one hand seized a bar, and by that means gained the second, though I think there were at least six or seven ranks between me and the window.

"In a few moments my pain, palpitation and difficulty of breathing ceased; but my thirst continued intolerable. I called aloud for "WATER FOR GOD'S SAKE:" had been concluded dead; but as soon as they heard me amongst them, they had still the respect and tenderness for me, to cry out, "GIVE HIM WATER, GIVE HIM WATER!" nor would one of them at the window attempt to touch it until I had drank. But from the water I found no relief; my thirst was rather increased by it; so I determined to drink no more, but patiently wait the event; and kept my mouth moist from time to time by sucking the perspiration out of my shirt-sleeves, and catching the drops as they fell, like heavy rain from my head and face: you can hardly imagine how unhappy I was if any of them escaped my mouth.

Thirst increased by water.

Strange refreshment.

"I came into the prison without coat or waistcoat; the season was too hot to bear the former, and the latter tempted the avarice of one of the guards, who robbed me of it when we were under the veranda. Whilst I was at this second window, I was observed by one of my miserable companions on the right of me in the expedient of allaying my thirst by sucking my shirt-sleeve. He took the hint, and robbed me from time to time of a considerable part of my store.

This plunderer, I found afterwards, was a worthy young gentleman in the service, Mr. Lushington, one of the few who escaped from death.

I mention this incident, as I think nothing can give you a more lively idea of the melancholy state and distress we were reduced to.

Delirium.

"By half an hour past eleven the much greater number of those living were in an outrageous delirium, and the others quite ungovernable; few retaining any calmness but the ranks next the windows. By what I had felt myself, I was fully sensible what those within suffered; but had only pity to bestow upon them, not then thinking how soon I should myself become a greater object of it.

Suffocation.

"They all now found that water, instead of relieving, rather heightened their uneasinesses; and, AIR, AIR, was the general cry. Every insult that could be devised against the guard, all the opprobrious names and abuse that the Nawab of Bengal, or the new native Governor of Calcutta,[1] could be loaded with, were repeated to provoke the guard to fire upon us, every man that could, rushing tumultuously towards the windows with eager hopes of meeting the first shot. Then a general prayer to heaven, to hasten the approach of the flames to the right and left of us, and put a period to our misery. But these failing, they whose strength and spirits were quite exhausted, laid themselves down and expired quietly upon their fellows: others who had yet some strength and vigour left, made a last effort for the windows, and several succeeded by leaping and scrambling over the backs and heads of those in the first ranks; and got hold of the bars, from which there was no removing them. Many to the right and left sunk with the violent pressure, and were soon suffocated; for now a steam arose from the living and the dead, which affected us in all its circumstances, as if we were forcibly held with our heads over a bowl full of strong volatile spirit of hartshorn, until suffocated; nor could the effluvia of the one be distinguished from the other, and frequently, when I was forced by the load upon my head and shoulders, to hold my face down, I was obliged, near as I was to the window, instantly to raise it again to escape suffocation.

[1] Raja Monikchund, appointed by the Nawab to be Governor of Calcutta.

"I need not, my dear friend, ask your commiseration, when I tell you that in this plight, from half an hour past eleven till near two in the morning, I sustained the weight of a heavy man, with his knees on my back, and the pressure of his whole body on my head. A Dutch serjeant, who had taken his seat upon my left shoulder, and a black christian soldier bearing on my right; all which nothing could have enabled me long to support, but the props and pressure equally sustaining me all around. The two latter I frequently dislodged, by shifting my hold on the bars, and driving my knuckles into their ribs; but my friend above stuck fast, and as he held by two bars, was immoveable. Half-past eleven till two o'clock in the morning.

"When I had bore this conflict above an hour, with a train of wretched reflections, and seeing no glimpse of hope on which to found a prospect of relief, my spirits, resolution, and every sentiment of religion gave way. I found I was unable much longer to support this trial, and could not bear the dreadful thoughts of retiring into the inner part of the prison, where I had before suffered so much. Some infernal spirit, taking the advantage of this period, brought to my remembrance my having a small clasp penknife in my pocket, with which I determined instantly to open my arteries, and finish a system no longer to be borne. I had got it out, when heaven interposed, and restored me to fresh spirits and resolution, with an abhorrence of the act of cowardice I was just going to commit: I exerted anew my strength and fortitude; but the repeated trials and efforts I made to dislodge the insufferable incumbrances upon me at last quite exhausted me, and towards two o'clock, finding I must quit the window, or sink where I was, I resolved on the former, having bore, truly for the sake of others, infinitely more for life than the best of it is worth. Suicidal temptation.

"In the rank close behind me was an officer of one of the ships, whose name was Carey, who had behaved with much bravery during the siege (his wife, a fine woman though country-born, would not quit him, but accompanied him into the prison, and was one who survived). This poor wretch Mr. and Mrs. Carey.

had been long raving for water and air; I told him I was determined to give up life, and recommended his gaining my station. On my quitting, he made a fruitless attempt to get my place; but the Dutch serjeant who sat on my shoulder supplanted him.

Death of Mr. Carey.

"Poor Carey expressed his thankfulness, and said he would give up life too; but it was with the utmost labour we forced our way from the window (several in the inner ranks appearing to me dead standing[1]). He laid himself down to die: and his death, I believe, was very sudden; for he was a short, full, sanguine man: his strength was great, and I imagine, had he not retired with me, I should never have been able to have forced my way.

Stupor.

"I was at this time sensible of no pain and little uneasiness: I can give you no better idea of my situation than by repeating my simile of the bowl of spirit of hartshorn. I found a stupor coming on apace, and laid myself down by that gallant old man, the Reverend Mr. Jervas Bellamy, who lay dead with his son the lieutenant, hand-in-hand, near the southernmost wall of the prison.

Loss of sensation.

"When I had lain there some little time, I still had reflection enough to suffer some uneasiness in the thought, that I should be trampled upon, when dead, as I myself had done to others. With some difficulty I raised myself, and gained the platform a second time, where I presently lost all sensation: the last trace of sensibility that I have been able to recollect after my lying down, was my sash being uneasy about my waist, which I untied and threw from me.

Interval of unconsciousness.

"Of what passed in this interval to the time of my resurrection from this hole of horrors, I can give you no account; and indeed, the particulars mentioned by some of the gentlemen who survived (solely by the number of those dead, by which they gained a freer accession of air, and approach to the windows) were so excessively absurd and contradictory as to convince me very few of them retained their senses; or

[1] Unable to fall by the throng and equal pressure round.

at least, lost them soon after they came into the open air, by the fever they carried out with them.

" In my own escape from absolute death the hand of heaven was manifestly exerted: the manner take as follows: When the day broke, and the gentlemen found that no intreaties could prevail to get the door opened, it occurred to one of them (I think to Mr. Secretary Cooke), to make a search for me, in hopes I might have influence enough to gain a release from this scene of misery. Accordingly Messrs. Lushington and Walcot undertook the search, and by my shirt discovered me under the dead upon the platform. They took me from thence; and imagining I had some signs of life, brought me towards the window I had first possession of. Carried to the window.

" But as life was equally dear to every man (and the stench arising from the dead bodies was grown intolerable) no one would give up his station in or near the window: so they were obliged to carry me back again. But soon after Captain Mills (now captain of the Company's yacht), who was in possession of a seat in the window, had the humanity to offer to resign it. I was again brought by the same gentlemen, and placed in the window. Recovery of consciousness.

" At this juncture the Nawab, who had received an account of the havock death had made amongst us, sent one of his Jemadars to inquire if the Chief survived. They shewed me to him: told him I had appearance of life remaining, and believed I might recover if the door was opened very soon. This answer being returned to the Nawab, an order came immediately for our release, it being then near six in the morning. Release ordered.

" The fresh air at the window soon brought me to life; and a few minutes after the departure of the Jemadar, I was restored to my sight and senses. But oh! Sir, what words shall I adopt to tell you the whole that my soul suffered at reviewing the dreadful destruction round me? I will not attempt it; and indeed, tears (a tribute I believe I shall ever pay to the remembrance of this scene, and to the memory of those brave and valuable men) stop my pen. Restoratio.

Slow opening of the door.

"The little strength remaining amongst the most robust who survived made it a difficult task to remove the dead piled up against the door; so that I believe it was more than twenty minutes before we obtained a passage out for one at a time.

Demands of the Nawab for hidden treasure.

"I had soon reason to be convinced the particular inquiry made after me did not result from any dictate of favour, humanity, or contrition; when I came out, I found myself in a high putrid fever, and, not being able to stand, threw myself on the wet grass without the veranda, when a message was brought me, signifying I must immediately attend the Nawab. Not being capable of walking, they were obliged to support me under each arm; and on the way, one of the Jemadars told me, as a friend, to make a full confession where the treasure was buried in the Fort, or that in half an hour I should be shot off from the mouth of a cannon.[1] The intimation gave me no manner of concern; for, at that juncture, I should have esteemed death the greatest favour the tyrant could have bestowed upon me.

Callous Nawab.

"Being brought into his presence, the Nawab soon observed the wretched plight I was in, and ordered a large folio volume, which lay on a heap of plunder, to be brought for me to sit on. I endeavoured two or three times to speak, but my tongue was dry and without motion. He ordered me water. As soon as I got speech, I began to recount the dismal catastrophe of my miserable companions. But he stopped me short, with telling me, he was well informed of great treasure being buried or secreted in the Fort, and that I was privy to it; and if I expected favour, I must discover it.

Nawab inexorable.

"I urged every thing I could to convince him there was no truth in the information; or that if any such thing had been done, it was without my knowledge. I reminded him of his repeated assurance to me, the day before; but he resumed the subject of the treasure, and all I could say seemed to gain no credit with him. I was ordered prisoner under the General of the Household Troops.

[1] A sentence of death common in Hindostan.

"Amongst the guard which carried me from the Nawab, one bore a large Mahratta battle-axe, which gave rise, I imagine, to Mr. Secretary Cooke's belief and report to the fleet, that he saw me carried out, with the edge of the axe towards me, to have my head struck off. This I believe is the only account you will have of me, until I bring you a better myself. But to resume my subject: I was ordered to the camp of the General's quarters, within the outward ditch, something short of Omichund's garden (which you know is above three miles from the Fort) and with me Messieurs Court, Walcot, and Burdet. The rest, who survived the fatal night, gained their liberty, except Mrs. Carey, who was too young and handsome. The dead bodies were promiscuously thrown into the ditch of our unfinished ravelin, and covered with the earth. Severe treatment.

"My being treated with this severity, I have sufficient reason to affirm, proceeded from the following causes. The Nawab's resentment for my defending the Fort, after the Governor, &c., had abandoned it; his prepossession touching the treasure; and thirdly, the instigations of Omichund[1] in resentment for my not releasing him out of prison, as soon as I had the command of the Fort: a circumstance, which in the heat and hurry of action, never once occurred to me, or I had certainly done it; because I thought his imprisonment unjust. But that the hard treatment I met with, may truly be attributed in a great measure to his suggestion and insinuations, I am well assured, from the whole of his subsequent conduct; and this further confirmed to me, in the three gentlemen selected to be my companions, against each of whom he had conceived particular resentment; and you know Omichund can never forgive. Reason for the Nawab's cruelty.

"We were conveyed in a hackery[2] to the camp the 21st of June, in the morning, and soon loaded with fetters, and stowed all four in a seapoy's tent, about four feet long, three wide, and about three high; so that we were half in, half out. Further sufferings.

---

[1] A great Hindu merchant of Calcutta.
[2] A coach drawn by oxen.

All night it rained severely. Dismal as this was, it appeared a paradise compared with our lodging the preceding night. Here I became covered from head to foot with large painful boils, the first symptom of my recovery; for until these appeared, my fever did not leave me.

Iron fetters.

"On the morning of the 22nd, they marched us to town in our fetters, under the scorching beams of an intense hot sun, and lodged us at the dock-head in the open small veranda, fronting the river, where we had a strong guard over us. Here the other gentlemen broke out likewise in boils all over their bodies (a happy circumstance, which, as I afterwards learned, attended every one who came out of the Black Hole).

Embark for Murshedabad.

"On our arrival at this place, we soon were given to understand, we should be embarked for Murshedabad,[1] where I think you have never been; and since I have brought you thus far, you may as well take this trip with us likewise. I have much leisure on my hands at present; and, you know, you may chuse your leisure for perusal.

Sufferings on the voyage.

"We set out on our travels from the dock-head the 24th in the afternoon, and were embarked on a large boat containing part of the plunder. She bulged ashore a little after we set off, and broke one of her floor timbers: however, they pushed on, though she made so much water she could hardly swim. Our bedstead and bedding were a platform of loose unequal bamboos laid on the bottom timbers: so that when they had been negligent in bailing, we frequently waked with half of us in the water. We had hardly any clothes to our bodies, and nothing but a bit or two of old gunny-bag, which we begged at the dock-head to defend us from the sun, rains, and dews. Our food only rice, and the water along-side, which, you know, is neither very clean, nor very palatable, in the rains; but there was enough of it without scrambling.

Poor diet a preservation.

"In short, Sir, though our distresses in this situation, covered with tormenting boils, and loaded with irons, will be

[1] The capital of Bengal.

thought, and doubtless were, very deplorable, yet the grateful consideration of our being so providentially a remnant of the saved, made every thing else appear light to us. Our rice-and-water diet, designed as a grievance to us, was certainly our preservation; for, could we (circumstanced as we were) have indulged in flesh and wine, we had died beyond all doubt.

"When we arrived at Hughly Fort, I wrote a short letter to Governor Bisdom (by means of a pencil and blank leaf of a volume of Archbishop Tillotson's sermons given us by one of our guard, part of this plunder) advising him of our miserable plight. He had the humanity to dispatch three several boats after us, with fresh provisions, liquors, clothes, and money; neither of which reached us. But, 'Whatever is, is right.' Our rice and water were more salutary and proper for us. Application to the Dutch at Chinsura.

"Matters ridiculous and droll abundantly occurred in the course of our trip. But these I will postpone for a personal recital, that I may laugh with you, and will only mention, that my hands alone being free from imposthumes, I was obliged for some time to turn nurse, and feed my poor distressed companions. Ridiculous incident.

"When we came opposite to Santipore, they found the boat would not be able to proceed further, for want of water in the river; and one of the guard was sent ashore to demand of the Zemindar[1] of that district light boats to carry prisoners of State under their charge to Murshedabad. The Zemindar, giving no credit to the fellow, mustered his guard of pykes, beat him, and drove him away. Refractory Zemindar.

"This, on the return of the messenger, raised a most furious combustion. Our Jemadar ordered his people to arms, and the resolution was to take the Zemindar and carry him bound a prisoner to Murshedabad. Accordingly they landed with their fire-arms, swords, and targets; when it occurred to one mischievous mortal amongst them, that the Attack on the Zemindar.

[1] A renter or proprietor of land.

taking me with them, would be a proof of their commission and the high offence the Zemindar had committed.

Holwell dragged through the sun.

"Being immediately lugged ashore, I urged the impossibility of my walking, covered as my legs were with boils, and, several of them in the way of my fetters; and intreated, if I must go, that they would for the time take off my irons, as it was not in my power to escape from them; for they saw I was hardly able to stand. But I might as well have petitioned tigers, or made supplication to the wind. I was obliged to crawl. They signified to me, it was now my business to obey, and that I should remember, I was not then in the Fort of Calcutta. Thus was I marched in a scorching sun, near noon, for more than a mile and half; my legs running in a stream of blood from the irritation of my irons, and myself ready to drop every step with excessive faintness and unspeakable pain.

Submission of the Zemindar.

"When we came near the Cutcherry of the district, the Zemindar with his pykes was drawn up ready to receive us; but as soon as they presented me to him as a prisoner of State, estimated and valued to them at four lakhs of rupees,[1] he confessed himself sensible of his mistake, and made no further show of resistance. The Jemadar seized him, and gave orders to have him bound and sent to the boat: but on his making a further submission, and promising to get boats from Santipore to send after us, and agreeing to pay them for the trouble he had caused, he was released, and matters accommodated.

Return march.

"I was become so very low and weak by this cruel travel that it was some time before they would venture to march me back; and the 'hard-hearted villains,' for their own sakes, were at last obliged to carry me part of the way, and support me the rest, covering me from the sun with their shields. A poor fellow, one of our Under-Gomastas of Santipore, seeing me at the Cutcherry, knew me, and, with tears in his eyes, presented me with a bunch of plantains, the half of which my guard plundered by the way.

---

[1] 50,000*l.*

"We departed from hence directly, in expectation of boats following us, but they never came; and the next day (I think the last of June) they pressed a small open fishing-dingy, and embarked us on that, with two of our guard only; for in fact, any more would have sunk her. Here we had a bed of bamboos, something softer, I think, than those of the great boat; that is, they were something smoother, but we were so distressed for room that we could not stir without our fetters bruising our own, or each other's boils; and were in woeful distress indeed, not arriving at Murshedabad until the 7th of July in the afternoon. We were all this while exposed to one regular succession of heavy rain, or intense sun-shine, and nothing to defend us from either. Re-embarkation.

"But then do not let me forget our blessings; for by the good-nature of one of our guard, we now and then latterly got a few plantains, onions, parched rice, with jaggree,[1] and the bitter green, called Curella: all which were to us luxurious indulgences, and make the rice go down deliciously. Small mercies.

"On the 7th of July, early in the morning, we came in sight of the French factory. I had a letter prepared for Mr. Law the Chief, and prevailed on my guard to put to there. On the receipt of my letter, Mr. Law, with much politeness and humanity, came down to the water-side, and remained near an hour with us. He gave the guard a genteel present for his civilities, and offered him a considerable reward and security, if he would permit us to land for an hour's refreshment: but he replied his head would pay for the indulgence. After Mr. Law had given us a supply of clothes, linen, provisions, liquors, and cash, we left his factory with grateful hearts and compliments. Humanity of Mr. Law, Chief of the French factory at Cosimbazar.

"We could not, as you may imagine, long resist touching our stock of provisions; but however temperate we thought ourselves, we were all disordered more or less by this first indulgence. A few hours after I was seized with a painful inflammation in my right leg and thigh. Over-indulgence.

---

[1] Molasses.

Arrival at Murshedabad.

"Passing by our fort and factory at Cossimbazar, raised some melancholy reflections amongst us. About four in the afternoon we landed at Murshedabad, and were conducted to, and deposited in an open stable, not far from the Nawab's palace in the city.

March through the city.

"This march, I will freely confess to you, drew tears of disdain and anguish of heart from me; thus to be led like a felon, a spectacle to the inhabitants of this populous city! My soul could not support itself with any degree of patience; the pain too arising from my boils, and inflammation of my leg, added not a little, I believe, to the depression of my spirits.

More sufferings.

"Here we had a guard of Moors placed on one side of us, and a guard of Hindus on the other; and being destined to remain in this place of purgatory, until the Nawab returned to the city, I can give you no idea of our sufferings. The immense crowd of spectators, who came from all quarters of the city to satisfy their curiosity, so blocked us up from morning till night, that I may truly say we narrowly escaped a second suffocation, the weather proving exceeding sultry.

Fever and gout.

"The first night after our arrival in the stable, I was attacked by a fever; and that night and the next day, the inflammation of my leg and thigh greatly increased; but all terminated the second night in a regular fit of the gout in my right foot and ankle; the first and last fit of this kind I ever had. How my irons agreed with this new visitor I leave you to judge: for I could not by any intreaty obtain liberty for so much as that poor leg.

Humanity of the French and Dutch.

"During our residence here, we experienced every act of humanity and friendship from Mons. Law and Mynheer Vernet, the French and Dutch Chiefs of Cossimbazar, who left no means unessayed to procure our release. Our provisions were regularly sent us from the Dutch Tanksal[1] and we were daily visited by Messrs. Ross and Ekstone, the Chief and Second there; and indeed received such instances of commiseration and affection from Mynheer Ross as will ever claim my most grateful remembrance.

---

[1] The Dutch mint near Murshedabad.

"The whole body of Armenian merchants too were most kind and friendly to us; we were not a little indebted to the obliging good-natured behaviour of Messrs. Hastings and Chambers, who gave us as much of their company as they could. They had obtained their liberty by the French and Dutch Chiefs becoming bail for their appearance. This security was often tendered for us, but without effect. Mention of Warren Hastings.

"The 11th of July the Nawab arrived in the city, and with him Bundoo Sing, to whose house we were removed that afternoon in a hackery; for I was not able to put my foot to the ground. Here we were confirmed in a report which had before reached us that the Nawab, on his return to Hughly, made inquiry for us when he released Messrs. Watts and Collet, &c., with intention to release us also; and, that he had expressed some resentment for having so hastily sent us up to Murshedabad. This proved a very pleasing piece of intelligence to us; and gave us reason to hope the issue would be more favourable to us than we expected. Better news.

"Though we were here lodged in an open bungalow only, yet we found ourselves relieved from the crowd of people which had stifled us at the stable, and once more breathed the fresh air. We were treated with much kindness and respect by Bundoo Sing, who generally passed some time or other of the day with us, and feasted us with hopes of being soon released. Hope of release.

"The 15th we were conducted in a hackery to the Killa,[1] in order to have an audience of the Suba, and know our fate. We were kept above an hour in the sun opposite the gate; whilst here we saw several of his ministers, brought out disgraced, and dismissed from their employs, who but a few minutes before we had seen enter the Killa in the utmost pomp and magnificence. Conducted to the Nawab's palace.

"Receiving advice that we should have no audience or admittance to the Nawab that day, we were deposited again at our former lodgings, the stable, to be at hand, and had the mortification of passing another night there. No audience.

[1] The seat of the Nawab or Suba's residence in the city of Murshedabad.

Disappointments.

"The 16th in the morning an old female attendant on the widow[1] of the late Aliverdi Khan paid a visit to our guard and discoursed half an hour with him. Overhearing part of the conversation to be favourable to us, I obtained the whole from him; and learned, that at a feast the preceding night the Begum had solicited our liberty, and that the Nawab had promised he would release us on the morrow. This, you will believe, gave us no small spirit; but at noon all our hopes were dashed by a piece of intelligence from the guard implying that an order was prepared, and ready to pass the seal, for returning us in irons to Raja Monikchund, governor of Allynagore, the name the Nawab had given to Calcutta.

Fears of the worst.

"I need not tell you what a thunderclap this proved to us in the very height of our flattering expectations; for I was, as to myself, well convinced I should never have got alive out of the hands of that rapacious harpy, who is a genuine Hindu, in the very worst acceptation of the word; therefore, from that moment, gave up every hope of liberty.

Despair.

"Men in this state of mind are generally pretty easy; it is hope which gives anxiety. We dined and laid ourselves down to sleep; and for my own part, I never enjoyed a sounder afternoon's nap.

Release.

"Towards five the guard waked me with notice that the Nawab would presently pass by to his palace of Mooteejeel. We roused, and desired the guard would keep the view clear for us. When the Nawab came in sight, we made him the usual salaam; and when he came abreast of us, he ordered his litter to stop, and us to be called to him. We advanced; and I addressed him in a short speech, setting forth our sufferings, and petitioned for our liberty. The wretched spectacle we made must, I think, have made an impression on a breast the most brutal; and if he is capable of pity or contrition, his heart felt it then. I think it appeared in spite of him in his countenance. He gave me no reply: but ordered two of his officers to see our irons cut off, and to

[1] The dowager princess, grandmother of Suraj-u-daula.

conduct us wherever we chose to go, and to take care we receive no trouble nor insult; and having repeated this order distinctly, directed his retinue to go on. As soon as our legs were free we took boat and proceeded to the Dutch Tanksall, where we were received and entertained with real joy and humanity.

Explanations.

"Thus, my worthy friend, you see us restored to liberty, at a time when we could entertain no probable hope of ever obtaining it. The foundation of the alarm at noon was this: Moneloll, the Nawab's Dewan, and some others, had in the morning taken no small pains to convince the Nawab that, notwithstanding my losses at Allynagore, I was still possessed of enough to pay a considerable sum for my freedom; and advised the sending me to Monikchund, who would be better able to trace out the remainder of my effects. To this, I was afterwards informed, the Nawab replied: 'It may be; if he has any thing left, let him keep it: his sufferings have been great; he shall have his liberty.' Whether this was the result of his own sentiments, or the consequence of his promise the night before to the old Begum, I cannot say; but believe, we owe our freedom partly to both.

Conclusion.

"Being myself once again at liberty, it is time I should release you, Sir, also from the unpleasing travel I have led you in this narrative of our distresses, from our entrance into that fatal Black Hole. And, shall it after all be said, or even thought, that I can possibly have arraigned or commented too severely on a conduct which alone plunged us into these unequalled sufferings? I hope not."

Demolition of the Black Hole in 1818.

The Black Hole was demolished in 1818. The accompanying extracts from a letter, signed "Asiaticus," which subsequently appeared in the Asiatic Journal of Bengal, will be read with interest.

Appearance of the Black Hole in 1812.

"The formidable Black Hole is now no more. Early in the year 1812 I visited it. It was situated in the old fort of Calcutta, and was then on the eve of demolition. Since that time the fort has come down, and on its site have been erected some extensive warehouses for the Company. I recollect forming one of a party in Calcutta, for the purpose of paying a last visit to this melancholy spot. It presented, on entering, the appearance of an oven, being long, dark, and narrow. One window (if I recollect right) was the utmost, and this secured by bars. The escape of even the small number who survived the horrid fate of the rest is surprising, and can only be accounted for by the accident of their being near the window, and the night air, which in Bengal is commonly damp, allaying the fever which consumed the rest."

List of the sufferers in the Black Hole.

The following is a list of the persons who perished in the Black Hole on the night of Sunday, the 19th of June 1756, appended to Holwell's Narrative. Sixty-nine soldiers are omitted from the list, as their names are unknown. It is supplemented by a list of the survivors.

VICTIMS.

Members of Council.

E. Eyre, Wm. Baillie, } Esqrs.; | The Reverend Jervas Bellamy.

Gentlemen in the Service.

Mr. Jenks.	Mr. Harod.
" Revely.	" P. Johnstone.
" Law.	" Ballard.
" Coastes, Ens. Mil.	" N. Drake.
" Valicourt.	" Carse.
" Jeb.	" Knapton.
" Toriano.	" Gosling.
" E. Page.	" Bing.
" S. Page.	" Dod.
" Grub.	" Dalrymple.
" Street.	

Military Captains.

Clayton.	Witherington.
Buchanan.	

Lieutenants.

Bishop.	Simson.
Hays.	Bellamy.
Blagg.	

Ensigns.

Paccard.	C. Wedderburn.
Scot.	Dumbleton, Ens. Mil.
Hastings.	

Serjeants, &c.

Sergeant-Major.	Abraham, Cartwright, Bleau, } sergeants of militia.
Quartermaster-Sergeant.	

Sea Captains.

Hunt.	Porter.
Osburne.	W. Parker.
Purnell, survived the night, but died next day.	Caulker.
Carey.	Bendall.
Stephenson.	Atkinson.
Guy.	Leech.
	&c., &c.

LIST OF THOSE WHO SURVIVED THE BLACK-HOLE PRISON.

Mr. Holwell.	Capt. Mills.
" Court.	" Dickson.
" Secretary Cooke.	" Moran.
" Lushington.	" John Meadows.
" Burdet.	And 12 military and militia blacks and whites, some of whom recovered when the door was open.
Ens. Walcot.	
Mrs. Carey.	

CHAPTER VIII.

FIRST GOVERNMENT OF CLIVE.

A. D. 1757 TO 1760.

Calcutta recovered, January 1757. Colonel Clive, Governor.

THE news of the disasters at Calcutta soon reached Madras. There was dismay at the capture of Calcutta. There were cries for vengeance on the murderers of Englishmen. Captain Clive had been away to England. He had returned with the commission of Lieutenant-Colonel from King George the Second. He had joined Admiral Watson in an expedition against Gheriah, a nest of Hindu pirates on the western coast of India. He had helped in the destruction of Gheriah. He had returned to Madras to hear of the capture of Calcutta and tragedy of the Black Hole. Colonel Clive and Admiral Watson were soon on their way from Madras to Calcutta. In January 1757 the English fleet reached Calcutta. The native Governor of Calcutta, who had been appointed by the Nawab, fled in a panic. After a very little fighting the English flag was hoisted over Fort William.

Attitude of the Nawab.

Calcutta was recovered on the second of January 1757; from this date Robert Clive was Governor of the English settlements in Bengal. Having recovered possession of the settlement of Calcutta, it was time to punish the Nawab for the massacre of Englishmen, and force him to make some compensation for the severe losses which had been sustained by the Company and the inhabitants of Calcutta. On the 10th of January the English attacked and captured the native town of Hughli. These movements aroused the young Nawab. He appeared in the neighbourhood of Calcutta with an army of forty thousand men. He feigned friendship: he promised redress; but it was difficult to believe him. Every demand made by the English was delayed or evaded. The presence of his army was a menace to the English at Calcutta; and some of his people were beginning to enter the Company's bounds.

Defeat of the Nawab by Clive, February 1757.

On the 4th of February Clive brought matters to a crisis. He called on the Nawab to withdraw his army. The Nawab refused. Clive had little more than two thousand men, but two-thirds were Europeans. He attacked the Nawab's camp at early morning. His success was marred by a fog, but it sufficed to frighten the enemy. The Nawab retreated from Calcutta and began to make overtures of peace.

Objections to peace.

There were objections to making a peace with the Nawab. Watson thought that he had not been sufficiently punished; and that the Nawab was only amusing the English in order to cover his retreat. The English generally were burning to avenge the atrocity of the Black Hole. But Clive was conscious of other dangers. Great Britain was on the eve of a war with France. The Nawab might form a league with the French at Chandernagore. If the Nawab's army was supported by a French force the English Company might find itself in danger. Under such circumstances Colonel Clive thought it would be best to make peace with the Nawab, secure compensation, and restore the Company's settlement to its old footing, rather than endanger the safety of the settlement by protracted hostilities for the sake of revenge.

Lavish promises of the Nawab.

Clive therefore began to negotiate with the Nawab. He found no difficulty as far as promises were concerned. The Nawab was ready to promise anything. He engaged to restore all the goods that had been taken from the English factories; he would pay for all that were lost or damaged ; he fixed the day on which full compensation was to be made. He granted all former privileges, and permitted the English to fortify Calcutta. A treaty was soon concluded ; the only question was whether the Nawab would fulfil its obligations.

Difficulties with the French at Chandernagore.

Peace having been made with the Nawab, the next question was how to deal with the French at Chandernagore. Clive proposed a neutrality in Bengal. But the French governor of Chandernagore could not pledge himself to a neutrality; he was bound to obey all orders he might receive from Pondicherry; should he be told to attack the English, he would have no option.

Increase of French influence in the Dekhan under Bussy.

This answer was perplexing; the English in Bengal had real grounds for alarm. French influence had increased in India. M. Bussy had set up a Nizam at Hyderabad, and was all powerful in the Dekhan. He had obtained the cession of a large territory for the maintenance of a French force; the new French dominion extended six hundred miles along the coast of Coromandel. It was certain that if M. Bussy joined the French at Chandernagore, the Nawab would court his friendship; and if the French supported the Nawab, there was every reason to fear that Calcutta would be overwhelmed.

Capture of Chandernagore.

Accordingly Clive asked the Nawab for permission to attack the French at Chandernagore. At first the Nawab refused. Then he was alarmed at rumours that the Afghans at Delhi were about to invade Bengal; and he naturally wanted Clive to help him to keep the Afghans out of Bengal. At last he gave the required permission to Clive to attack the French. In March Chandernagore was captured by the English.

The Nawab inclines towards the French.

Clive was now bent upon rooting the French out of Bengal. Some fugitives from Chandernagore had fled to Cossimbazar, and found refuge in the French factory under M. Law. Clive demanded the surrender of the refugees. But the Nawab had already begun to lean towards the French. He had given money and arms to the French refugees. When Clive became more pressing, the Nawab gave the French more money, and sent them away up country towards Patna, under pretence of banishing them from his dominions. To crown all, authentic reports were received by

Colonel Clive that M. Bussy was marching a large force towards Bengal; it was also discovered that the Nawab was sending friendly letters and presents to M. Bussy.[1]

Alarming proceedings of the Nawab.

By this time Clive found that he could not trust the Nawab. Mr. Watts, a Company's servant, was sent to reside at Murshedabad. He reported that the Nawab was not only intriguing with the French, but evading the fulfilment of the treaty. The conduct of the Nawab was suspicious and threatening. One day he would tear up Clive's letters and threaten to put Mr. Watts to death; the next day he would beg pardon of Mr. Watts. He sent an army to Plassey, under the command of his prime minister, with the evident object of threatening the English at Calcutta. Clive requested him to withdraw the army. In reply the Nawab sent a further reinforcement to Plassey under the command of Meer Jaffier.

Difficulties of Clive.

Clive was now placed in a most difficult and trying position. He was hurried on by force of circumstances into a line of action which no one had foreseen. On recovering possession of Calcutta he would have been content with a certain amount of redress and compensation. All he wanted was to inflict such a punishment on the Nawab as would prevent him from making any future attempt on Calcutta.

[1] The determination of the Nawab to break with the English was obvious in other directions. English merchants going to the Factories up country were arrested and sent back by the Nawab's orders. This was contrary to treaty, but the merchants were told that the Nawab would not regard the treaty.—See Verelst's Bengal, page 17.

But the war with France introduced new complications. The Nawab had been inclined to pit the French against the English; he had given an unwilling consent to the English capture of Chandernagore; he was inviting the French in the Dekhan to drive the English out of Bengal. The capture of Chandernagore had silenced the French for a while; but nothing short of the destruction of the Nawab would prevent a renewal of the struggle between the French and English in Bengal.

The state of Bengal in 1757 thus bore a strong resemblance to the state of the Carnatic a few short years before. Had there been a Dupleix in Bengal, he would have supported Suraj-u-daula as a French Nawab, and gone to war with the English. In like manner Clive was prepared to set up an English Nawab in Bengal, to counteract any joint efforts that might be made by the French in the Dekkan and Suraj-u-daula to drive the English out of Calcutta. **French and English in Bengal.**

Fortune played into the hands of Clive. The grandees at Murshedabad were already disgusted with the insolence of the Nawab. Many of them were alarmed at his threats. At last they formed a conspiracy to dethrone him. Jugget Seit, the Hindu banker, was a leader in the conspiracy; so was the prime minister who commanded the army at Plassey; so was Meer Jaffier who had joined the army at Plassey. The conspirators were timid after the manner of Bengalees; they wanted Clive to help them; they made overtures through Omichund, **Native conspiracy at Murshedabad.**

the Hindu[1] contractor who had formerly served the Company.[2]

Clive makes terms with the conspirators.

It is needless to dwell upon the plot. Clive made secret terms with the conspirators. Mr. Watts escaped from Cossimbazar. The Nawab marched all his forces to Plassey, whilst Clive moved up from Calcutta. Clive and the Nawab met at Plassey. The battle was fought in June 1757, just a twelvemonth after the loss of Calcutta. Meer Jaffier had promised to go over to Clive; but he only looked on and did nothing. Clive utterly routed the Nawab's army. The Nawab fled away, a helpless fugitive. Subsequently he fell into the hands of his enemies, and was put to death by a son of Meer Jaffier.

Clive makes Meer Jaffier Nawab. Presents and compensation.

Clive went on to Murshedabad and placed Meer Jaffier on the throne. The new Nawab was profuse with presents and promises. The treasures of Suraj-u-daula had been estimated at forty millions sterling. In reality they only amounted to a million and a half. Meer Jaffier engaged to pay a million to the Company; three-quarters of a million as

---

[1] See *ante*, page 224. Omichund subsequently threatened to divulge the whole plot to the Nawab, unless he was paid about three hundred thousand sterling. Clive duped him with a sham copy of a treaty, purporting to have been made between the Company and Meer Jaffier, stipulating that the money should be given to Omichund. The real treaty contained no such clause. This trick, by which Clive personally profited nothing, has done more harm to his reputation than any other charge that has been brought against him.

[2] Meer Jaffier and Meer Cossim have become such current names in the Government records as well as in the Parliamentary debates, that it would be inexpedient to change them into modern spelling; otherwise they should be styled Jafir Mír and Mír Kazim, or Amír Jaffir and Amír Kazím.

compensation to the inhabitants of Calcutta, native and European; also presents to Clive and members of Government. Half the money was paid down at once, and the remainder was promised at an early date. Boats went down the river from Murshedabad to Calcutta laden with treasure to the value of eight hundred thousand pounds sterling.

Joy and triumph at Calcutta.

Few events in history have created a greater revulsion of feeling than the victory at Plassey. The people of Calcutta had been depressed, not only by the capture of the Factory, but by the utter loss of all their worldly goods. But now the disgrace was forgotten in the triumph; the poverty was forgotten at the sight of the treasure. Orme says that the whole settlement was intoxicated with joy; quarrels were forgotten and enemies became friends.

Wealth of Clive.

Clive received a vast money reward from Meer Jaffier. Large as it was, the time came when he expressd his surprise that he had not taken more. He had placed Meer Jaffier on the throne of the three provinces at a time when the trembling grandee might have expected death and destruction for his inaction at Plassey. For the moment, the grandees at Murshedabad regarded Clive as the symbol of power, the arbiter of fate, the type of omnipotence who could protect or destroy at will. One and all were eager to propitiate Clive with presents; such has been the instinct of orientals from the remotest antiquity. They are ever ready to propitiate men in power with flatteries and presents, just as they seek to avert the wrath or implore the protection of deity by praises and sacrifices. Clive refused to accept any present, saving what came from the hands of Meer Jaffier.

Meer Jaffier drives the Hindus into rebellion.

In due course Clive returned to Calcutta. He soon had cause for anxiety. The new Nawab began to enter upon a dangerous course of policy. Hitherto the Nawabs of Bengal, and of every other province under Moghul rule, had employed Hindu ministers and renters in preference to Muhammadans. The Hindus were a check upon the kinsmen and retainers of the Nawab. They were more subservient and amenable to the Nawab. Meer Jaffier reversed this state of things; he sought to remove the Hindu prime minister, and some of the more powerful of the Hindu governors, and replace them by his own kinsmen. The result was that four different rebellions broke out at the same time. To make matters worse the Nawab of Oude was threatening to invade Behar and take possession of the three provinces of Bengal, Behar, and Orissa.

Nawab of Oude threatens Bengal.

The Nawab of Oude played an important part in the subsequent history of British India. His name was Shuja-u-daula. His territories extended from Behar to the neighbourhood of Delhi; from the banks of the Jumna to the mountains of Nepal.

Clive averts the danger.

Clive was once more driven on by the force of circumstances. He had set up a new Nawab, who was equally incapable of keeping the peace in Bengal, or of keeping invaders out of the province.

Unless he interfered in the administration of affairs, Bengal would go to rack and ruin, and the Company's settlements be swamped in the general anarchy. He suppressed the rebellions within the three provinces by guaranteeing the safety of the Hindu officials. The prime minister escaped to Calcutta and was taken under English protection. Clive especially guaranteed the Hindu governor of Behar, named Ram Narain. This man ruled the country between Bengal proper and the dominions of the Nawab of Oude. By giving him a guarantee, he was kept from deserting Meer Jaffier and going over to the Nawab of Oude. The fear of an invasion, however, was soon over; the Nawab of Oude was called away by troubles in the North-West.

Difficult position of Clive.

Meer Jaffier was forced to respect the guarantees of Clive, but he was very jealous of the interference. Clive, however, could not help his position. He already saw that he had no alternative but to exercise a paramount power or abandon the country. If Behar was invaded from without, the Nawab had no one to look to but Clive. Meanwhile, had the rebellions of the Hindu governors continued in the provinces, they would have laid the country open to invasion.

Authority of the Nawab exercised by Clive.

Meer Jaffier was well aware of his weakness. He knew that he was helpless without Clive. Still his mortification was none the less. Before the capture of Calcutta, no Englishmen appeared at Murshedabad, except as supplicants for trading privileges. Since the battle of Plassey, the English were lords and masters. The Hindu grandees were making their court to Clive, just as the English merchants during the previous century had been accustomed to make their court to the Nawab and his great men.

Mahrattas and Moghuls court Clive.

The victories of Clive had made him famous in India, before he went to Bengal. Before the battle of Plassey, the Mahrattas of Poona offered to help him against the Nawab of Bengal. After the battle, as will be seen hereafter, he received flattering overtures from the Moghul court at Delhi.

Ruin of the French interest in the Dekhan.

Whilst Clive was trying to keep the peace in Bengal, the French were making war in the Southern Peninsula. The declaration of war in 1756 between Great Britain and France had revived the old struggle between the English and French in the Carnatic. A large French force landed at Pondicherry under the ill-fated Count Lally. Clive sought to create a diversion, by sending an expedition under Colonel Forde to drive the French out of the Dekhan. The story of the expedition has lost its interest. It will suffice to say that French influence in the Dekhan was ruined by Lally. He recalled Bussy from the Dekhan. The consequence was that Forde succeeding in expelling the French from the Dekhan. Subsequently Lally laid siege to Madras, but was compelled to raise it. He was next utterly defeated at Wandewash by Sir Eyre Coote. Pondicherry was taken by Coote and Lally returned to France, where he was condemned to death, and most unjustly executed.

Meantime the English in Bengal had troubles of their own. In the beginning of 1759 there was a storm from the north-west. At Delhi, the King, or Padishah, was entirely in the hands of his Vizier, and was in danger of his life. His eldest son, known as the Shahzada, fled from Delhi to escape from the Vizier. After many adventures and wanderings, the Shahzada appeared on the border of Behar. He gave out that his father, the King, had given him the government of Bengal, Behar, and Orissa. He was soon at the head of a large army.

The Shahzada threatens Bengal.

Clive marched to the frontier and soon disposed of the Shahzada. Meer Jaffier expressed much gratitude for this service. The Vizier at Delhi was equally pleased at the overthrow of the rebel prince. He sent the letters or sunnuds of investiture to Meer Jaffier, as Nawab of Bengal, Behar, and Orissa. He also sent a title of honour to Clive; subsequently the Nawab gave a jaghire to Clive for the maintenance of the title. It was given out that the grant of the jaghire was an act of gratitude on the part of the Nawab for the defeat of the Shahzada.[1]

Defeated by Clive.

---

[1] This title led to the celebrated acquisition known as Clive's jaghire. In India under the Moghuls it was customary to give a grant of land with a title; the recipient farmed out the lands at a comparatively high annual rate, and paid a smaller yearly quit-rent into the imperial treasury. After the battle of Plassey, the Nawab had ceded a large territory on the bank of the river Hughli to the English Company. The Company paid a quit-rent of thirty thousand pounds to the Nawab, and farmed out the lands for a hundred thousand pounds. The Nawab made over this quit-rent to Clive, which was henceforth known as Colonel Clive's jaghire.

War with the Dutch.

In 1759 Clive was involved in hostilities with the Dutch. A Dutch armament suddenly arrived from Batavia and sailed up the Hughli River. It turned out that whilst Meer Jaffier had been flattering Clive, he had been intriguing with the Dutch at Chinsura; and the Dutch had arranged to help him with a fleet against the English. There was no war between Great Britain and Holland, and consequently it was difficult for Clive to decide how to act; yet it was obvious that the Dutch armament at Batavia threatened Calcutta; that if the armanent effected a junction with the Dutch force at Chinsura, the two combined might overwhelm Calcutta. Clive took upon himself all the responsibilities of a war; he fought against the Dutch, as it were with a halter round his neck. He barred the advance of the Dutch; he left them to begin the attack; he then routed them utterly. He compelled the Dutch to acknowledge themselves the aggressors and to pay compensation for all losses and damages. The Dutch government in Europe made loud complaints, but they had no remedy. Clive had beaten them both at diplomacy and at arms.

Meer Jaffier frightened.

The complicity of Meer Jaffier in the Dutch expedition was beyond all doubt. Indeed it might be conjectured that Clive got his jaghire, not because he had defeated the Shahzada, but because Meer Jaffier was in mortal terror lest Clive should punish him for his intrigues with the Dutch. It seems far more likely that the jaghire was given as a peace-offering than as an act of gratitude.

In 1759-60 the Shahzada again threatened Behar, supported by the Nawab of Oude. Clive sent a force against the invaders under the command of Major Calliaud. The first administration of Clive was drawing to a close. He embarked for England in February 1760. He was in the zenith of his fame at the early age of thirty-five. **Clive returns to England, 1760.**

The policy of Clive at this period may be gathered from a remarkable letter which he addressed to William Pitt, dated the 7th of January 1759.[1] He told Pitt that no trust or reliance could be placed upon the Nawab, and still less upon the heir apparent to the throne at Murshedabad. A strong European force in Bengal was therefore indispensable, and Clive thought that two thousand European soldiers would put an end to all alarm. If the Nawab or his successor proved troublesome, such a force would enable the English to assume the sovereignty of the country. It would be easy to obtain letters of confirmation from the Court at Delhi by engaging to send a yearly tribute to the King, as His Majesty's share of the revenue of the province. The people of the country would rejoice at the change of rulers.[2] **Policy of Clive: his letter to Pitt.**

---

[1] See Malcolm's Life of Clive, volume II, page 119.

[2] Clive estimated the gross revenues of Bengal, Behar, and Orissa at three or four millions sterling. In the early years of the reign of Aurangzeb, the imperial share of the revenue of Bengal amounted to fifty-five lakhs, or more than half a million sterling. In 1665-66 Tavernier saw this amount of money being carried in hard cash from Bengal to Delhi. (See *ante*, page 154.) Neither Tavernier, nor any one else, could estimate the gross revenue. Forty years later, when Nawab Murshed Kuli Khan was trying to ingratiate himself with the Moghul Court at Delhi, he sent more than a million sterling to the imperial treasury as the king's share of the revenue of Bengal.

Clive offered the post of Dewan by the Moghul Court: reasons for refusing.

Clive further told Pitt that the Vizier at Delhi had already sounded him on this point. The Vizier had offered Clive the post of Dewan, or Collector of the revenue of Bengal, Behar, and Orissa. Originally the post of Dewan had been distinct from that of Nawab or Nazim. The Dewan was the financial minister who collected the revenue in the name of the Emperor; paid all the official salaries from that of the Nawab Nazim downwards; and remitted the surplus to the imperial treasury at Delhi. The Nawab Nazim was the military commander of the province, who was supposed to keep the peace, and help the Dewan to collect the revenue. But the two posts of Dewan and Nawab Nazim had become united in one man ever since the days of Murshed Kuli Khan. Clive declined the separate post of King's Dewan. It would have excited the jealousy of Meer Jaffier, and he had not a sufficient European force in Bengal to enable him to carry out the measure in the teeth of the Nawab.[1]

Previous scheme of Colonel Mill.

Strange to say, Clive's scheme for the government of Bengal resembles one which had been drawn up twelve years previously by a Colonel James Mill. In all probability Clive never saw it.[2] Colonel James Mill had lived twenty years in India. He projected the conquest of the three provinces

[1] It will be seen hereafter that the post of King's Dewan was subsequently accepted by Clive in behalf of the English Company.

[2] No historian, as far as I am aware, has referred to Mill's scheme. It lies buried in an appendix to Bolt's Affairs in Bengal. The original is very diffuse, like most English in the eighteenth century. The remarks in the text give all the points in Mill's memorandum.

of Bengal, Behar, and Orissa, under the flag of the Emperor of Germany. In 1746 he submitted his scheme to Francis of Lorraine, the husband of Maria Theresa.

"The Moghul empire," says Colonel Mill, "is overflowing with gold and silver. She has always been feeble and defenceless. It is a miracle that no European prince with a maritime power has ever attempted the conquest of Bengal. By a single stroke infinite wealth might be acquired, which would counterbalance the mines of Brazil and Peru.

"The policy of the Moghuls is bad; their army is worse; they are without a navy. The empire is exposed to perpetual revolts. Their ports and rivers are open to foreigners. The country might be conquered, or laid under contribution, as easily as the Spaniards overwhelmed the naked Indians of America.

"A rebel subject, named Aliverdi Khan, has torn away the three provinces of Bengal, Behar, and Orissa from the Moghul empire. He has treasure to the value of thirty millions sterling. His yearly revenue must be at least two millions. The provinces are open to the sea. Three ships with fifteen hundred or two thousand regulars would suffice for the undertaking. The British nation would cooperate for the sake of the plunder and the promotion of their trade. The East India Company should be left alone. No Company can keep a secret. Moreover, the English Company is so distracted as to be incapable of any firm resolution."

Clive's ideas of conquest.

It has been said that Clive conquered Bengal for the sake of the late Company. From his letter to Pitt it would seem that he did nothing of the kind. He wished all conquests in India to be transferred to the British nation; and he suggested to Pitt that the surplus revenue might be appropriated to the payment of the national debt.

Pitt's objections.

Pitt concurred with Clive as regards the practicability of the scheme, but he saw difficulties in the way. The Company's charter would not expire for twenty years. The Judges had been already consulted, and decided that the conquests in India belonged to the Company and not to the Crown. Moreover, if the conquests were transferred to the Crown, Pitt was of opinion that they might endanger the public liberties. It is a curious coincidence that a single century should have precisely intervened between the day when Clive penned his letter, and the day when the direct government of India was assumed by the Crown.[1]

---

[1] Only eight weeks were wanting to complete the century. Clive wrote on the 7th of January 1759. The proclamation of the Queen's assuming the direct Government of India was made on the 5th of November 1858.

CHAPTER IX.

CALCUTTA RECORDS: CHANGING NAWABS.

1760 TO 1763.

Critical state of Bengal.

THE departure of Clive from Bengal was followed by what may be termed the revolutionary period. Clive had foreseen that the existing status could not last. He had propounded his scheme of government to Pitt; but the famous war minister had raised objections. Some decided step was absolutely necessary. Delay might be attended with serious danger. Hindustan was swarming with adventurers, Mahratta and Afghan. A helpless Nawab with a rabble army would never repel the warlike bands from the north-west who were carving out principalities in India. An English force could hold Bengal against all comers; but there was no money to pay for it. The revenues of the Nawab were swallowed up by his rabble following; and it was impossible to expect that the Company should provide for the defence of Bengal out of their profits as merchants. Fortunately Mahrattas and Afghans were at war against each other in the Upper Provinces, or Bengal might have been overwhelmed at any moment, and all the advantages gained by the battle of Plassey might have been sacrificed at a single blow.

Governors Holwell and Vansittart.

Clive was succeeded for a few months by Mr. Holwell as Governor of Calcutta. Holwell was the man who had written an account of his sufferings in the Black Hole. He was naturally spiteful against all Nawabs, and especially so against Nawab Jaffier. He was succeeded by Mr. Vansittart, a well-meaning man, who was soon called upon to take serious action.

Bengal threatened.

The Shahzada and Nawab of Oudh were turning up again under novel circumstances. The King of Delhi had been murdered by the Vizier. The Shahzada proclaimed himself King under the name of Shah Alam, and appointed the Nawab of Oudh to be his Vizier. They raised an army and began to threaten Behar.

Nawab Jaffier deposed.

The dethronement of Nawab Jaffier was thus perhaps a political necessity; a stronger man was wanted for the place. Meer Cossim was pitched upon; he had married a daughter of Nawab Jaffier, and was known to be a soldier of capacity. There was no difficulty as to terms. The Calcutta Council expected a donation of twenty lakhs of rupees to be distributed amongst themselves. Meer Cossim was ready to promise payment, but Vansittart refused to take the money. Indeed so large a sum, equal to more than two hundred thousand pounds sterling, could scarcely have been forthcoming out of an empty treasury, with a dangerous enemy on the frontier.[1]

[1] Mr. Mill, and every historian after him, says that Mr. Vansittart took the money and distributed it. It will be seen hereafter that the charge was a calumny as far as Vansittart and Warren Hastings are concerned.

Nawab Cossim was placed upon the throne without the slightest opposition. Meer Jaffier yielded to his fate, and gave up the post to his son-in-law. The people of Bengal cared nothing about the change of Nawabs, and thus the English could already depose and set up Nawabs at will. Installation of Nawab Cossim.

The English and Nawab Cossim took the field against the King and Nawab Vizier. The details of the military operations are of no moment. It will suffice to say that the enemy was utterly routed. The Nawab Vizier fled back to Oudh. Shah Alam surrendered to the English, and took up his abode at Patna, the capital of Behar. Invasion repelled.

The records in the Home Office at Calcutta begin about this period. The letters which passed between the Governor and Council at Calcutta and the Court of Directors at London form the most valuable portion. The Governor and Council at Calcutta reported the progress of events. In reply the Court of Directors reviewed what had happened and passed their orders. These records are diffuse but intelligible; they tell the actual state of affairs; at the same time they show that neither the Board at Calcutta, nor the Directors at London, were able to read between the lines. Records of the Home Office at Calcutta.

It is obvious from the records, assisted perhaps by a knowledge of after events, to see that from the first, Meer Cossim was bent on emancipating himself from the English. He did his best to withdraw from all intercourse with English. He put a stop to all money disputes with his allies by ceding Designs of Meer Cossim.

three districts,[1] yielding a yearly revenue of half a million sterling. He was under the impression that this revenue would satisfy the English once and for all, as it would suffice to maintain an English force in time of war, and to fill the coffers of the Company in time of peace. He left the English to administer the affairs of these three districts as they pleased. He thus entered upon the undisturbed possession of the remainder of the three provinces. Moreover, he moved his capital from Murshedabad to Monghyr. Murshedabad was not much more than a hundred miles from Calcutta. Monghyr was nearly three hundred miles. At Monghyr Nawab Cossim could train and discipline an army without observation; and it will appear from the sequel that he formed an army at Monghyr that fought against the English with an obstinate bravery far exceeding that of any native army encountered by Clive.

Shah Alam at Patna.

All this while Shah Alam was living in a very anomalous position at Patna. He was nominally a rebel when he was defeated by Clive and Nawab Jaffier. He was nominally a King when he was defeated by the English and Nawab Cossim. In reality he had hitherto been a puppet in the hands of the Nawab Vizier of Oudh; and now he had surrendered himself to the English and Nawab Cossim,

[1] The three districts were Burdwan, Midnapore, and Chittagong. For some years no change was made in the native administration of the three districts. The Company's servants merely took the nett collections from the zemindars, or farmers of the revenue, and left the native zemindars to collect the revenues after their own fashion, and administer justice in their own way.

and was living on their bounty at Patna. But for all this Shah Alam was King, and might have mounted the throne at Delhi, if he could only have got there.

English propose conducting Shah Alam to Delhi.

The state of Delhi at this period is beyond anything that can be imagined from European experiences. The anarchy and confusion was not brought about by the struggles of internal parties but by conflict between foreign enemies. For years Delhi had been a bone of contention between Mahrattas and Afghans. In 1759 the Vizier, supported by Mahrattas, had murdered the King, the father of Shah Alam. Since then the Vizier had been driven out of Delhi by the Afghans under Ahmad Shah Abdali. In January 1761, the Afghans under Ahmad Shah Abdali had crushed the Mahrattas at Panipat. The defeat was followed by a massacre of Mahrattas, which left Ahmad Shah Abdali undisputed master of Hindustan.

Afghan influences predominating at Delhi.

Ahmad Shah Abdali was anxious to place Shah Alam upon the throne of Delhi. He raised a son of Shah Alam to the throne, until Shah Alam should himself arrive at Delhi. Shah Alam was then most anxious for the English to conduct him to Delhi. What the English thought of this proposal may be gathered from the following extract of a general letter sent by Mr. Vansittart and Council at Calcutta to the Court of Directors.

Extracts from Calcutta records.

The President and Board at Calcutta are thus speaking, as it were, to the Court of Directors in London:—

King Shah Alam returns towards Delhi; fails to

"The first thing that occurs under the head of Country Powers is the Proclamation of Shah Alam (formerly known obtain the help of the English.

by the name of the Shahzada) as King of Delhi. He remained at Patna till the beginning of June, and was extremely desirous of having a body of English forces accompanying him to his capital; but as we were uncertain of Colonel Coote's regiment coming down from the coast,[1] and the security of your possessions in Bengal was first to be regarded, we found it impossible to spare a sufficient detachment for undertaking so distant and so important a service. The King, therefore, being pressed by his relations at Delhi to proceed thither with all expedition, and Shuja-u-daula, the Nawab of Oude, whom he has appointed his Vizier, having advanced to the borders of this Province to meet him, he determined not to wait longer for our assistance. The Nawab Meer Cossim supplied him with considerable sums of money during his residence at Patna, and at the time of his departure caused Sicca Rupees to be struck in his name throughout these provinces; of which having advised the President, it was agreed that the Siccas in the name of Shah Alam should also be struck in our Mint on the 15th of July, which was accordingly done, the usual notice being first given. Shah Alam is not, however, as yet generally acknowledged. The late Vizier [at Delhi] has engaged some of the chiefs of the empire in his party, and has formed a considerable army to oppose the King and Shuja-u-daula on their way to Delhi. These last were by our freshest advices about ten days' march on this side of Agra, which was in the hands of the late Delhi Vizier, so that upon the whole the event of this affair is very doubtful.[2]

"We hope, however, that none of the contending parties will return this way, and that Bengal will continue to enjoy a state of tranquillity."

---

[1] The "coast" always refers to the Coromandel Coast; in other words, to the Madras Presidency. Thus the Calcutta letter means that the Governor and Council were uncertain whether Colonel Coote would bring up his European regiment from Madras. Had they been assured on this point, an English force would even at this early period have been sent to Delhi to place Shah Alam on the throne. What the result would have been, few can divine.

[2] General letter to Court, 12th November 1761, paras. 56 to 71.

Designs of Nawab Cossim upon the King.

It ultimately turned out that neither the English nor Nawab Cossim would help Shah Alam. At the same time both were anxious to get what they could out of him. The name of Padishah, or King, was still held in profound respect throughout Hindustan; and his sign manual sufficed for the grant of provinces. Meer Cossim had been made Nawab of Bengal, Behar, and Orissa by English prestige. He was anxious to get letters of investiture from the King, under the King's seal. It would not only confirm his right to the three provinces, but render him independent of the English. He would be Nawab, not by the nomination of foreigners, but by the favour of the King. Shah Alam, on the other hand, insisted upon the payment of the old annual tribute as the imperial share of the revenue of the three provinces. He would not give the letters of investiture without some guarantee that the imperial share would be paid. In the end Nawab Cossim agreed to pay the King an annual tribute of twenty-four lakhs, or two hundred and forty thousand pounds sterling; and by this large sacrifice of revenue secured the letters of investiture.

Designs of the English upon the King.

Mr. Vansittart heard that Nawab Cossim had got letters of investiture for Bengal, Behar, and Orissa, and naturally followed the example. He asked the King for letters of investiture for the jaghire lands granted by Nawab Jaffier, and for the three districts ceded by Meer Cossim; he also asked for similar letters investing Mahomed Ali, the English Nawab of Arcot, with the government of the Carnatic.[1] Mr. Vansittart evidently thought that the request for the letters was a very simple one; but he was told that no letters of investiture would be granted, unless the imperial share of the revenues of the Carnatic, as well as that of the three districts in Bengal, was sent to the King. He was evidently taken aback by the refusal. It will be seen hereafter that the Directors were equally offended with the King; they thought the King ought to have granted the letters of investiture out of gratitude to the English. The following extract from the letter to the Court already quoted sufficiently details the facts:—

"By the Nawab Cossim's letter to the President, which he laid before the Board the 12th October, we are advised of his having received from Shah Alam the Sunnuds [*i. e.*, letters of investiture] for the three provinces.

The English apply to Shah Alam for other Sunnuds.

"We directed Major Carnac and Mr. McGuire, and afterwards Colonel Coote and Mr. McGuire, to apply, as soon as Shah Alam should be acknowledged King, for Sunnuds for the Company's possessions and privileges in Bengal, *viz.* :—

"The zemindari of the pergunnahs or lands about Calcutta granted by Meer Jaffier.

"The jaghires of the districts of Burdwan, Midnapore, and Chittagong, granted by the present Nawab, and the confirmation of the freedom of our Mint.

Also for Sunnuds for their Nawab at Arcot.

"We directed also application to be made at the same time for the Sunnuds for the Provinces of Arcot in the name of the Nawab Mahomed Ali Khan, with whom we have been so long allied. These requests were made by Major Carnac, who was detached by Colonel Coote to escort the King to the borders of the Province; and the King wrote upon the

[1] See *ante*, page 146.

papers of requests that they should be granted whenever a proper tribute was remitted. The Major transmitted to us copies of the said papers of requests with the King's superscription, and advised us at the same time that the King had offered to confer on the Company the Dewani of Bengal on condition of our being answerable for the Royal Revenues; but as we were sensible that our accepting of this post would cause jealousy and ill-will between us and the Nawab, we thought it more prudent to decline it."[1]

Designs of Nawab Cossim against the Hindu grandees.

The next move of Nawab Cossim betrays the same desire to get rid of English interference which he had shown ever since he became Nawab. Clive had put an end to rebellions by giving guarantees of protection to Hindu grandees. Mr. Vansittart withdrew the guarantees. The subject was one of bitter controversy at the time. The general letter may be left to tell its own story:—

Non-interference with the Nawab's servants: question as regards Ram Narain.

"In your commands of the 13th March 1761,[2] you have favoured us with your opinion in general as to our conduct with the country government. We are very happy in the confidence you are pleased to express in our management, and shall endeavour to conform to those views of economy and good order you therein recommend. Our sentiments with respect to protecting the servants of the country government agree perfectly with yours. Those who have received such protections have proved in general false friends to us, of which the transactions of Roy Doolub and Nundcomar,[3] mentioned in our advices of last season, may be

[1] This offer of the Dewani is a repetition of the offer already made to Clive. In 1765 it was accepted by Clive, as will be seen in the account of his second administration of Bengal. It was offered in 1761 on the condition that the English would conduct Shah Alam to Delhi.

[2] Not at Calcutta.

[3] Roy Doolub was the Hindu Prime Minister of Meer Jaffier; Nundcomar was the Hindu Governor of Hughli. The lives of both, as well as that of Ram Narain, had been guaranteed by Clive.

esteemed a proof. Those two, however, do remain under our protection, but we shall take care that the number of them does not increase. Our Select Committee's address of the 29th December 1759, which you take notice of, does not mention the particulars of the engagements that subsisted between Ram Narain [Nawab of Behar or Patna];[1] nor can we find them anywhere. We could, therefore, construe them no otherwise than as justice and equity and the constitution of the country would admit. We supposed them accordingly to be of this nature, that he should have the protection of the English as long as he should duly give an account of his administration to the Subah[2] of Murshedabad, and be answerable to him for the revenues of the Behar Province according to their real produce, or at least according to the terms agreed with the late Nawab Jaffier Ali Khan, which were extremely easy. Upon this footing we were determined still to support him, and sent orders accordingly to Major Carnac early in the month of March, which orders we afterwards repeated several times, and endeavoured to the utmost of our power to bring him to an adjustment of his accounts with the Nawab [*i. e.*, Subahdar of Bengal]; but more than four months having elapsed, and none of his accounts delivered in, the Nawab grew extremely uneasy, and insisted on dismissing Ram Narain, and placing another in the administration of the affairs of the Behar Province in his room, which we thought improper longer to oppose; and we were accordingly acquainted on the 10th of August that Rajbullub was appointed to that Government. Ram Narain continues with the Nawab at Patna, and we are informed that since he was turned out he has paid some part of the balance due from him.

---

[1] Ram Narain is styled Nawab in the records. Properly speaking, he was Naib, or Deputy Nawab.

[2] This was the name sometimes given to the Nawab. Properly, Subah was the name of the province; the Governor was known as Subahdar. The term "Subah of Murshedabad" is identical with that of Nawab of Bengal, Behar, and Orissa.

"It is with great concern that we must request your perusal of so large a number of pages in our Consultation Book filled entirely with disputes which began at Patna between Major Carnac and the Nawab (Meer Cossim), and continued afterwards between Colonel Coote and the Nawab; complaints and remonstrances made by the Nawab in consequence; and dissents of nine of the Members of the Board from the opinion of the majority on those subjects. In the Proceedings of the Select Committee you will see the beginning, the continuation, and we hope the end of these dissensions, which have been by so much the more disagreeable as in some instances the great object of the Company's interest and the tranquillity of the country seems to be lost in unbecoming personal invectives. By the examination which has been made since into the Nawab's complaints laid before the Board the 26th June, we imagine his fears on this head to have proceeded from his uneasiness at our protection of Ram Narain, and from the jealousy which many ill-disposed people made it their business to excite in him by giving him secret intelligence that we had a design to procure the Dewani for the Company.[1]

Major Carnac and Colonel Coote wished to protect Ram Narain, Governor of Behar, against Meer Cossim.

"As we all have the highest respect for the character of Colonel Coote, and a due sense of how much the Company owe to his services, it has been a matter of particular concern to us that anything should have happened in the course of these disputes to give him uneasiness. We shall avoid repeating here anything that might tend to inflame the minds afresh."

Regrets the dispute with Colonel Coote.

The miscellaneous incidents recorded in the general letter call for no preliminary explanation; the extracts may be left to speak for themselves:—

Miscellaneous incidents.

"By two vessels which have sailed lately for Pegu, the President wrote to the King (of Burma), and sent a trifling present in order to obtain leave for the timbers to be brought

Troubles in Burma.

[1] The new Nawab, Meer Cossim, had already found out the design which Colonel Clive communicated to Mr. Pitt. See ante, page 267.

away from the Negrais. It would be much more agreeable to us, if an opportunity offered, to assert our rights after a different manner, and demand satisfaction for the massacre of Mr. Southby and the people who were with him; but it is vain to make such demands without being well able to enforce them.

Distress amongst French families in Bengal.

"There being a great number of French families, chiefly women and children, dispersed at Chandernagore, Chinsurah, and Serampore, who, having spent what little they had left after the capture of their settlement, were reduced to the utmost distress, we could not help giving some attention to the representation which was made to us; and we hope you will approve of our resolution to divide amongst them for their subsistence the sum of one thousand Arcot rupees per month.

State of affairs with the Dutch.

"We have this year had no disputes with the Dutch Government in Bengal; but upon a vague report brought here from out of their settlements upon the coast of a probability of a war between England and Holland, they sent a deputation from their Council with a letter proposing our entering into a neutrality in the Ganges. We wrote them in answer that they were too hasty in giving credit to a report so ill-founded; but, in case of such an event, our conduct must be guided by the orders of our superiors.

Remonstrance with the Dutch respecting the West Coast.

"Being informed of some unwarrantable proceedings of the Dutch upon the West Coast of Sumatra since the capture of your settlements there, and imagining that a representation from hence, when their possessions are so much in our power, may have weight with the General and Council at Batavia, we have wrote a remonstrance to them, which we shall send through the hands of the gentlemen of Bencoolen, and hope it may be of use in preventing any interruption being given by the Dutch in the re-establishment of your settlements. They have indeed been suffered too long to tyrannize in that part of India.

Deputation of Mr. Warren Hastings to

"The Nawab continues still in the Behar Province, and we have reason to suspect that some busy persons have been

Nawab Meer Cossim: question of the twenty lakhs, 1762.

endeavouring to form out jealousies between us, and to fill him with apprehensions that we are not well inclined towards him. Our desire to preserve the tranquillity of the country, and to discover the authors of this jealousy, have induced us to depute Mr. Hastings on a visit to the Nawab to make him those assurances on our part, to advise him to be careful whose reports he trusts to, and to punish with severity any of the people about him whom he finds to be endeavouring to create a misunderstanding between us. Instructions for this purpose being prepared, Mr. Amyatt proposed another clause should be added, directing Mr. Hastings to demand of the Nawab to pay to the Company the sum of twenty lakhs of rupees, which he offered at the time the treaty was made him, to present to the gentlemen of the Select Committee then in Calcutta. Messrs. Carnac, Johnstone, and Hay joined with Mr. Amyatt in this clause; but the President[1] objected to it, and refused to join in it, because himself and the other gentlemen of the Select Committee did absolutely reject this offer, as he (the President) has often since mentioned, and particularly in consultation 12th January 1761. He gave it therefore as his opinion that neither the Company, nor he, nor any other person, have any just claim upon the Nawab on account of the said offer.[2] The reasons of the several Members of the Board in support of their respective opinions are entered on the minutes of the consultations of the 22nd ultimo.[3]

Disputes in the Calcutta Council.

"The President, referring to the 96th paragraph of your commands of the 1st April 1760,—where you are pleased to direct that all applications to, or disputes with, Country Powers should pass through his authority alone,—observed to the Board on this occasion that he thought his opinion in such a case ought to have more weight than the common voice of a Member of the Board. This, however, was not admitted,

---

[1] Mr. Henry Vansittart.

[2] This paragraph contradicts the statement of Mr. Mill, who asserts that the twenty lakhs were actually divided.

[3] Separate letter, dated 18th April 1762, not classified like the others. In same volume as general letter for 1761.

and we are to request your directions on this subject. Also that you will explain to us more particularly on what occasion it is your meaning that Colonel Coote and Major Carnac should be Members of the Board, as this also was a matter of debate in consultation the 22nd ultimo.

Charge of treachery against Ram Churn: suspected forgery.

"On the 27th April we received from Mr. Johnstone, then at Jelasore, a packet of letters intercepted by one of his servants which contained some letters under the seal of Ram Churn, formerly the Banian of Colonel Clive, then of Colonel Calliaud, and now of Mr. Vansittart. These letters were addressed to Kunder Khan, the chief of the rebellious zemindars in the Patna Province. In the same packet were letters under the seal of Kunder Khan to Ram Churn in answer to fore-mentioned, and some letters to other persons referring to the same. Some circumstances appeared on the first enquiry which made us suspect they were forged. We used our utmost endeavours to come to a certainty by either discovering the authors of the invention or the reality of the correspondence, but could not succeed so fully as we could wish. Time perhaps may bring it to light. In the meanwhile, we have sent you our proceedings in this enquiry in a separate book of consultations, which conclude with the opinions of the different members upon the whole. It may not be improper in this place to observe to your Honors, that the manner of doing business in this country seems to be purposely contrived to evade all enquiry; for the letters are never signed, and are put under a cover which is secured only with paste, and sealed with a seal which any engraver can counterfeit. Thus, on the one hand, a guilty man has it in his power to deny letters really his own; and, on the other, an innocent man is subject to be accused of having wrote letters which he never saw. In such cases it is only from circumstances and the views and interest of the person accused that a judgment can be formed.

Bequests of Omichund to the Magdalen and Foundling.

"The late Omichund having left a considerable part of his fortune to be laid out in charities in all parts of the world, his executor, Huggoor Amul, has requested us to remit by this conveyance the sum of fifteen hundred current rupees, or pounds sterling one hundred and seventy-five, to the Governors of the Magdalen House, and the like sum to the Governors of the Foundling Hospital, for the uses of those charities respectively; and further, that we would receive into your cash the sum of thirty-seven thousand five hundred current rupees, there to remain for ever, and the interest to be remitted annually to the before-mentioned charities."[1]

Meanwhile news of the proclamation of Shah Alam as King of Delhi had reached the Court of Directors, and they proceeded to express themselves to the following effect:— Despatches from the Court of Directors reviewing events.

"Governor Hutchinson (Governor of St. Helena) informs us that the *Lord Anson* left Bengal the 23rd of March, and brought the news of the Shahzada's being proclaimed Emperor; that a faction, of which the late Delhi Vizier is at the head, had set up a nephew of the Shahzada to oppose him; and that it was therefore supposed a detachment of the forces at Calcutta will join and march to Delhi with the troops the Shahzada can raise, and place him upon the throne.[2] News of Shah Alam received *viâ* St. Helena.

"Although the *Lord Anson* has not yet arrived with your advices, yet we have great reason, from the care Mr. Hutchinson always takes to send us any material intelligence he can collect upon the arrival of our shipping, that what we have quoted from him as before mentioned is fact. We own, if your endeavours for setting the Shahzada upon the throne of his ancestors could be carried into execution without risk to the Company, and at a moderate expense, it may secure him in our interest, and be the means of settling the peace and quiet of the kingdom; but, as a transaction of this kind depends upon many circumstances and unforeseen events, and you have most probably already embarked in this undertaking, we are entirely at a loss to give you any directions, Circumstances under which the Directors would have helped Shah Alam.

[1] Separate letter dated 8th April 1761.

[2] Despatch, dated London, 30th September 1761. *Postscript*, dated 7th October 1761.

or even our sentiments thereupon, in other than these general terms, that we hope you have acted, and will act, with the utmost caution on considering all circumstances with that prudence and attention which an affair of such a serious and important nature requires.

Remarks of the Directors on Bengal revolutions in general.

"This is the third revolution in Bengal wherein the very being of the Company has been, and from their consequences may still be, at stake. Your advancing Jaffier Ali Khan to the Nawabship in the room of Suraj-u-daula was undoubtedly a necessary measure, as well for the good of the country in general as the interest of the Company in particular. Your afterwards deposing Jaffier Ali Khan and setting Cossim Ali Khan in his room, we hope was done also with the same view. Upon this presumption and confidence that no other motives whatever had any influence upon you, we must look upon the measures pursued upon this occasion to be unavoidable. At the same time we cannot help observing that it is to the great regard the Company have always had to a faithful observance of their agreements, they have acquired and hitherto preserved a reputation with the Natives of India. We would have wished, therefore, the situation of affairs would have admitted keeping terms with Jaffier Ali Khan; that even the least handle for a pretence might not have offered to prejudiced people to make use of to throw any reflections upon this transaction.

Colonel Calliaud charged with an attempt to assassinate the Shahzada.

"It is strongly reported that Colonel Calliaud, with the Chuta Nawab (*i. e.*, Meer Cossim)[1] signed a paper offering a reward of Rs. 50,000, or some such sum, to several black persons to assassinate the Shahzada. It is further reported that this paper was carried to Mr. Amyatt, the then chief of Patna, for him to sign, which he refused as a most infamous measure. It is also added that this very paper is in the hands of a Sayyid in Bengal. We have always had the highest opinion of Colonel Calliaud, and have given many proofs of our regard to his merit and services. But this

[1] Meer Cossim was called Chuta Nawab, or Little Nawab, before he was placed upon the throne of Bengal, Behar, and Orissa.

is an imputation of so extraordinary and serious a nature that we think it highly necessary it should be cleared up, as well in vindication of Colonel Calliaud's character, as the honor, good name, and interest of the Company, which are essentially interested therein. We, therefore, positively direct that you make the most strict and impartial enquiry into this affair; and, should it be possible that Colonel Calliaud is guilty of such a crime (which we heartily hope will not be the case), he is immediately to be dismissed our service and sent to England by the first conveyance that offers. But, should he be at Madras, and he proves guilty of what is here laid to his charge, you are to signify these our orders to our President and Council there, which are on no pretence to be evaded.

"If Colonel Calliaud should, contrary to our hopes, be found culpable, you are to make our resentment of so high a crime as public as possible, even to the Shahzada himself; that all the world may know how jealous we are of the honor and reputation of the Company; and that we shall always, to the utmost of our power, preserve the same unsullied by the severest resentment against any of our agents, of whatsoever rank or station, who shall violate the same. Punishment if guilty.

"Should any other Europeans, either in our service, or residing under our protection, be concerned in or accessory to the crime imputed to Colonel Calliaud, they are also, upon being found guilty, in like manner to be sent home immediately; and, should any Natives of India be concerned therein, they are to be treated with the utmost severity.[1] Other Europeans, if implicated, to be punished in like manner.

"In our letter of the 30th September last we gave you our sentiments in general upon the late revolutions in Bengal, since which we are further informed of the Shahzada's defeat, his throwing himself upon your protection, and the immense expense of his maintenance out of the Company's money, of no less than one thousand rupees a day, and of some views of Complaints of the heavy cost of revolution.

[1] It will suffice to say that the necessary explanations were furnished, and that Colonel Calliaud was fully and honourably acquitted of the charges brought against him.

placing him upon the throne of Delhi. It is alleged, indeed, that care will be taken that the Nawab defrays the said daily expense, which we hope will be the case, or at least that some other certain means be fixed upon to reimburse that expense and all other expenses on his account.[1] Upon a view of the frequent revolutions, the great designs proposed to be executed, and the consequent heavy expenses too justly to be apprehended, we are filled with the utmost anxiety lest the events should turn out to the prejudice of our affairs; and, in particular, the scheme of assisting the Shahzada, we hope has been well considered, and, if entered upon, carried out with that prudence as may leave no room to impeach your conduct.[2]

Tranquillity in Bengal most desirable.

"It is from a quiet situation of affairs only in Bengal that we can hope to have the benefit of the large revenues we are at present in possession of. A permanent tranquillity, therefore, must be the constant object in view; for, extensive as our territories and revenues are, they must be exhausted by the army, which, by your treaty with the present Nawab, is to be paid out of the produce of them.

Revenue of fifty lakhs yearly under the treaty with Meer Cossim most satisfactory.

"The three districts granted to the Company by the treaty with the present Nawab, you say, will in time of peace, under proper regulations, produce an annual revenue of fifty lakhs and upwards.[3] This is a noble object and well worth your utmost care and attention, more especially at this time, when our wants are so great and our expenses so heavy. We shall accordingly depend upon your taking such prudent measures as may secure to us the quiet possession of those territories, and the collection of the revenues to as large an amount as may be consistent with the ability of the inhabitants, and

---

[1] The amount was paid by Nawab Cossim. The money was probably spent for the purpose of securing letters of investiture of the post of Nawab of Bengal, Behar, and Orissa.

[2] General letter from 19th February 1762.

[3] This was the estimated revenue of the three districts of Burdwan, Midnapore, and Chittagong, which had been ceded to the Company by Meer Cossim on his accession. Fifty lakhs, roughly stated, are equivalent to about half a million sterling.

that humane lenity which we would always have observed on such occasions.

"It gives us pleasure to observe that the King of the Burmas, who caused our people at the Negrais to be so cruelly massacred, is since dead, and succeeded by his son, who seems to be of a more friendly and humane disposition. However, the intention of withdrawing all the remaining people and effects from thence is a right measure, especially as the country is so much involved in troubles as you represent it. We have reason to think the late King would not have proceeded to such a cruel extremity without some provocations. The President and Council of Fort St. George, under whose more immediate cognisance the affairs of that country fall, appear by their last advices to be making some enquiries into the causes of the King's indignation against the English. We therefore defer giving our sentiments thereon until we have the final result of those enquiries. We cannot omit observing, however, that it has been alleged the people belonging to some of the country ships had taken part with the Peguers and behaved in a hostile and violent manner. We hope by this time our President and Council have gone through the enquiry; and, if they find any truth in this allegation, that the persons concerned have been duly censured, for we will never suffer our affairs to be embroiled by the indiscretions and bad conduct of private persons residing in India under our protection. You will be informed from Fort St. George whether any persons belonging to Calcutta have been any way guilty in this affair, and we shall expect you will resent this behaviour as it shall appear to deserve.

Real cause of the massacre of the English in Burma.

"It is very disagreeable to us to find so many pages in your diaries filled with dissents and disputes in the transacting some interesting part of our affairs pointed out in your letter of the 12th November 1761. We have read and re-considered the whole very attentively, and must express the great dissatisfaction it has given us to find our interest and the general welfare lost in these warm altercations."[1]

Highly dissatisfied with the disputes in the Calcutta Council.

---

[1] Separate letter of 66 paras., dated 17th December 1762.

Further despatches to the Court of Directors.

The foregoing extracts may appear somewhat tedious to modern readers, but they reveal the enormous difficulties under which the English laboured during this troubled period. The Court of Directors were anxious that the conduct of their servants should be governed by right principles, but they were hasty in their conclusions. Meantime the President and Board at Calcutta were despatching further information to the Court of Directors. The extracts from the general letters to England tell their own story :—

Results of the mission of Warren Hastings to Meer Cossim.

"We acquainted Your Honors in our address of the 8th April that Mr. Hastings was gone on a deputation to the Nawab with a view chiefly to confirm the friendship between us, and remove some little apprehensions that we had reason to imagine he had received from some false reports that had been industriously spread in the country; and with further instructions from the majority of the Board to make a demand of the twenty lakhs he had offered the President and the other gentlemen present of the Select Committee at the time of concluding the treaty for making him Nawab. To the first of Mr. Hastings' instructions, the Nawab answered that the little disputes which fell out between his people and ours, and which would sometimes unavoidably happen, did not weaken his confidence in our friendship, upon which he rested his chief dependence. To the second, he absolutely refused to comply with the demand for twenty lakhs, urging that he had fulfilled all his engagements, and was under no obligation to give such a sum or any sum to the Company or any person whatever. For further particulars we beg leave to refer your Honors to our correspondence with Mr. Hastings during his absence, and the memorial delivered to him by the Nawab, entered in Consultation of the 14th June.[1]

[1] General letter, Fort William, 30th October 1762.

Proposed alliance with the Rajah of Munipur against the King of Burma.

"In Consultation of the 4th October, the President sent to the Board a letter which he had received from Mr. Verelst at Chittagong, containing an invitation which had been made to him and his Council by the Rajah of Meckley[1] to assist him in obtaining redress for some grievance he complained to have suffered from the Burmas, and enclosing a paper of articles of alliance which the Rajah had tendered to be executed between him and us for this purpose; which letter and articles of alliance being taken into consideration, it was the opinion of the Board that the articles were very favourable, and that the opportunity would be no less so if we could with propriety come into the scheme for obtaining reparation from the Burmas for the repeated ill-treatment of our factory at Negrais; but, as it was judged necessary and proper, before we proceeded further, to call for the opinion of Colonel Coote and Major Carnac upon the subject, the Secretary was ordered to summon them to the next consultation.

Application of Shah Alam for help to recover Delhi.

"At our next consultation the Colonel (Coote) being indisposed could not attend, but the President and Major (Carnac) being both present, the consideration of this affair was resumed, when the President laid before the Board translates of some letters which he had received from the King and Shuja-u-daula, earnestly soliciting the assistance of a large body of troops to enable the King to gain possession of the capital. This application, we are informed by a letter from Mr. Ellis to the President laid before the Board at the same time, has been, owing to a powerful alliance made by the former Vizier, Ghazi-ud-din Khan,[2] against Shuja-u-daula. As we cannot yet foresee what revolutions and troubles may be produced from this alliance, and how far they may affect Bengal, we judged it improper for the present to detach any Europeans to so distant a quarter as Meckley (*i. e.*, Munipur); but it being likeiwse thought prudent not to lose the opportunity of contracting an alliance with the Rajah of Meckley, it was resolved to detach a force of six Companies of Sepoys, commanded

---

[1] Meckley is a province about 250 miles to the eastward of Chittagong, and Moneypoor (*i. e.*, Munipur) is the capital of the said province.

[2] Ghazi-u-din was the Vizier who put to death the father of Shah Alam.

by three Officers, to take a post there, and under the direction of Mr. Verelst or one of his Council, make themselves acquainted with the strength, nature, and dispositions of the Burmas, and of this intelligence to send us advice, but to proceed to no hostilities without our positive directions. We are hopeful that this undertaking will open to us a road for obtaining satisfaction for the many injuries we have suffered from the Burmas; and, in case nothing disturbs our tranquillity to the northward, we shall certainly embrace it.

Reply to Shah Alam: Mr Vansittart proposes seeing the King at Monghyr.

"In answer to the King's application for troops, the President has wrote him a complimentary letter, informing him of his intended journey up the country, and that he will again pay his more immediate respects to him when he arrives at Monghyr. When the President arrives there, he purposes conferring with the Nawab on this subject; and, having by this means gained time to be further informed of the views and connections of the several chiefs, we shall pursue such measures as shall seem most proper for preserving the tranquillity of these provinces, and securing the Company's possession and interests under our care.

Mr. Vansittart will also conciliate Meer Cossim.

"With this view, as well as for the sake of a change of air, the President set out a few days past for Monghyr, where he will have an interview with the Nawab, and concert with him the most necessary measures for obtaining those salutary ends. This meeting, which the Nawab has frequently urged and requested, will, we are hopeful, have the effect of removing entirely all those idle reports which a few busy people have industriously propagated about the country, with the design of alarming and making him uneasy; as likewise those mutual jealousies which it has not failed to cause between our people and the government in most parts of the country to the interruption of the private trade.

Further enquiries about Ram Churn; implication of Nundcoomar in the forgery.

"In our address of the 8th April 1762 by the *Godolphin*, we informed you of an enquiry we had had before us concerning a parcel of letters stopped on the road to Cuttack, and said to be a correspondence between Ram Churn and Kunder Khan; and in our packet by that ship we transmitted our proceedings at length in the said enquiry. We remarked to Your Honors in our said address that several strong circumstances appeared to give reason to believe that the whole packet was a forgery. Fresh circumstances appearing since to confirm the said belief, we entered into a further examination of this matter, our proceedings wherein are likewise transmitted in the *Godolphin's* packet. This further examination has fully convinced us that the letters were forged: and there is great reason to think that Nundocoomar was contriver thereof, with a design of ruining Ram Churn. We cannot say there are such direct proofs as to fix the crime upon him with an absolute certainty; nor, indeed, is it possible there should be positive proofs while he and his Munshi (the only persons supposed to be present when the letters were forged) have resolution enough to persist in denying it.

"The before-mentioned Nundcoomar is the same person who was convicted some time ago of carrying on a correspondence with the Burdwan Rajah of a nature inconsistent with his duty and hurtful to your interest. We find also that the same Nundcoomar was instrumental in carrying on a correspondence between the Shahzada and the French Governor General before the capture of Pondicherry. This information was given to the President, and by him being laid before the Board, was proved by such positive evidence as to leave no room to doubt of the fact. The least we could conclude upon such crimes was, that Nundcoomar, being a person improper to be trusted with his liberty in your settlement, and capable of doing mischief if he was permitted to go out of this province, either to the northward or towards the Dekhan, should therefore be kept confined to his own house under so strict a guard as to prevent his writing or receiving letters."

Dangerous character of Nundcoomar.

Subsequently the Court of Directors reviewed the events above recorded at considerable length, and expressed themselves to the following effect[1] :—

Despatches from the Directors.

"It gives us great pleasure to find that the country enjoys a perfect tranquillity. We earnestly recommend that you

Highly gratified with the general tranquillity and prosperity.

[1] General letter with headings, London, 8th March 1763, 128 paras.

use your best endeavours to keep it so, as the only means to secure to us the advantages we may hope for, and which we have in some degree experienced by the investment you have made; and in the agreeable assistance you have given Madras and Bombay to furnish money for our China ships which were to be despatched from them; and as your sentiments respecting the conduct to be held towards the Country Government, and adopted by you, coincide so fully with our orders, we shall not enlarge on this subject.

An advance to Delhi would be most injudicious: the best policy is isolation and neutrality.

"From the general view you have given us with respect to your transactions with the Shahzada who has been proclaimed King at Delhi, as well as from the several proceedings on the same subject, which appear at large in your Select Committee's Diary, we observe Major Carnac and Colonel Coote were both very solicitous to have engaged in the project of accompanying the King to the capital with a body of our forces. However, we are better pleased that the King left the province without our being obliged to engage in such a hazardous enterprise; and, had Colonel Coote's regiment arrived before the urgency of the King's affairs required his [*i. e.*, the King's] moving forward to the capital, yet we should have hoped you would not, even then, have been tempted to engage in so distant an undertaking, but have contented yourselves with the right step you have taken in treating that Prince with all due respect during his stay in the Province of Bengal, and escorting him with a proper force to the borders. For, in short, our sentiments are, that, if we can secure our present possessions and privileges in Bengal, preserve the peace of the province, and the Nawab in the government, and prevent the borders from being invaded or disturbed by the neighbouring Rajahs or other Powers, we shall be fully satisfied, and think our forces judiciously employed in answering these principal points. For we are by no means desirous of making further acquisitions, or engaging our forces in very distant projects, unless the most absolute necessity should require it to answer one or other of the principal views before mentioned.

Nawab Meer Cossim ought to have been better supported in claiming the Sunnuds for Bengal, Behar, and Orissa from Shah Alam.

"The Sunnuds being sent by the King to the Nawab for the three provinces is a very agreeable circumstance. But although you do not mention in the general advices any complaints that the Nawab made on his being obliged to purchase those grants at a much greater expense to him after the King passed the borders, than he would have had to pay for them while the King was at Patna, if the Nawab had been properly supported in his pretensions by our Commanding Officer then there, yet something of this appears in your diaries; and if true, surely our force and influence were not so effectually applied as they might have been. And, although we are unwilling to pass a censure on any particular person on this point, yet we hope to have no occasion in future even for a doubt that the interest of a Prince[1] we are so closely connected with by treaty has been slighted. For, if the difficulties are multiplied upon him, and his power and influence not supported by us when he wants our assistance, he must suffer by such measures, as our interest must likewise do in the end.

Approve of the refusal of the Dewani offered by Shah Alam: ingratitude of the King.

"Your refusal of the Dewani of Bengal offered by the King was right, and we are well satisfied with the just and prudent reasons you give for declining that offer. However, it seems something extraordinary to us that, at the time the King makes this advance, he should return the applications made to him for the Sunnuds to confirm our privileges and possessions in Bengal, in so loose and unsatisfactory a manner, and even to require a present before he passes the order in due form. The great services we had rendered His Majesty, and the generous treatment he met with from us, as well as from our ally the Nawab, during his stay at Patna, surely claimed a more distinguished treatment, and at least a full grant of our requests, without such an expensive demand annexed. The time and manner of the refusal seems likewise very extraordinary; your applications being returned at the very juncture Major Carnac was escorting him to the River Karamnassa, or borders of the province, a service which

[1] By Prince is meant the Subahdar or Nawab in Bengal.

must then be fresh in the King's memory; and therefore there is reason to apprehend the King is not so cordially attached to us as we might have expected. However, if you judge the obtaining such Sunnuds to be absolutely necessary, you have, we doubt not, continued your application to have them perfected. It was a prudent consideration in you to add to your applications on this subject our ally the Nawab of Arcot, which we suppose you have or will continue to do when you think it proper to move again in this affair; and if the King should succeed in his pretensions to the throne, the sooner the grants are obtained, the less we apprehend will be the expense attending it.

Surprised at the unwarrantable demand of twenty lakhs from the Nawab.

"We cannot comprehend on what grounds the majority of the Council, contrary to the remonstrances made by the President against it, could venture to authorise Mr. Hastings to demand of the Nawab in our name twenty lakhs of rupees, upon the bare pretence that he had made an offer of that sum to Mr. Vansittart and the Select Committee at the time of making the treaty for his accession, and which had been then so properly and so honorably refused. We rejoice at the just and spirited refusal he gave to that unwarrantable demand.[1]

Full apologies to be tendered to the Nawab in the name of the Company.

"And that we may vindicate ourselves in the mind of the Nawab from such unfavourable impressions which this demand, or other unfavourable circumstances, must naturally have left upon him, we direct that the President in your name do in the most respectful manner by letter acquaint him that we are truly sorry that the conduct of any of our servants has given him umbrage, or created in him a moment's distrust of the sincerity of our friendship; that we totally disapprove, and shall properly resent, all such misbehaviour; and to assure him that it is our most earnest wish, and our positive orders to you (which we strictly direct), that our servants join him in every reasonable measure for his support and welfare, and observe every engagement entered into

[1] Separate letter, dated London, 13th May 1763.

with him. You will acquaint him, likewise, that we shall have the honor to give him these assurances by letter the next opportunity; the ship *Pitt* being upon the point of her departure, we have not leisure to do it now."

Weak capacity of Mr. Vansittart.

It will be seen from the foregoing records that Mr. Vansittart was a man of good intentions. He had refused to receive any of the money offered by Meer Cossim; yet Mill's History, on very doubtful evidence, says that the twenty lakhs were paid at the time, equivalent to two hundred thousand pounds sterling, and that Mr. Vansittart received five lakhs, or fifty thousand pounds. But whilst Mr. Vansittart proves himself to have been strictly honourable, it is certain that he lacked the capacity and strong will of Clive. It is a grave question whether he was justified in abandoning Ram Narain to the tender mercies of the Nawab; as a matter of fact, the Hindu grandee was deprived of all his wealth and put to death. Clive was bitterly incensed at the violation of his guarantee; he declared that it set every Hindu in the three provinces against the English.

CHAPTER X.

CALCUTTA RECORDS: PRIVATE TRADE.

A. D. 1763.

Bengal gomastas.

THE next batch of Calcutta records refers to events quite as revolutionary as those connected with the change of Nawabs. It refers to proceedings which were unquestionably lawless; but the lawlessness was not that of Europeans, but that of their native agents or gomastas. This quarrel, so petty in its rise, led to the most lamentable results; to a war between the English and the Nawab, which led to the dethronement of Meer Cossim and the restoration of Meer Jaffier.

Private trade.

The servants of the English Company derived their chief wealth from their private trade. Their official salaries were almost nominal. They had carried on this private trade in the eastern seas from the earliest days of the British settlements in India. Every one traded in some way or other, from the governor of a settlement to the lowest servant of the Company, not excluding the chaplain and schoolmaster.

Extension of private trade inland.

Hitherto this private trade had been confined to the seaports. When the English became masters in Bengal, they sought to extend it inland. They began to deal in country commodities, such as salt, betel-nut, and tobacco. They claimed to be free of all duties of every kind, by virtue of the privileges which had been guaranteed in unqualified language by existing treaties.

English flag and dustuck.

When the English Company originally obtained from the Moghul the privilege of trading duty free, the officers of the Nawab insisted upon searching every boat and every person in the boat. Subsequently it was agreed that whenever the boat showed the English flag and Company's dustuck or permit, no search was to be made, and all goods in the boat were to be passed duty-free.

Native respect for the English

After the battle of Plassey, the English had grown all-powerful in Bengal. The grandees bent before them; the natives regarded them with respectful awe. No one ventured to offer resistance. Those who had the best reason to hate them were the foremost to flatter and propitiate them, and only plotted against them in dark and secret ways. So long as Nawab Jaffier was reigning, every native of position sought the favour and protection of the English. When Jaffier was deposed, he refused to stay at Murshedabad. He begged that he might go either to Mecca or Calcutta; he could not, he said, be safe in Bengal excepting under English protection.[1] There are no traces of any complaint of the harshness or injustice of the English; their honesty and good faith in all commercial dealings

[1] Malcolm's Life of Clive, Vol. II, page 268, *note*. When deposed, the Nawab wanted his case to be referred to the judgment of Clive.

had won general confidence. The Vizier at Delhi, as already seen, was ready to entrust the collection of the revenues of Bengal, Behar, and Orissa to the English Company as represented by Clive.[1]

Native agents or gomastas.

It was not the English, but the native servants of the English, that terrified the people of Bengal. The employment of native agents or gomastas was already familiar to the English. In 1753 the Company had ceased to employ native contractors, and had dealt direct with weavers and artisans through the medium of these gomastas. The servants of the Company employed gomastas in like manner to carry on the inland trade. The gomastas were entrusted with the English flag and Company's dustuck; they bought and sold duty free. Under such circumstances, the inland trade of Bengal soon grew into a vast monopoly in the hands of the servants of the Company and their gomastas.

Complaints against the gomastas.

The monopoly was bad enough; the conduct of the gomastas was far worse. Native servants of European masters are generally inclined to be pretentious and arbitrary towards their own countrymen. It is easy to understand how they would conduct themselves in remote districts, when invested with the emblems of authority, and when the English name was regarded with awe. Bengallees of no character or position, who had been seen at Calcutta walking in rags, were sent out as the

---

[1] See *ante*, page 268.

gomastas of English merchants, factors, or writers. They assumed the dress of English sepoys, lorded it over the country, imprisoned ryots and merchants, and wrote and talked in an insolent manner to the Nawab's officers. Nawab Cossim complained that the gomastas plundered his people, injured and disgraced his servants, and exposed his government to contempt. The gomastas, he said, thought themselves the equals of the Company. In every district, village, and factory they bought and sold salt, betel-nut, ghee, rice, straw, bamboos, fish, ginger, sugar, tobacco, opium, and other native commodities. They forcibly took away the goods of ryots and merchants for a fourth part of their value, and obliged the ryots to give five rupees for articles which were not worth one.[1]

Pretensions of Nawab Cossim.

Nawab Jaffier never ventured to make such complaints. He depended solely upon the English for support; he was the nominee of the English; without them he was nobody and nowhere. Nawab Cossim had taken warning by his example to sever himself as much as possible from the English. He had withdrawn to Monghyr, secured letters of investiture from the King, disciplined his army, wreaked his vengeance on the grandees who had been protected by the English in the time of Nawab Jaffier, and was in every respect prepared for the collision. He still made a show of friendship towards Governor Vansittart and Warren

[1] Verelst's View of Bengal.

Hastings, a member of the Board. He ordered his officers not to hinder the gomastas of his friends, but to thwart the gomastas of his enemies. He raised the question of whether the Company's servants had the right to carry on the inland trade duty free. No doubt he had the abstract right to levy duties as an independent ruler; but he had abandoned this right by treaty; and no exception whatever had been made as regards the duties on inland trade. It would have been expedient for the English servants of the Company to have abandoned that right, but in so doing they would have sacrificed the bulk of their incomes for the public service, and this was the point on which the question mainly turned.

The records may now be left to tell the progress of the struggle:—

Recriminations between the English and the Nawab's officers respecting the inland trade.

"The President having laid before the Nawab the complaints of the gentlemen of Chittagong, Dacca, and Luckipore, concerning the stoppage of several of their boats at different chokeys (*i. e.*, custom houses), also received from him a multitude of complaints from his (the Nawab's) officers in several parts of the country against the English gomastas, but particularly those at Rungpoor, Silhet, Rangamutty, and other distant parts of the country, employed chiefly in the trade of salt, tobacco, betel-nut, and some few other articles of inland trade, which he urged we were restrained from before the troubles. The Nawab enlarged much upon the detriment his revenues suffered by the authority exercised by our gomastas in carrying on their trade in those distant parts, where we had no government to restrain them, and his was too weak to do it; urging finally that he thought we had no right to deal in those articles.

"The President and Mr. Hastings being of opinion that the trade in such articles ought not to be carried on to the prejudice of the revenues of the Country Government, and that rules should be laid down for the conduct of our gomastas and the officers of the Government, respectively, proposed to the Nawab articles for this purpose. The Nawab declined binding himself by these articles, but represented again in a letter to the President, just before his departure from Monghyr, the grievances before mentioned; and the President wrote him an answer concerning the regulations before proposed, and some other articles, and assuring him that the inland trade should be carried on upon that footing only, and our gomastas to be subjected in the manner therein mentioned to the officers of the Government. The rest of the gentlemen of the Council at Calcutta did not approve of the articles proposed in the letter before mentioned from the President and Mr. Hastings, nor of the President's letter to the Nawab, which had been transmitted them from the factory at Dacca, and determined, therefore, to call all the members of the Board to Calcutta, excepting those at Patna and Chittagong, whose great distance would make it inconvenient, that they might consider this affair. Certain it is, the officers of the Country Government have made a very ill use of the concessions made in their favour, and the restraints laid upon our agents and gomastas, as they have in many places stopped our trade entirely, and grossly insulted our agents and gomastas. The members of the Board called down on this occasion being arrived, we shall take this affair into consideration tomorrow, and lay down such rules for carrying on the inland trade, and for the conduct of our gomastas towards the Country Government, as shall appear most equitable and expedient for removing the grievances of both parties. In the meantime the President has represented strongly to the Nawab the insolence of his officers, and told him that till full and sufficient regulations are agreed on, our trade in any articles must not be interrupted; and if any attempts are made to the contrary, we shall use our own force to remove all such obstructions."

Discussion in the Board: all the Directors summoned to Calcutta.

Meeting of the full Board at Calcutta.

Under the foregoing circumstances a full Board of all the members of Council was held at Calcutta. The proceedings began in February 1763 and lasted till the following April. The following extracts from a letter sent to the Court of Directors, dated 18th April 1763, will explain the nature and scope of the Consultations:—

Consultations, 15th February: Majors Adams and Carnac summoned.

"Previous to our entering upon business, motions were made for summoning Major Adams and Major Carnac to sit at the Board on this occasion; which motions being approved by the majority, those gentlemen were accordingly summoned.

Measures for preventing disorders during the interval.

"Major Adams, being then at the cantonments near Ghyrottee, could not be present that day. All that we concluded therefore at this meeting was, upon a due and serious consideration of the several letters received, to issue orders to the different subordinates, instructing them, until they should receive our further directions, to carry on both the Company's and private business in the same manner as before, paying such duties on certain articles in the latter branch as they usually did pay previous to the late regulations; and on this footing to prevent, as far as possible, any violence being committed either by our people or the Governments; but that, if any such insolencies should be attempted as to oblige them to make use of force, to endeavour to seize the principal person who might have thus endeavoured to injure us. And to prevent all pleas of ignorance, which might in such cases be urged on the part of the Government, the President at the same time wrote circular letters to the several Foujdars, informing them, as far as was necessary, of these regulations and orders.

Consultations, 19th February: translation ordered of all Firmans, Husboolhookums, and Treaties.

"We met again on the 19th with an intention to consider the first article of the said plan compared with our Firmans, Husboolhookums, and subsequent Treaties; but many of these exact translations being previously required to enable us to judge properly on the question, we ordered translations to be accordingly prepared, and for that day proceeded on the second article of the plan, relative to the Nawab's having shut up one of the gates of the city of Patna and ran an entrenchment into the river, which prevented the tracking of boats on the side of the factory. Our opinions and determination on these points, as well as regarding a gunge or wharf belonging to the said factory, which the Nawab wanted to remove, are entered at large on the face of the consultation, to which therefore we refer you.

Consultations, 22nd February: matter in dispute reduced to questions.

"The translations and other necessary papers ordered to be prepared being laid before us, were entered on the face of the next consultation agreeable to the order in which they were read; and, being likewise fully considered and debated on at the Board, the substance of the whole was reduced into a set of questions, on which the several members were desired to deliver in their opinions in writing against the Tuesday following.

Consultations 1st March: majority agreed on the freedom from all duties: cede the duty on salt to the Nawab.

"Accordingly, they were delivered in; and it was found to be the opinion of the majority that, from the tenour of our Firmans, Husboolhookums, and Treaties, we had an absolute right to carry on our trade, as well foreign as inland, in the Provinces of Bengal, Behar, and Orissa, by means of a dustuck (or permit) free of all duties or customs to the Country Government. But that the Nawab might have no room left for complaint, or to think that we intended pressing our rights harder upon him than we had done on former Nawabs, it was agreed to continue to him a certain consideration in the article of salt. And by the sum of the answers to the question, 'What that consideration should be?' It was resolved, in consultation of the 2nd March, to allow him 2½ per cent. upon the Hughly market price; and that salt was the only article of trade which should pay any customs whatever to the Country Government.[1]

---

[1] The Consultations for 1762-63, which have been preserved in the Home Office, are in a very imperfect state. The correspondence and minutes are not entered in the Consultation volumes, but are only preserved in the bundles, and much is wanting. It appears, however, that the Firmans from the King had granted to the English Company absolute freedom from all duties; that these terms had been agreed to, both by Jaffier Ali Khan and

Merits of the question submitted to the Directors.

"This being become here an established and fixed resolution, it now remains with Your Honors to judge of the justness of it, as well as of the validity of the arguments made use of on both sides on the occasion.

Consultations, 5th March: regulations for the mutual restraint of English agents and the Nawab's servants.

"Having determined that our gomastas or agents should be under no actual control of the officers of the Nawab's Government, but restrained by certain regulations which should be laid down, we proceeded to settle such regulations as we thought necessary for restraining accordingly our agents and gomastas from interfering with any affairs of the Country Government, injuring the people or being injured by them, and for deciding disputes which might arise between them. For these ends we determined that a gomasta being aggrieved by any dependant upon the Government should first make his application to the officer of the Government residing on the spot; from whom, if he did not receive immediate satisfaction, he should send his complaint to the Chief of the nearest factory, who should be empowered to take cognisance of the same, and demand or exact, if necessary, the satisfaction which the case might require. On the other hand, where the Government's people should have reason to complain against English gomastas or agents, we determined that they should be directed to give the said agent or gomasta notice of the complaint in writing, and require and recommend him to turn

---

Cossim Ali Khan; that Mr. Vansittart had given up these privileges, excepting as regards goods bought for exportation; that he had agreed that English merchants should pay a duty of nine per cent. *ad valorem* to the Nawab on all articles of inland trade, such as salt, tobacco, and betel-nut; and that he had suggested that all complaints should be settled by the Nawab's own officers.

The majority of the Board over-ruled these proceedings of Mr. Vansittart. It was urged that he had no right to abandon privileges which had been freely granted. The idea of having questions settled by the Native Courts was especially denounced. If an Englishman or his agent gained a suit he would be obliged to pay the expenses of the Court, *plus* a chout of twenty-five per cent. on the money recovered. If he refused to pay, he never gained another suit, as it could then be the interest of the Native Judge to decide against him. Native merchants were sensible of the impossibility of carrying on business under such restrictions, and purchased the protection of some higher native official.

to settle the same in an equitable and amicable manner; which if the gomasta or agent should refuse or neglect to do, that the Government's officer should then transmit an account of it to the Chief of the nearest English factory, who should be required to examine strictly into the affair, and decide it according to justice. Likewise, to render the whole everywhere effectual, we appointed a member of the Cossimbazar Factory Resident at Rungpoor, to take cognisance of the complaints and decide the disputes which might arise in the districts too distant from any of the established factories, and who should, at the same time, carry on and endeavour to improve the Company's silk investment made at that place.

Mr. Vansittart's correspondence with the Nawab, 7th March.

"During the course of these deliberations, the President wrote frequently to the Nawab, first, to inform him that the regulations he had proposed could not take place, and afterwards, of the many complaints which arrived from all quarters against his officers, and for which we should expect to receive ample reparation. The first answer of any consequence to these letters arrived with us in Council the 7th of March. In the one of them he contained his answer with respect to trade in three propositions or demands, which are extracted and entered at length in the body of the consultation.[1] In the other there appeared throughout a general disinclination to give us any satisfaction for the interruptions and ill-usage which we had received from the officers of his Government. And both letters, on the whole, seemed rather an evasion than any answer to the President's representation.

Deputation of Messrs. Amyatt and Hay to the Nawab.

"It was, therefore, agreed that a letter should be immediately wrote him, containing our opinion of his letters, and

[1] The three demands of the Nawab are set forth in a letter entered upon the Consultations of the 7th March 1863. They were to the following effect :—

(1).—That the Nawab should correspond only with the President and have nothing to do with the other members of the Board.

(2).—That the English should abstain from all inland trade, and confine their trade to exports and imports.

(3).—That the English gomastas or agents were to be amenable to his (the Nawab's) own officers.

giving him a full account of what had hitherto been resolved on by the Board in consequence of the reference made to the Firmans, Husbulhookums, and Treaties, by the tenour of which the Board were determined to abide. It was at the same time resolved that Messrs. Amyatt and Hay should be deputed to the Nawab, to explain to him more fully the justice of those rights and pretentions, and settle with him the rule for levying the custom which we had agreed should be paid him; and that for the former purpose they should be furnished with copies of the said Firmans, Husbulhookums, and Treaties. Of this resolution likewise the Nawab was now advised; and further acquainted that, as we should examine into all the complaints against English agents and gomastas and cause them to make amends for whatsoever injustice it might appear they had committed, so we should insist upon justice against all those officers of his Government who might prove guilty of the obstructions and extortions laid to their charge, and that they should be obliged to make reparation for all losses occasioned thereby.

Question of corresponding through the President or through the whole Board.

"As the first of the before-mentioned propositions from the Nawab implied an ignorance of the nature of our Government, and the powers of the Council, Mr. Johnstone moved that a public letter should be wrote to him, explaining these points, and re-demanding the President's letter, which contained the regulations; and that such letter should be signed by the whole Board, and go under the Company's seal. But the majority of the Council dissenting to the latter part of this motion, it was agreed that the point mentioned by Mr. Johnstone should be expressed in two additional paragraphs to the letter before ordered to be wrote under the sign and seal of the President.

Abolition of all duties by the Nawab, 22nd March.

"On the 22nd March Mr. Johnstone laid before the Board copy of a sunnud and perwanna of the Nawab's which he had received in private letters from Patna, the former containing an exemption of all duties whatever within his Government for the space of two years, and the latter to the Naib of Patna enjoining the strictest compliance with the term of this sunnud. On these Mr. Johnstone desired the opinions of the Board might be collected, and a resolution come to before Messrs. Amyatt and Hay should proceed on their deputation.

Consultations, 24th March: determination to remonstrate with the Nawab.

"This was accordingly done next council day, for the majority of the Board being of opinion that the Nawab as Subah had no authority to take such a step; that it was done with a view to prejudice the Company's business, and counteract the measures which the Board had been taking for the welfare of trade in general; it was therefore resolved that a paragraph should be added to Messrs. Amyatt and Hay's instructions, directing them to represent this to the Nawab, and insist upon his revoking the sunnuds and collecting duties as before.

Consultations, 30th March: Nawab refuses to receive the deputation.

"Messrs. Amyatt and Hay now remained ready to set out when the Nawab's answer should arrive; but, on receipt thereof, it was found to contain rather a refusal than an acceptance of the visit, so far as we should regard the public business, from a conception, that his having abolished all kinds of duties rendered any further conference or regulations respecting trade altogether unnecessary. The further substance of his further letters congested is a repetition of his former remonstrances and retorts, and a refusal to give us the satisfaction required for the losses sustained by the disturbances. The several members were therefore desired to deliver in their opinions on those letters, whether they thought Messrs. Amyatt and Hay should proceed, or what other measures should be taken to bring these disputes to a conclusion.

Consultations, 1st April: deputation sent to Monghyr: Nawab told that his refusal might bring on a rupture.

"Accordingly, in consultation, the 1st of April, the opinions were given in and read; and the matter being also fully considered and debated on, it was resolved, in conformity to the voice of the majority, that the Nawab should be again written to, to insist on his receiving the intended deputation for treating upon business; and that Messrs. Amyatt and Hay should proceed to and wait his answer at Cossimbazar. The President therefore addressed him, under that date, representing the indecent style of his letters and the impropriety of his conduct; that these had been already such as would fully justify our coming to a rupture: but, to show him how distant such a proceeding was from our thoughts, we acquainted him at once with our intentions that, with a view of settling the disputes in the country in the most effectual and speedy manner, and to avoid coming to extremities, we deputed Messrs. Amyatt and Hay to confer with him at Monghyr; and that this commission treated on many other points, besides that of duties, tending to the welfare of his Government, as well as the Company's. That he accordingly ought to regard such an appointment as that of two gentlemen of the Board as the strongest mark of our friendship and confidence paid him; and that it therefore behoved him to write us immediately that he would receive the deputation in a suitable manner to treat upon business. That, if he refused so reasonable a demand, it would not be in our power to remove the suspicions and jealousies which he harboured in his mind; and, as the alarms in all parts of the country must be attended with very great loss and detriment, both to his affairs and the Company's, that a breach of the friendship between us would infallibly ensue. That we once more assured him of our hearty resolution to support and assist him in every branch of his Government; but that if he refused to receive the present deputation, it would be regarded in no other light than a declaration on his side of his intention to come to a rupture with us.

Consultations, 11th April: Nawab persistently refuses to receive the deputation.

"Since the departure of Messrs. Amyatt and Hay, we have received two more letters from the Nawab, in one of which he still declines receiving those gentlemen upon business for the reasons he had before given. But, as we had already resolved to be determined in our measures from the answer which he shall send to our letter of the 1st April, we thought it unnecessary to reply to those, and only transmitted copies of them to Messrs. Amyatt and Hay for their information.

Nawab asked for definite charges against Mr. Ellis.

"In one of the President's letters to the Nawab he had desired him to write what particular accusations he had to lay to the charge of Mr. Ellis; as also to point out to him any particular instances of the losses which he had sustained through the oppression and bad behaviour of English gomastas. But we find from his answer, which is one of the above letters, that all he has to allege against Mr. Ellis, are the complaints which happened in the course of last year; and as to the last he refuses to discuss the affair further."

Court of Directors condemn the Calcutta Board.

The most important point in the foregoing extracts is the action taken by the Nawab to evade the pretensions. The English persisted in maintaining the privilege of carrying on the inland trade without the payment of duties. The Nawab abolished the payment of all duties for the space of two years. By thus abandoning all duties he broke up the monopoly by placing the native merchants on the same footing. No one could deny the right of the Nawab to abolish duties, excepting such as were blinded by their own interest. The Court of Directors, having no interest whatever in the question, were enabled to see the matter in a just light. They strongly condemned the action taken by the Board at Calcutta. They administered rebukes to almost every one excepting Vansittart and Warren Hastings. The following extracts will sufficiently illustrate their feelings at this time:—

The Nawab to be informed accordingly.

"Unwilling as we always are to place too much confidence in private informations, yet these are too important to pass unnoticed. If what is all stated is fact, it is natural to think that the Nawab, tired out and disgusted with the ill-usage he has received, has taken this extraordinary measure, finding that his authority and government are set at nought and trampled upon by the unprecedented behaviour of our servants and the agents employed by them in the several parts of the Nawab's dominions. If we are right in our conjecture, we positively direct, as you value our service, that you do immediately acquaint the Nawab, in the Company's name, that we disapprove of every measure that has been taken in real prejudice to his authority and Government, particularly with respect to the wronging him in his revenues by the shameful abuse of Dustucks; and you are further to inform him that we look upon his and the Company's interest to be so connected that we wish for nothing more than to have everything put on such a footing that the utmost harmony may be promoted and kept up between us.[1]

Colonel Calliaud honourably acquitted.

"Having considered with the greatest attention every circumstance of your proceedings with respect to the allegation against Colonel Calliaud for consenting to a proposal of the late Nawab Jaffier Ali Khan to cause the Shahzada to be seized or cut off, we are unanimously of opinion that he stands honourably acquitted of any design or intention upon or against the life of that Prince.

Disapproval of every measure taken against the Nawab.

"Although we have not received any letter from you since that which bore date the 14th February 1763, which gave us some general account of very disagreeable altercations with the Nawab, yet private advices have been received which take notice that the Nawab having made repeated complaints of the notorious abuse of Dustucks by which he lost great part of his customs, and having obtained no redress, he at once overset the Company's servants by declaring all goods custom free, so that their Dustucks are of no use.

All the Nawab's grievances to be redressed.

"In order to promote this harmony, you are most heartily and seriously to take under your consideration every real grievance the Nawab lays under, to redress them to the utmost of your power and prevent such abuses in future. And, with respect to the article of Dustucks in particular, you are hereby positively directed to confine this privilege as nearly as possible to the terms granted in the Firmans; and you are to give the Nawab all the assistance you can to

[1] Separate letter, London, 30th December, 1763.

reinstate him in the full power of collecting and receiving his revenues, which as Subah he is justly entitled to.

"We are impatient for your next advices, that we may be informed of your proceedings with respect to this important affair, and that we may give you our sentiments thereupon in a more full and explicit manner, which we hope will be before the despatch of our last letters this season. **Impatient for further intelligence.**

"One great source of the disputes, misunderstandings, and difficulties which have occurred with the Country Government, appears evidently to have taken its rise from the unwarrantable and licentious manner of carrying on the private trade by the Company's servants, their gomastas, agents, and others, to the prejudice of the Subah, both with respect to his authority and the revenues justly due to him, the diverting and taking from his natural subjects the trade in the inland parts of the country, to which neither we nor any persons whatever dependent upon us, or under our protection, have any manner of right, and consequently endangering the Company's very valuable privileges. In order, therefore, to remedy all these disorders, we do hereby positively order and direct— **Private trade the chief cause of all the misunderstandings with the Nawab.**

"That, from the receipt of this letter, a final and effectual end be forthwith put to the inland trade in salt, betel-nut, tobaccos, and in all other articles whatsoever produced and consumed in the country; and that all Europeans and other agents or gomastas who have been concerned in such trade be immediately ordered down to Calcutta, and not suffered to return or be replaced as such by any other persons. **All inland trade to be abolished.**

"That as our Firman privileges of being duty free are certainly confined to the Company's export and import trade only, you are to have recourse to, and keep within, the liberty therein stipulated and given as nearly as can possibly be done. But, as by the connivance of the Bengal Government and constant usage, the Company's covenant servants have had the same benefit as the Company with respect to their export and import trade, we are willing they should enjoy the same, and that Dustucks be granted accordingly. But herein **Export and import trade alone to be duty free.**

the most effectual care is to be taken that no excesses or abuses are suffered upon any account whatsoever, nor Dustucks granted to any others than our covenant servants as aforesaid. However, notwithstanding any of our former orders, no writer is to have the benefit of the Dustuck until he has served out his full term of five years in that station. Free merchants and others are not entitled to or to have the benefit of the Company's Dustucks, but are to pay the usual duties.

All agents to be abolished. All trade to be carried on through the Company's Factories.

"As no agents or gomastas are to reside on account of private trade at any of the inland parts of the country, all business on account of licensed private trade is to be carried on by and through the means of the Company's Covenanted Servants, resident at the several subordinate Factories, as has been usual.

All persons acting contrary to orders to be dismissed the service.

"We are under the necessity of giving the before-going orders in order to preserve the tranquillity of the country and harmony with the Nawab. They are rather outlines than complete directions, which you are to add to, and improve upon, agreeably to the spirit of, and our meaning in, them, as far as may be necessary to answer the desired purpose. And, if any person or persons are guilty of a contravention of them, be they whomsoever they may, if our own servants, they are to be dismissed the service; if of others, the Company's protection is to be withdrawn, and you have the option of sending them forthwith to England if you judge the nature of the offence requires it.

Nundcoomar to be kept under surveillance.

"From the whole of your proceedings with respect to Nundcoomar, there seems to be no doubt of his endeavouring by forgery and false accusations to ruin Ramchurn, that he has been guilty of carrying on correspondence with the Country Powers hurtful to the Company's interest, and instrumental in conveying letters between the Shahzada and the French Governor General of Pondicherry. In short, it appears that he is of that wicked and turbulent disposition that no harmony can subsist in a society where he has the opportunity of interfering. We therefore most readily concur with you, that Nundcoomar is a person improper to be trusted with his liberty in our settlements, and capable of doing mischief if he is permitted to go out of the province, either to the northward or towards the Dekhan. We shall therefore depend upon your keeping such a watch over all his actions as may be the means of preventing his disturbing the quiet of the public or injuring individuals for the future.[1]

"We are well pleased that you have engaged no further in assisting the Rajah of Meckley (*i. e.*, Munipur) for obtaining redress for some grievances he complained to have suffered from the Burmas. For, although the advantage offered by the Rajah may be specious, and you might have an opportunity of getting redress for the repeated ill-treatment of our settlement at the Negrais, yet the distance of the object, the general weakness of our forces, and the uncertainty of success, surely are sufficient reasons for not proceeding upon new hostilities. We do not disapprove, however, of your ordering the detachment of six companies of sepoys to take part at Munipore under the direction of the Chief and Council of Chittagong; provided it may have been the means of cultivating a friendship with the said Rajah, and giving you an opportunity of being acquainted with the strength, nature, and dispositions of the Burmas; that such future use may be made of these circumstances as may be really and essentially necessary for the Company's interest, and on no other account whatsoever. But we shall still be always well pleased with and applaud your endeavours for opening any new channels of commerce."

Glad that no help was given to the Rajah of Munipur.

It would be tedious to proceed further with the extracts. It will suffice to briefly refer to the manner in which the question was misunderstood in England. There was no question as to the treaty right of the English to trade free of duty. There may have been a question whether the right was

Current errors.

---

[1] General letter, London, 22nd July 1764.

conferred only upon the trade of the Company, or whether it extended to the private trade of the Company's servants. But that was a question which did not affect the Nawab. The Company ask with some inconsistency why they, the masters, had not been allowed to share in a trade which had become so lucrative to their servants. But that was a paltry dispute between master and servant, with which history has nothing to do.

Treaties only hurried agreements.

The plain truth was that the so-called treaties were mere agreements patched up on the eve of a revolution. The English were in a position to demand anything; the Nawab expectant could refuse nothing. There was not even a show of deliberation, for there was no time to haggle over terms. The term "duty free" meant anything or everything.

Necessity for a dictator.

The crisis was one of those epochs in history when nothing could stop the quarrel but the strong arm of absolute power. Had Clive been in Bengal, he would have made himself arbiter in the dispute; and both the Nawab and the English would have been compelled to submit to his dictation. As it was, the moderate counsels of men like Vansittart and Warren Hastings were thrown to the winds, because they were wanting in authority. No one heeded them; both parties were bent on effecting their respective objects by force of will.

Suspects the English.

Meantime Meer Cossim began to suspect the designs of the English. He had inklings of the negotiations between the English and the young King, Shah Alam. He knew that Vansittart and Warren

Hastings were supporting his pretensions. Doubtless he ascribed their conduct to weakness; especially when he saw that the English Governor was thwarted by a majority of his own Council, an opposition which few Asiatics in the eighteenth century could have been made to understand.

Meer Cossim must have been more sure of the support of his grandees than his immediate predecessor. He had despoiled some of the high Hindu officials; but the blame fell upon the English, who permitted him to break the guarantee which had been given by Clive. The Hindu grandees were estranged from the English by the withdrawal of the guarantee; and community of interests led them to make common cause with the Nawab. Meantime the quarrel of the Nawab with the English only served to strengthen his position. The people were regarding the English as their oppressors, and looking to the Nawab for protection. Reliance of the Hindu grandees.

CHAPTER XI.

CALCUTTA RECORDS: PATNA MASSACRE.

A. D. 1763.

English audacity.

AT this time the English never contemplated meeting any real resistance from Nawab Cossim. They expected that he would yield to threats. They had long ceased to fear him; they treated him as a creature of their own creation. As for themselves, they never doubted their personal security, either at Calcutta, or at the more remote factories up-country. Patna, for instance, was in the heart of Behar. It was cut off from Calcutta by the Nawab's capital at Monghyr. Yet Mr. Ellis, the Chief of the English factory at Patna, had all along been one of the most violent opponents of the Nawab and his officials.

Ill-timed mission to Monghyr.

It was under such circumstances that the English Commissioners, Messrs. Amyatt and Hay, proceeded from Calcutta to Monghyr. They were expected to induce the Nawab to withdraw his orders for the abolition of all inland duties. The Nawab was so angry that he would hardly give them a hearing. He rejected every proposition that they made to him. To make matters worse, an English boat attempted to pass Monghyr with a supply of arms for the factory at Patna. The Nawab was furious at the news, and stopped the boat at Monghyr.

Imperious action of the English.

The English at Calcutta were equally furious at the action of the Nawab. Messrs. Amyatt and Hay received orders from Calcutta to leave Monghyr unless the Nawab allowed the arms to go on to Patna. This, however, was easier said than done. Mr. Hay was detained at Monghyr as a hostage for the safety of the Nawab's officers who had been arrested by the English. Mr. Amyatt was permitted to return to Calcutta.

Terrible results.

Such was the course of events when a tragedy was enacted at Patna, almost as terrible as that of the Black Hole. It raised an outcry in England like that which followed the massacre at Cawnpore during the mutiny. In the present day the story of Patna has been forgotten; but it may be revived by extracts from the journals of the sufferers, for it is a lesson for all time.

Mr. Amyatt leaves Patna.

Mr. Amyatt left Monghyr in good spirits. The Nawab entertained him with a nautch the night before he went away, and he seems to have had no sense of danger. The story of his murder by the Nawab's retainers will appear hereafter.

English factory at Patna.

Whilst Mr. Amyatt was at Monghyr, he carried on a correspondence with Mr. Ellis at Patna. When he left Monghyr, Mr. Ellis took the alarm. There was an English force at the factory; but the factory itself was untenable. Accordingly it was resolved by Mr. Ellis and the English at the factory to attack Patna and occupy the town.

Diaries at Patna.

The following extracts from the journal of a gentleman at Patna describe the operations which followed:—

Anniversary dinner of the battle of Plassey.

"*June 23rd, 1763.*—This day I dined at the Factory with most of the Officers, &c., in commemoration of the Battle of Plassey, when I observed by the private conferences of Messrs. Ellis, Carstairs, &c., that the public embroils which had been long threatening appeared to be coming near to a crisis, which made me take Carstairs aside and ask him whether he thought I was safe to stay longer in the city; he told me, for that night I may, but no longer, and invited me out to his garden.

Contemplated attack on the town of Patna.

"*24th.*—This morning I employed myself in settling matters with my Banian and getting my things sent out to Captain Carstairs's; dined at the Factory, where the gentlemen kept everything very private; arrived at Carstairs's about four o'clock. Upon enquiry of him, understood that they intended attacking the city to-morrow morning, but he had just received a chit from Mr. Ellis, wherein he mentioned he had received intelligence by the foot post that Mr. Amyatt had been entertained by the Nawab with a nautch and came home highly pleased; wherefore he thought their intentions of attack should be deferred till he heard from Mr. Amyatt himself, which he expected that evening, and should then give him immediate notice. Betwixt eight and nine a message arrived that he had heard from Mr. Amyatt, and that he had leave of the Nawab to proceed to Calcutta on the 24th; wherefore he ordered the attack should be made on the morning. As they formerly agreed, most of the Officers supped with Carstairs, and I came into the Factory betwixt eleven and twelve, and found all the gentlemen making all preparations for the attack.

Patna taken and lost.

"*25th.*—The Army moved from Bankipore at two o'clock in the morning, and they judged in the Factory that the Army would reach the city before four. Accordingly, about a quarter before four we heard a firing, upon which a party of sepoys who were stationed on the top of the Factory house were ordered to keep up a constant fire upon the rampart of the wall next the Factory, and two 3-pounders, which were also there, were ordered to play away upon the same rampart, and the two 24-pounders below kept up an incessant fire till daylight (all this period very little firing was returned from the city, as I believe they were all asleep when attacked). We now observed all the walls lined with our colours and sepoys, which to be sure in our situation was very agreeable, and every minute furnished us with the agreeable news of everything going before us; in short, by nine we were confidently assured that we were in possession of every post; then our great folks began to look into the administration of the province; perwannahs[1] were issuing out to the Foujdars[2] to continue their former obedience in sending in provisions, &c., to the city as formerly; Nuzzurs[3] were coming in plenty to the Chief, and joy reigned in the face of everybody. Biscuits, wine, &c., were sent in to the Officers to refresh them; numbers of wounded men were now coming out of the city, which employed Messrs. Fullarton, Anderson, and self for the day; surmises now passed that we had not as yet got possession of the Fort, and by twelve was confirmed. About two o'clock Carstairs and Kinch came to the Factory and acquainted us that we were beat out of the city, and that it was not in their power to make one man stand; which was the case, for by all accounts less than a hundred men drove our whole Army out, and this sad misfortune was entirely owing to the plundering of our sepoys and soldiers, which turned their courage into avarice, and every one of them thought of nothing but skulking off with what they had got. By three o'clock most of the scattered Army returned into the Factory.

"After this melancholy accident everybody was greatly nonplused what was the most prudent step to be taken: as

Flight of the English towards Oude.

---

1 Perwannahs were letters conveying orders.

2 Foujdars were military officers in charge of towns, villages, or districts in behalf of the Nawab.

3 Nuzzurs were complimentary offerings on occasion of rejoicing.

W

in such case numbers of schemes were proposed, and none could determine what was the most advisable; at last it was fixed to proceed to Shuja-u-daula's province, [*i. e.*, Oude,] but a great difficulty arose in the procuring of boats. At last with much trouble there were collected as many as we thought would do, and agreed to set off the next evening."

Surrender of the English to Meer Cossim.

The English had captured Patna; but soldiers and sepoys were alike wanting in discipline, and the town was recovered by the Nawab's troops the same day. The English were in a dilemma. They could not remain at the factory, for they could not hold it against the enemy. They could not go down the river to Calcutta, for they would certainly be stopped by the Nawab at Monghyr. They had no alternative but to go up the river into Oude. They made the attempt, but it failed; the stream was against them, and indeed everything was against them. In the end they surrendered to the Nawab. Some were imprisoned at Patna; others, including Mr. Ellis, were imprisoned at Monghyr.

Diary of an English prisoner at Patna.

Extracts from the journal of an English prisoner at Patna throw further light on the progress of affairs:—

News from Monghyr.

"*August 6th.*—Mr. Roach's boy arrived from Monghyr; brings news of Mr. Amyatt's head being brought there some time ago; that Mr. Chambers and some of the Cossimbazar Factory people are there also. Hear that we were thrice repulsed in the attack of the city of Muradabad, but the fourth attack carried everything; that the old Nawab Meer Jaffier is declared.

Murder of Mr. Amyatt and Ensign Cooper.

"*11th.*—Messrs. Bennet and Thomson were to-day brought to us; they give us an account of Mr. Amyatt and Ensign Cooper being killed at Muradabad as follows:—They had embarked all the party, and sent the horses, &c., with the syces by land. Meeting with contrary winds, it was ten days ere they reached Muradabad, when at once they saw troops drawn upon each side of the river with some great guns; they hailed them and desired them to come to, but not taking notice of them some of them fired, on which some of our sepoys began to fire also and killed somebody on the shore, on which great guns and volleys were fired, which induced them to put to the opposite shore where was the least fire. Mr. Amyatt, notwithstanding the fire, landed with a pair of pistols; he took the Nawab's perwannah in one hand and held it up to them, and a pistol in the other, and advanced to the top of the bank, where he was shot in the leg, and soon after cut to pieces. Ensign Cooper met with the same fate in making resistance, but the other gentlemen they can give no account of, but expect they were sent to Monghyr with Mr. Chambers and the others from Cossimbazar. They also inform us Mr. Hay and Mr. Gulston were left at Monghyr, and remain there yet. These gentlemen have suffered greatly, being put in irons, and brought up in one boat without cover and scarcely victuals or necessaries to cover them, being in all twenty-seven persons. The Nawab here allows ten rupees per day to the twenty-seven people left, and an addition of two rupees per day to us on account of these two gentlemen.

"*23rd.*—As His Excellency[1] still continues at Monghyr, it gives us reason to think our troops are not yet in possession of the upper pass. Nawab at Monghyr.

"*24th.*—Hear for certain our troops are at Shahabad; that the enemy are repairing what of Monghyr they had destroyed; that everything was in the greatest confusion in His Excellency's camp; that Somru had the management of everything. His Excellency had not eaten for three days, nor allowed his Nazir to be beat; that he himself and Somru were at Monghyr and his army advanced to Gulgot Nullah, so that we may hourly expect some news.

[1] The Nawab Meer Cossim.

Murder of Europeans.

"*26th.*—This evening heard that ten Europeans at Bar had been tied and thrown into the river, so that from this we may guess what we are to expect; have also an account that some perwannahs have arrived here to several jemadars of His Excellency's camp; some think he will be laid hold of by his own people.

Nawab marches from Mongyr to Patna.

"*29th and 30th.*—Hear that His Excellency is two coss this side Ruinulla, and Somru with the Armenians at the nullah; that his people are going off daily, and he is in great fear of his life; that about three weeks ago he proposed cutting us all off, but was prevented by Somru, the Armenians, and some of his jemadars.

"*Tuesday, 4th.*—To-day, His Excellency arrived at Ram Narain's gardens, and to-morrow comes into the city. They have been very busy to-day mounting guns on the bastions of this place. Heard that Meer Jaffier's brother had made his escape.

"*Wednesday, 5th.*—Hear the Setts were cut off near Barr.

Horrible rumours.

"*Thursday, 6th.*—Heard this morning that Mr. Ellis and forty-seven gentlemen were cut off last night, so that doubtless our fate must be sealed in twenty-four hours, for which God prepare us all."

Diary of Mr. Fullarton, sole survivor.

An English surgeon, named Fullarton, was the sole survivor of the massacre. He had been a medical attendant upon the Nawab Meer Cossim, and never seems to have been in danger. When hostilities began Mr. Fullarton was at Monghyr. Subsequently he was sent to Patna, and was present there at the time of the massacre. The following extracts from his narrative show the course of events at Monghyr and Patna:—

"*July 6th.*—Mr. Ellis with the rest of the gentlemen were brought to Patna. I petitioned to be sent to them, or be suffered to see them, both which were refused.

"*The 8th.*—Mr. Ellis with the rest of the gentlemen were sent to Monghyr and there confined; there was Rs. 45,000 of the Company's cash on board the budgerow when Mr. Ellis was taken, and some plate which was given to him, but in the care of some of the Nawab's people, to be given him when he wanted it; some time it remained with Coja Petruss, afterwards with Mamodom Khan.

"*The 16th.*—I was sent down to Monghyr and there confined separately from the rest of the gentlemen, as I afterwards understood they were all well used, though strictly confined. We had victuals sent us by the Nawab regularly twice a day.

August 10th.—The Nawab left Monghyr, and the fort was left in charge of Mamodom Khan; he treated us with the greatest lenity to appearance, and pretended to carry on a treaty with Mr. Ellis, but it was all a sham, for he never was in earnest. I was allowed to see the gentlemen on account of Captain Turner being ill, who afterwards died of a flux.

"*September 13th.*—Mr. Ellis and the rest of the gentlemen were sent from Monghyr; Messrs. Ellis and Greentree were in palankeens; Lushington, Smith, Lieutenant Bowen, Ensign McLeod, and one other gentleman whom I don't remember, were on horseback; the rest were in irons, some in dooleys, and some in hackeries, and after their arrival at Patna were confined in Haji Ahmad's house.

"*September 19th.*—I was sent from Monghyr to Patna and confined alone in the Killa.

"*October 5th.*—Mr. Ellis with the rest of the gentlemen were inhumanly butchered by Somru, who came that evening to the place with two companies of sepoys (he had the day before sent for all the knives and forks from the gentlemen); he surrounded the house with his people and went into a little outer square and sent for Messrs. Ellis, Hay, and Lushington, and with them came six other gentlemen, who were all terribly mangled and cut to pieces, and their bodies thrown into a well in the square and it filled up; then the sepoys were sent into the large square and fired on the gentlemen there, and, rushing upon them, cut them into

Massacre at Patna by Somru.

pieces in the most inhuman manner, and they were thrown into another well, which was likewise filled up.

Excesses and threats of the Nawab.

"*The 7th.*—The Nawab sent for me and told me to get myself in readiness to go to Calcutta, for that he had been unlucky in the war, which, he asserted with great warmth, had not been of his seeking, nor had he been the aggressor, reproaching the English with want of fidelity and breach of treaty, but he said he had still hopes of an accommodation; he asked me what I thought of it; I told him I made no doubt of it. When some of his people then present mentioned the affair of Mr. Amyatt's death, he declared that he had never given any orders of killing Mr. Amyatt, but after receiving advice of Mr. Ellis's having attacked Patna, he had ordered all his servants to take and imprison all the English in his provinces wherever they could find them; he likewise added that if a treaty was not set afoot, he would bring the King, the Mahrattas, and Abdulla[1] against us, and so ruin our trade, &c.; he had finished his letters, and ordered boats and a guard to conduct me, when, upon the advice of some of his people, he stopped me and said there was no occasion for me to go. After his sending for me at first he ordered the sepoys in whose charge I was to go to their quarters; two Moguls and twelve hurkaras to attend me, but to let me go about the city where I pleased. I then applied for liberty to stay at the Dutch Factory, which was granted.

Flight of the Nawab.

"*The 14th.*—On the approach of our army Nawab Cossim decamped with his troops in great confusion, and marched five coss to the westward of the city. The hurkaras that were with me having no orders about me, I gave them some money which made them pretty easy.

Escape of Dr. Fullarton.

"*The 25th.*—After giving money to a jemadar that had the guard to the westward of the Dutch Factory by the river side, I set out in a small boat, and got safe to the boats under command of Captain Wederburn that were lying opposite to the city on the other side of the river, and at

[1] Ahmud Shah Abdali, the sovereign of the Afghans.

eleven o'clock that night arrived at the army under the command of Major Adams, laying at Jutly."

It is needless to dwell on the disaster. It will suffice to say that fifty-one English gentlemen were slaughtered in cold blood at Patna, together with a hundred others of inferior rank. The order was given by Nawab Cossim, but the massacre was directed by a deserter from the French army named Somru[1] who had entered the service of the Nawab. The massacre rendered accommodation impossible. The war which followed led to the utter ruin of the Nawab. Meer Cossim was utterly beaten; his threats were vain and futile; he fled away to Oude and took refuge with the Nawab Vizier. Ruin of Meer Cossim.

The Nawab Vizier of Oude was prepared to take advantage of the confusion of the times. He was still accompanied by the King, Shah Alam; he still hoped to get possession of Behar, Bengal, and Orissa. The military operations have lost their interest; there was a mutiny of the sepoys in the English army; it was the first on record; it was suppressed by blowing twenty men from their guns. Then followed the battle of Buxar; it was fought on the 23rd October 1764; it settled the fate of the English in India; it placed the whole of Oude and the North-West Provinces at the feet of the English at Calcutta. To Decisive battle of Buxar, 1764.

[1] The real name of this man was Walter Reinhardt. He deserted to the English and took the name of Summer; the soldiers changed his name to Sombre because of his evil expression. Subsequently he entered the Nawab's service as stated in the text.

all outward appearance, the English had become the paramount power, not only in Bengal, but in all Hindustan, from the left bank of the Jumna to the slopes of the Himalayas.

Restoration of Meer Jaffier.

Meanwhile Meer Jaffier was restored to the throne of Bengal, Behar, and Orissa. Mr. Vansittart returned to England and was succeeded by a Mr. Spencer as Governor of Bengal. Lord Clive had been raised to the peerage and appointed Governor of Bengal. A Select Committee of five members, with Lord Clive at their head, was formed for the exclusive management of all political affairs. All these arrangements were reported to Calcutta in 1764. In 1765 Lord Clive was sailing up the Bay of Bengal with two of the members of the new Committee, for the purpose of taking over the supreme control of affairs.

CHAPTER XII.

SECOND GOVERNMENT OF CLIVE.

1765—1767.

Plans of Lord Clive.

LORD CLIVE landed at Calcutta in May 1765. On his way up the Bay he had touched at Madras, and heard that Meer Jaffier had died the previous February. He was delighted at the news. He was anxious to introduce the new system for the government of the Bengal provinces, which he had unfolded to Pitt more than seven years before. He would set up a new Nawab who should be only a cypher. He would leave the administration in the hands of native officials. The English were to be the real masters; they were to take over the revenues, defend the three provinces from invasion and insurrection, make war and conclude peace. But the sovereignty of the English was to be hidden from the public eye. They were to rule only in the name of the Nawab and under the authority of the Moghul Emperor.

Setting up an infant Nawab.

Lord Clive had no misgivings as to his new scheme. He knew that there were two claimants to the Nawab's throne, an illegitimate son of Meer Jaffier aged twenty, and a legitimate grandson aged six. He would place the child of six on the throne at Murshedabad. He would carry out all his arrangements during the minority, without the possibility of any difficulty or opposition.

Forestalled by Governor Spencer.

On reaching Calcutta, Lord Clive found that he had been forestalled. Governor Spencer and Members of Council had refused to await the arrival of Lord Clive and the Select Committee. They were anxious to make fortunes by installing a new Nawab. Directly they heard of the death of Meer Jaffier, they sent a deputation of four of their number to the city of Murshedabad. The deputation made a hurried bargain with a clever native grandee, named Mahomed Reza Khan. It was agreed that the young man of twenty should be made Nawab; that Mahomed Reza Khan should exercise all real power under the name of Naib Subah, or Deputy Nawab; that twenty lakhs of rupees, or more than two hundred thousand pounds sterling, should be distributed amongst the Governor and Council at Calcutta; and to prevent any unpleasantness, like that which led Meer Cossim to withhold the twenty lakhs, the money was paid over at once in cash and bills obtained from Hindu bankers, and the deputation returned to Calcutta in great joy and exultation.

A puppet Nawab and Native Mentor.

Complaints of the new Nawab.

Lord Clive did not hear all this at once. He was sufficiently exasperated at the news that the young man of twenty had been made Nawab instead of the child of six. A few days after his arrival at Calcutta, he received a letter from the young Nawab. The prince was weak and stupid; chafing at the loss of the twenty lakhs, and impatient of his state of pupilage under Mahomed Reza Khan. He complained to Lord Clive that he had been treated with insult and indignity; that the money had been paid to the English gentlemen against his will; that the treasury at Murshedabad had been unequal to the demand; that most of the money had been raised by a forced loan extorted from the Seit bankers.

Wrath of Lord Clive.

Lord Clive was excessively angry. He declared that blacks and whites had united together to plunder the Nawab's treasury. Governor Spencer and his Council asserted that they had only followed the example set by Clive himself after the battle of Plassey. They forgot that circumstances had entirely changed. At Plassey Clive had rendered great public services to the Nawab and the Company, whilst there was no law whatever against the receipt of presents. At the death of Meer Jaffier, Spencer and his Council had rendered no services whatever; moreover, stringent orders had been passed by the Court of Directors against the receipt of presents. Covenants to that effect had been received at Calcutta; and the execution of the covenants had been purposely delayed by Governor Spencer and his Council until the English gentlemen had received the money. It is needless to dwell upon the scandal. Most of the gentlemen were returning to England, and Lord Clive left their conduct to be dealt with by the Court of Directors.

Provisional measures.

Lord Clive did not set aside the Nawab. The prince had been installed by the English deputation, and the arrangement had been ratified by the Governor and Council. But he restricted the authority of Mahomed Reza Khan. He associated two Hindu grandees with Mahomed Reza Khan, and thus distributed the powers of the Naib Subah amongst a council of three.

Treaty with the King and Nawab Vizier.

Shortly afterwards, Lord Clive was called away from Calcutta to conclude a treaty with the King Shah Alam and the Nawab Vizier. The negotiations were of a complex character. There were three important questions which called for early settlement:—

1st.—The future status of Oude and the Nawab Vizier.

2nd.—The future relations between the English and the King, or Padishah.

3rd.—The future status of the Nawab of Bengal, Behar, and Orissa with regard to the King and the English.

Settlement of Oude.

The first business was the settlement of Oude. This territory extended from Behar almost to Delhi. It formed a barrier between the three Bengal provinces on one side, and the Mahrattas on the south and Afghans on the north-west.

Conflicting policy of Spencer and Clive.

At this moment Delhi was in the hands of the Afghans. Governor Spencer had wanted to treat with the Afghans for the cession of Oude to the Afghan invaders, and restoration of the King to the throne of Delhi. Lord Clive set his face against this policy. He would have nothing to do with Delhi or the Afghans. He sought to restrict the

English to the three provinces of Bengal, Behar, and Orissa, and to guard against their interference in the countries beyond. He was willing to restore the territory of Oude and the guardianship of the King to the Nawab Vizier.

Lord Clive's idea was to establish the English ascendancy in Bengal, Behar, and Orissa under the authority of Moghul sovereignty. In so doing he resuscitated some of the forms in the Moghul imperial system. He sought to maintain the King by a settled yearly charge on the revenues of Oude and Bengal, which might be regarded as the King's share, and serve to strengthen the King's authority. Objects of Clive.

Lord Clive gave back Oude to the Nawab Vizier. He only insisted that the King should receive the yearly revenue of the districts of Allahabad and Korah as his share of the revenue of Oude. So far the imperial sovereignty of the King was recognised in Oude. The King continued to reside at Allahabad, under the guardianship of the Nawab Vizier. In reality he was waiting for the turn of fortune which should carry him on to Delhi. Restoration of Oude to the Nawab; provision for the King.

Lord Clive next arranged the future government of Bengal, Behar, and Orissa. He accepted the post of King's Dewan for the three provinces in the name of the English Company. The English Company, as King's Dewan, took over all the revenue of the three provinces; they engaged to pay the King a yearly rent of twenty-six lakhs, or at the existing rate of exchange, about three hundred The Dewani of Bengal, Behar, and Orissa.

thousand pounds sterling, as the imperial share. They were left to deal with the surplus revenue as they thought fit, and to make their own terms with the Nawab of Murshedabad.

Provision for the Nawab Nasim.

Lord Clive next went to Murshedabad. He required the young Nawab to disband his rabble army. He arranged to take over the whole revenue of the three provinces. He agreed to pay a yearly stipend of fifty-three lakhs to the Nawab.[1] In this manner the English Company came into possession of the yearly revenues of Bengal, Behar, and Orissa. They paid twenty-six lakhs to the King, and fifty-three lakhs to the Nawab. The yearly payments were thus something less than a million sterling. The yearly receipts, however, were estimated at three or four millions. Out of the surplus they provided for the defence of the country and maintenance of the public peace. The balance was so large that the Company appropriated it to the purchase of goods and manufactures in India and China. The

---

[1] Henceforth the Nawab was known as the Nawab Nazim. The outward form of the Government of Bengal, Behar, and Orissa resembled that which prevailed in the reign of Aurungzeb. There was a Nawab Nazim, who was responsible for the defence of the three provinces and the maintenance of the public peace, as well as for the administration of justice and enforcing obedience to the law. There was a King's Dewan, who received the yearly revenues of the three provinces, and was responsible for all disbursements, as well as for the payment of the surplus to the King as his imperial share.

The outward form adopted by Lord Clive was only a veil to conceal the real transfer of power. Lord Clive had taken away all military power from the Nawab Nazim and reduced him to a cypher. The Company as King's Dewan took possession of all the surplus revenue. In the time of Aurungzeb and his immediate successors, the yearly remittances to the King amounted to a million sterling. In Lord Clive's time the King was only too glad to receive three hundred thousand pounds sterling.

result was that within a few years the three Bengal provinces were literally drained of rupees.[1]

Exposition of the policy by the Select Committee at Calcutta.

The nature and results of this grant of the Dewani to the Company are fully set forth in the correspondence between the Select Committee at Calcutta and the Court of Directors. The letters to England explain the policy of Lord Clive. The letters from England expound the views of the Directors. The Select Committee begins[2]:—

Existing status.

"The time now approaches when we may be able to determine, with some degree of certainty, whether our remaining as merchants, subjected to the jurisdiction, encroachments, and insults of the country government, or supporting your privileges and possessions by the sword, are likely to prove most advantageous to the Company. Whatever may be the consequence, certain it is, that after having once begun, and proceeded to such lengths, we have been forced to go on, step by step, until your whole possessions were put to the risk by every revolution effected, and by every battle fought. To apply a remedy to those evils, by giving stability and permanency to your government, is now and has been the constant object of the serious attention of your Select Committee.

Necessity for accepting the Dewani.

"The perpetual struggles for superiority between the Nawabs and your Agents, together with the recent proofs before us of notorious and avowed corruption, have rendered us unanimously of opinion, after the most mature deliberation, that no other method can be suggested of laying the axe to the root of all those evils, than that of obtaining the Dewanny of Bengal, Behar, and Orissa, for the Company. By establishing the power of the Great Mogul, we have likewise established His rights; and his Majesty, from principles

[1] The curious phenomena which followed these financial arrangements will be explained in the next chapter.

[2] Despatch of Select Committee at Fort William, dated 30th September 1765. Also despatch from the same, dated 31st January 1766.

of gratitude, of equity, and of policy, has thought proper to bestow this important employment on the Company, the nature of which is, the collecting all the revenues, and after defraying the expenses of the army, and allowing a sufficient fund for the support of the Nizamut, to remit the remainder to Dehli, or wherever the King shall reside or direct. But as the King has been graciously pleased to bestow on the Company, for ever, such surplus as shall arise from the revenues, upon certain stipulations and agreements expressed in the Sunnud, we have settled with the Nawab, with his own free will and consent, that the sum of fifty-three lakhs[1] shall be annually paid to him, for the support of his dignity and all contingent expenses, exclusive of the charge of maintaining an army, which is to be defrayed out of the revenues ceded to the Company, by this royal grant of the Dewanny; and indeed the Nawab has abundant reason to be well satisfied with the conditions of this agreement, whereby a fund is secured to him, without trouble or danger, adequate to all the purposes of such grandeur and happiness as a man of his sentiments has any conception of enjoying; more would serve only to disturb his quiet, endanger his government, and sap the foundation of that solid structure of power and wealth, which, at length, is happily reared and completed by the Company, after a vast expense of blood and treasure.

Prospective advantages.

"By this acquisition of the Dewanny, your possessions and influence are rendered permanent and secure, since no future Nawab will either have power or riches sufficient to attempt your overthrow, by means either of force or corruption. All revolutions must henceforward be at an end, as there will be no fund for secret services, for donations, or for restitutions. The Nawab cannot answer the expectations of the venal and mercenary, nor will the Company comply with demands injurious to themselves, out of their own revenues. The experience of years has convinced us that a division of power is impossible without generating discontent and hazarding the whole: all must belong either to the Company or to

[1] 662,500*l* at the current rate of exchange.

the Nawab. We leave you to judge which alternative is the most desirable and the most expedient in the present circumstances of affairs. As to ourselves, we know of no other system we could adopt, that would less affect the Nawab's dignity, and at the same time secure the Company against the fatal effects of future revolutions than this of the Dewanny. The power is now lodged where it can only be lodged with safety to us, so that we may pronounce with some degree of confidence, that the worst which will happen in future to the Company will proceed from temporary ravages only, which can never become so general as to prevent your revenues from yielding a sufficient fund to defray your civil and military charges, and furnish your investments."

"The more we reflect on the situation of your affairs, the stronger appear the reasons for accepting the Dewanny of these provinces, by which alone we could establish a power sufficient to perpetuate the possessions we hold, and the influence we enjoy. While the Nawab acted in quality of Collector for the Mogul, the means of supporting our military establishment depended upon his pleasure. In the most critical situations, while we stood balancing on the extreme border of destruction, his stipulated payments were slow and deficient, his revenues withheld by disaffected Rajahs, and turbulent Zemindars, who despised the weakness of his government; or they were squandered in profusion, and dissipated in corruption, the never-failing symptoms of a declining constitution and feeble administration. Hence we were frequently disappointed of those supplies, upon the punctual receipt of which depended the very existence of the Company in Bengal." Self-preservation

The letter from the Court of Directors approving of this arrangement is very valuable. It lays down with much precision what were to be the relations between the Nawab Nazim and the English President and Council. It shows that at this period there were strong objections to any interference in Approval of the Court of Directors.

the native administration. An English Resident was continued at Murshedabad; he was to take over the monthly payments from the Nawab's officers; his chief duty was to protect the native administration from the encroachments of the Company's servants. The following extracts are historical[1] :—

Sentiments.

"We come now to consider the great and important affair of the Dewanny, on which we shall give you our sentiments, with every objection that occurs to us.

Danger of the crisis.

"When we consider that the barrier of the country government was entirely broke down, and every Englishman throughout the country armed with an authority that owned no superior, and exercising his power to the oppression of the helpless native, who knew not whom to obey; at such a crisis, we cannot hesitate to approve your obtaining the Dewanny for the Company."

Definition of the office and power of King's Dewan.

"We observe the account you give of the office and power of the King's Dewan, which in former times was 'the collecting of all the revenues, and, after defraying the expenses of the army, and allowing a sufficient fund for the support of the Nizamat, to remit the remainder to Delhi.' This description of it, is not the office we wish to execute; the experience we already have had in the province of Burdwan convinces us, how unfit an Englishman is to conduct the collection of the revenues, and follow the subtle native through all his arts, to conceal the real value of his country, and to perplex and elude the payments. We therefore entirely approve of your preserving the ancient form of government, in the upholding the dignity of the Subah.

Limitations of the authority exercised by the Company.

"We conceive the office of Dewan should be exercised only in superintending the collections, and disposal of the revenues; which, though vested in the Company, should officially be executed by our Resident at the Durbar, under

[1] Despatch from the Directors to the Select Committee, dated 17th May 1766.

the control of the Governor and the Select Committee. The ordinary bounds of which control, should extend to nothing beyond the superintending the collection of the revenues, and the receiving the money from the Nawab's treasury to that of the Dewanny, or the Company, and this we conceive to be neither difficult nor complicated: for at the annual Poonah the government settles with each Zemindar his monthly payments for the ensuing year; so the monthly payments of the whole from the Nawab's Dewan, is but the total of the monthly payment of each Zemindar; which must be strictly kept up, and if deficient, the Company must trace what particular province, Rajah, or Zemindar, has fallen short of his monthly payments; or, if it is necessary to extend the power farther, let the annual Poonah, by which we mean the time when every landholder makes his agreement for the ensuing year, be made with the consent of the Dewan or Company. This we conceive to be the whole office of the Dewanny. The administration of justice, the appointment of officers, Zemindarries,—in short, whatever comes under the denomination of civil administration,—we understand is to remain in the hands of the Nawab or his ministers.

"The Resident at the Durbar being constantly on the spot, cannot be long a stranger to any abuses in the government, and is always armed with power to remedy them. It will be his duty to stand between the administration and the encroachments always to be apprehended from the agents of the Company's servants, which must first be known to him; and we rely on his fidelity to the Company, to check all such encroachments, and to prevent the oppression of the natives."

The Nawab Nazim died in May 1766. The event was reported home by the Select Committee in the following terms. They show that the Nawab Nazim was already of no moment in the administration:— Death of the Nawab Nazim.

"We are sorry to acquaint you, that on the 8th day of May, his excellency the Nawab Nudjum al daulal breathed Report of the Select Committee.

his last, after a short illness, incurred by some intemperance in eating, and increased by a gross habit, and unsound constitution. As he was a prince of mean capacity, bred up in total ignorance of public affairs, this event, which formerly might have produced important consequences in the provinces, can at present have no other effect than that of exhibiting to the eyes of the people a mere change of persons in the Nizamut. Nudjum al daulah dying without issue, his brother Syef al daula succeeded to his dignities; and promises, from the mildness and pliancy of his disposition, to answer all the purposes of a Nawab to the people and to the Company. At present he is a youth not exceeding the age of sixteen, which more immediately and naturally brings the administration into the hands of persons in whom we can repose confidence[1]."

Private trade.

The minor details of Lord Clive's second administration have lost their interest. He did not put a stop to the private trade; and it was only stopped in after years by a general increase of salaries.

Mutiny of the Civil Servants.

Lord Clive had to encounter a curious mutiny amongst the civil servants. The massacre at Patna had carried off many of the seniors. Many juniors were appointed to posts for which they were unfit. The Secretary's department was made over to a youth of only three years' standing. The post of Paymaster to the Army was held by another young writer, whilst three hundred thousand pounds sterling lay in his hands for months. The business of these offices was really transacted by natives;

[1] As the Nawab Nazim had been reduced to the position of a pageant the necessity for maintaining an expensive state ceremonial gradually died out. Accordingly, on the accession of the new Nawab Nazim, the yearly allowances were reduced from fifty-three lakhs to forty-one lakhs; in 1770 they were reduced to thirty-one lakhs; and in 1772 to sixteen lakhs. Since 1772 there has been no further reduction.

the most secret concerns were known in the bazar; and serious abuses prevailed in all directions.

Outsiders from Madras.

Lord Clive called up four civilians from the Madras establishment and gave them vacant seats in the Bengal Council. The results of this measure may be given in what appears to be Lord Clive's own words[1]:—

Opposition of Bengal Civilians.

"We are sorry to find that our endeavours to serve the Company in a manner the least injurious to your servants here, should be misconstrued. As soon as this measure became known, by reports from Madras, and previous to our laying any proceedings before the Board, the young gentlemen of the settlement had set themselves up for judges of the propriety of our conduct, and the degree of their own merit: each would think himself qualified to transact your weighty affairs in Council, at an age when the laws of his country adjudge him unfit to manage his own concerns to the extent of forty shillings. They have not only set their hands to the memorial of complaint, but entered into associations unbecoming at their years, and destructive of that subordination without which no government can stand—All visits to the President are forbidden—All invitations fr om him and the members of the Select Committee are to be slighted—The gentlemen called down by our authority from Madras are to be treated with neglect and contempt—Every man who deviates from this confederacy is to be stigmatised and avoided—In a word, the members are totally to separate themselves from the head, decorum and union are to be set at defiance, and it becomes a fair struggle whether we or the young gentlemen shall in future guide the helm of government. Look at their names, examine their standing, inquire into their services, and reflect upon the age of four-fifths of the subscribers to this bill of grievances, who now support the association, and you will be equally surprised with us at the

[1] Despatch from Select Committee, dated 31st January 1766.

presumptuous intemperance of youth, and convinced that a stop of three or four years in the course of promotion is indispensably necessary, if you would have your Council composed of men of experience and discretion.

Determination of Clive.

"From this sketch of the behaviour of your servants, you will perceive the dangerous pitch to which the independent and licentious spirit of this settlement hath risen; you will then determine on the necessity and propriety of the step we have taken: in the mean time we are resolved to support it, or we must submit to the anarchy and confusion consequent on subjecting the decrees of your Select Committee to the revisal and repeal of young gentlemen just broke loose from the hands of their schoolmasters."

Mutiny of the Bengal Military officers.

Lord Clive had next to contend against a mutiny of the officers of the army. The Bengal army had been regimented, and formed into three brigades; one was at Monghyr, a second at Patna, and a third at Allahabad.

Abolition of double batta.

After the battle of Plassey the officers of the Bengal army received an additional allowance from the Nawab, known as double batta. The Directors, when they took the place of the Nawab, refused to continue the double batta. The double batta was abolished from the first of January 1766. The officers of the three brigades formed a secret league for throwing up their commissions on a certain day unless the double batta was restored. They raised subcriptions for the purpose; and some of the civil servants subscribed to the fund.

Triumph of Clive.

The story is nearly obsolete; but the energy and genius of Lord Clive were never more conspicuous. The Bengal officers relied on forcing the Governor and Council to restore the batta, for the army was about to take the field against the Mahrattas. Lord Clive, however, accepted every commission that was tendered. He gave commissions to deserving soldiers. He called up officers from Madras. He sent many officers under arrest to Calcutta, where they were afterwards shipped for England. At last the tide turned; many officers began to repent. Lord Clive displayed as much leniency as he could, and the mutiny was brought to a close.

Lord Clive left India in the beginning of 1767. He was only in his forty-second year; he never returned to India. He died six years afterwards at the early age of forty-eight. Before he left India he penned an able state paper in which he expounded his policy, domestic and foreign. The following extracts are worthy of permanent record :—

Lord Clive leaves India, 1767.

Policy for the future.

"The first period in politics which I offer to your consideration is the form of government. We are sensible that since the acquisition of the Dewanny, the power formerly belonging to the Subah (*i. e.*, Nawab) of these provinces is totally, in fact, vested in the East India Company. Nothing remains to him but the name and shadow of authority. This name, however, this shadow, it is indispensably necessary we should seem to venerate; every mark of distinction and respect must be shown him, and he himself encouraged to show his resentment upon the least want of respect from other nations.

Authority of the Nawab of Bengal reduced to a shadow.

"Under the sanction of a Subah, every encroachment that may be attempted by foreign powers can effectually be crushed, without any apparent interposition of our own authority, and all real grievances complained of by them can, through the same channel, be examined into and redressed.

Nawab to be retained to satisfy foreign nations.

Be it, therefore, always remembered that there is a Subah; that we have allotted him a stipend which must be regularly paid in support of his dignity; and that, though the revenues belong to the Company, the territorial jurisdiction must still rest in the chiefs of the country acting under him and this Presidency in conjunction. To appoint the Company's servants to the offices of Collectors, or, indeed, to do any act by an exertion of the English power which can equally be done by the Nawab at our instance, would be throwing off the mask,—would be declaring the Company Subah of the provinces. Foreign nations would immediately take umbrage, and complaints preferred to the British Court might be attended with very embarrassing consequences. Nor can it be supposed that either the French, Dutch, or Danes would readily acknowledge the Company's Subahship, and pay into the hands of their servants the duties upon trade or the quit-rents of those districts which they may have long been possessed of by virtue of the Royal firman or grants from former Nawabs. In short, the present form of government will not, in my opinion, admit of variation. The distinction between the Company and Nawab must be carefully maintained, and every measure wherein the country government shall even seem to be concerned must be carried on in the name of the Nawab and by his authority. In short, I would have all the Company's servants, the supervisors excepted,[1] confined entirely to commercial matters only, upon the plan laid down in the time of Aliverdy Khan.

Revenue not to be increased; evil of a drain of silver.

"It will not, I presume, be improper in this place to observe that you ought not to be very desirous of increasing the revenues, especially where it can only be effected by oppressing the landholders and tenants. So long as the country remains in peace the collections will exceed the demands; if you increase the former, a large sum of money will either lay dead in the Treasury or be sent out of the country, and much inconvenience arise in the space of a few years. Every nation trading to the East Indies has usually

[1] The duties of supervisors will be duly set forth in the next chapter.

imported silver for a return in commodities. The acquisition of the Dewanny has rendered this mode of traffic no longer necessary for the English Company; our investments may be furnished; our expenses, civil and military, paid; and a large quantity of bullion be annually sent to China, though we import not a single dollar. An increase of revenue, therefore, unless you can in proportion increase your investments, can answer no good purpose, but may in the end prove extremely pernicious, inasmuch as it may drain Bengal of its silver; and you will undoubtedly consider that the exportation of silver beyond the quantity imported is an evil, which, though slow, and, perhaps, remote in its conseqnences, will nevertheless be fatal to the Indian Company. This point, therefore, I leave to your constant vigilance and deliberation.

No offensive wars except for the defence of Bengal, Allahabad and Oude.

"The subject of moderation leads me naturally into a few reflections upon military affairs. Our possessions should be bounded by the provinces: studiously maintain peace,—it is the groundwork of our prosperity: never consent to act offensively against any powers, except in defence of our own, the King's or the Nawab Vizier's dominions, as stipulated by Treaty; and, above all things, be assured that a march to Delhi would be not only a vain and fruitless project, but attended with certain destruction to your army, and perhaps put a period to the very being of the Company in Bengal.

Political relations with Shuja-u-daula, the Nawab Vizier of Oude.

"Shuja-u-daula, the Nawab Vizier of Oude, we must observe, is now recovering his strength, and although I am fully persuaded from his natural disposition, which is cautious and timid, and from the experience he has had of our discipline and courage, that he will never engage against us in another war, yet, like most of his countrymen, he is ambitious, and I am of opinion that, as soon as he shall have formed an army, settled his country, and increased his finances, he will be eager to extend his territories, particularly by the acquisition of the Bundelcund district, formerly annexed to the Subahship of Allahabad. It is even not improbable that he will propose an expedition to Delhi and desire our assistance, without which, I think, he has not courage to risk such an undertaking. Here, therefore, we must be upon nor guard, and plainly remind the Vizier that we entered into an alliance with him for no other purpose than the defence of our respective dominions, and that we will not consent to invade other powers unless they should prove the aggressors by committing acts of hostility against him or the English, when it will become necessary to make severe examples in order to prevent others from attacking us unprovoked. With regard to his Delhi scheme, it must be warmly remonstrated against and discouraged. He must be assured, in the most positive terms, that no consideration whatever shall induce us to detach our forces to such a distance from this country, which produces all the riches we are ambitious to possess. Should he, however, be prevailed upon by the King to escort His Majesty to that capital without our assistance, it will then be our interest to approve the project, as it is the only means by which we can honourably get rid of our troublesome royal guest.

Three powers alone worthy of attention: the Vizier, the King, and the Mahrattas.

" The Rohillas, the Jauts, and all the northern powers are at too great a distance ever to disturb the tranquillity of these provinces. Shuja-u-daula's ambition, the King's solicitations, and the Mahrattas, these are the three grand objects of policy to this Committee, and by conducting your measures with that address of which you are become so well acquainted by experience, I doubt not that the peace of Bengal may be preserved many years, especially if a firm alliance be established with the Subah of the Deccan, and Januji, the Nagpore Rajah, be satisfied with the chout proposed, to which, I think he is in justice and equity strictly entitled.[1]

Mahrattas divided into two States, Poona and Nagpore.

" The Mahrattas are divided into two very great powers, who at present are at variance with each other, *viz.*, first, those Mahrattas who possess a large part of the Deccan, whose Chief is Ram Rajah, well known by the Presidency of Bombay, and whose capital is Poona, about thirty coss from Surat. Secondly, those Mahrattas who possess the extensive province of Berar, whose Chief is Januji, and whose capital, Nagpore, is distant from Calcutta about four hundred coss. These last are called

[1] Lord Clive's idea of paying chout to the Mahrattas of Berar occasioned much political controversy in after years.

Rajpoot Mahrattas, and are those who, after the long war with Aliverdy Khan, obliged him to make over the Ballasore and Cuttack countries and to pay a chout of twelve lakhs of Rupees."

Lord Clive's information respecting the Mahrattas of the Dekhan is imperfect. Ram Raja was a puppet prince of the dynasty of Sivaji; he was a state prisoner at Satara. The sovereign power was wielded by a hereditary line of Mahratta ministers who reigned at Poona under the name of Peishwas.

"With Januji it is our interest to be upon terms of friendship, for which purpose a Vakeel has been dispatched as appears upon the Committee proceedings; and I would recommend your settling of the chout with him agreeably to the plan I have proposed, *viz.*, that we shall pay sixteen lakhs upon condition that he appoint the Company Zemindar of the Ballasore and Cuttack countries, which, though at present of little or no advantage to Januji, would in our possession produce nearly sufficient to pay the whole amount of the chout. Whatever the deficiency may be, it will be overbalanced by the security and convenience we shall enjoy of free and open passage by land to and from Madras, all the countries between the two Presidencies being under our influence; but I would not by any means think of employing force to possess ourselves of those districts; the grant of them must come from him with his own consent, and if that cannot be obtained, we must settle the chout upon the most moderate terms we can.

Mahrattas of Nagpore, *i. e.*, Berar, to be reconciled by a grant of chout.

"The Mahrattas of the Deccan can only be kept quiet and in awe by an alliance with Nizam Ali of Hyderabad, which has already in part taken place; and I have not the least doubt that the Subah's own security, and the perpetual encroachments of the Mahrattas, will soon make him as desirous as we are of completing it. When this measure is

Mahrattas of Poona, *i. e.*, Western Dekhan, to be overawed by an alliance with the Nizam.

brought to perfection, not only the Deccan Mahrattas, but Januji also, will have too much to apprehend from our influence and authority so near home to be able to disturb far distant countries, and Bengal may be pronounced to enjoy as much tranquillity as it possibly can, or at least ought to enjoy, consistent with our main object—security.

"With regard to all other powers, they are so distracted and divided amongst themselves, that their operations can never turn towards Bengal."

Objections of the Court of Directors.

This policy did not meet the views of the Court of Directors. In two general letters, dated respectively 20th November 1767, and 16th March 1768, they remark as follows:—

No security to be obtained by alliances with Native Princes.

"From what appears in your proceedings, we think we discern too great an aptness to confederacies or alliances with the Indian powers, on which occasion we must give it you, as a general sentiment, that perfidy is too much the characteristic of Indian Princes for us to rely on any security with them; but should you enter into a treaty to act in concert with them in the field, one of our principal officers is to command the whole—a pre-eminence our own security and our superior military skill will entitle us to."

The Nizam not to be supported as a balance of power against the Mahrattas.

"We entirely disapprove the idea adopted, of supporting the Subah of the Deccan as a balance of power against the Mahrattas. It is for the contending parties to establish a balance of power among themselves. Their divisions are our security; and if the Mahrattas molest us, you must consider whether an attack from Bombay, when being near the capital of their dominions, may not be preferable to any defensive operations with the country powers on your side of India."

Failure of the foreign policy of isolation.

The foreign policy of Lord Clive and the Court of Directors calls for no further remark. It was a policy of isolation. The English were to lie snugly ensconced in the three provinces of Bengal,

Behar, and Orissa. The frontier of Oude was to form a permanent barrier against all further progress. Within a single decade this policy was thrown to the winds.

The domestic policy of Lord Clive was in like manner doomed to fall. The "double government," as it was called, of the English and the Nawab shared the fate of political shams. It was found useful, but only as bridging over the interval between Native administration and British administration. Meantime a solemn farce was played every year at Murshedabad. The annual Poona was held, when every landholder made his agreement as regards his payments of revenue for the coming year. The Nawab Nazim was seated on the throne at Murshedabad, as Subahdar of Bengal, Behar, and Orissa; and the English Governor stood on his right hand, as representative of the Honorable Company in the quality of King's Dewan.

Failure of the domestic policy of "double government."

There is a strange significance in Lord Clive's scheme of a puppet Nawab. The same political sham was going on in every native court in India. In the imperial system of the Moghuls, the King had become a puppet and the Vizier was sovereign ruler. In the Moghul provinces the King's name was the symbol of authority, whilst Subahdars and Nawabs were sovereign princes. In the imperial system of the Mahrattas, the nominal King was a State prince at Satara, whilst the Peishwa, a hereditary minister, reigned in full sovereignty at

Puppet sovereignties throughout India.

Poona.[1] The double government of Lord Clive was thus the outturn of political exigencies, which were producing the same results elsewhere throughout all India.

---

[1] The Mahratta empire was a series of anomalies. Every Peishwa in succession received investiture from the imprisoned Raja at Satara. All the later Peishwas affected to consider themselves as the servants of the Moghul Kings of Delhi. The Mahratta confederacy was a sham. The Peishwa was regarded as the head; but each of the confederate powers—Scindia, Holkar, the Guikowar of Baroda, and the Bhonsla of Berar—intrigued to get the better of him and of each other.

CHAPTER XIII.

BEGINNING OF BRITISH ADMINISTRATION.

A. D. 1767 TO 1770.

THE political system laid down by Lord Clive was warmly approved by the Directors. Indeed it was perfect in theory. By retaining a native administration it relieved the English of all the responsibilities of government. By the rigid adherence to a policy of isolation it stopped all dealings with native states outside the frontier. By taking over the surplus revenue, ample provision was made, not only for the maintenance of an army, but for the purchase of all commodities in India and China. Clive's system perfect in theory;

This political system, so perfect in theory, was soon found to be impossible in practice. Before Lord Clive left Calcutta, he modified the three principles it involved. He appointed English supervisors, as noticed in his own memorandum, to check the native collectors of revenue in the districts.[1] He proposed to form an alliance with the Nizam of Hyderabad against the Mahrattas; and although this step was forbidden by the Court of Directors, yet even they admitted the possible necessity of making war upon the Mahrattas from the side of Bombay. Last of all, Lord Clive Impossible in practice.

[1] See *ante*, page 344.

discovered that the appropriation of the surplus revenue to the trade with China was draining the Bengal provinces of rupees, and creating a silver famine.

Mr. Verelst, Governor of Bengal: advanced policy.

Lord Clive was succeeded by Mr. Verelst as Governor of Bengal. Verelst was forced by circumstances to depart still further from Lord Clive's original platform. The administration of Verelst has been overlooked by historians; yet it has an interest for all time. Verelst was taught by experience to adopt views and recommend measures which modified those originally expounded by Lord Clive, and led to still further modifications by his successors. He saw that by appropriating the revenue of the country, the English had become responsible for the rightful government of the people in every branch of the administration. He saw that the English would soon be forced to hold the balance of power between the native states in Hindustan.

Character of Verelst.

Verelst was a different man from Lord Clive. He was not a soldier-statesman, ruling the Bengal provinces by the force of will. He was a civilian, mindful of the welfare of the native population. Lord Clive's experiences were derived from life in camp, or negotiation with native officials and grandees. Verelst's experiences were derived directly from the masses. He knew the people well. He had passed through the several grades of the Company's commercial service. He had gained great credit as supervisor of the collection of the revenues in the three districts ceded by Meer Cossim.[1] Altogether he was nearly twenty years in India, and seems to have been well versed in the thoughts and ways of the people at large.

Revolutions of a decade, 1757-67.

The rise of British power in Bengal is the story of a single decade. It begins with the battle of Plassey in 1757, and ends with the departure of Lord Clive in 1767. It is one of the revolutionary episodes in the eighteenth century. It may not dazzle the imagination like the later annals of conquest which built up the British empire; but it is more startling to the actors; and it effected far greater changes in the social and political relations between Englishmen and natives.

Verelst's experiences of the mercantile period.

Verelst served his apprenticeship in Bengal during the old mercantile period. He was familiar with the times when the English in Bengal were all traders, and nothing but traders. Stories were told of fights with petty Rajas about tolls and transit duties; but the ambition of merchants was to make good bargains and push their trading interests in Bengal. They made municipal laws and administered justice within their little zemindary; but they took no heed of what was going on outside the Company's bounds unless it affected trade.

Sudden accession of the English to wealth and power.

After the battle of Plassey, the English rose to wealth and power at a single bound. Successes followed one after the other with such bewildering rapidity that neither the English at Calcutta nor the Directors in London could realise their real

[1] See *ante*, page 274.

position. Before one revolution was accomplished it was upset by another. One Nawab was deposed because he was too weak; his successor was deposed because he was too strong. Then followed the massacre at Patna, a disaster as terrible as that of the Black Hole. Next came the victory at Buxar as glorious and decisive as that of Plassey. The battle of Plassey had made the English masters of Bengal. The battle of Buxar and capture of Lucknow had carried them into the heart of Hindustan.

Era of peace.

The second administration of Lord Clive was an era of peace. So far his foreign policy was a success. By giving back Oude to the Nawab Vizier he raised a barrier between Bengal and the Mahrattas, which remained undisturbed for years.

Experimental political system of Lord Clive.

The domestic policy of Lord Clive was necessarily an experiment. Neither he, nor any of the merchants or military officers, knew anything or cared anything for the native administration of the country. Lord Clive thought it best to leave the native administration alone; at any rate until some experience should be gained of its actual workings. Political considerations compelled him to be cautious. The East India Company would have alarmed native princes and European powers by the premature assumption of the sovereignty of Bengal. The nominal sovereignty of the Moghul still overshadowed the land. The conservatism of the people of India was satisfied by the preservation of Moghul forms. No other European power could possibly interfere, so long as the Company acted only as

King's Dewan, and the native administration was carried on in the name of the Nawab Nazim. No harm could accrue from governing Bengal in the name of the Moghul, although the representative of the Moghul was living in empty and idle state at Allahabad. In like manner, no harm could accrue from exercising suzerainty in the name of a pageant Nawab, who wasted his days in the same empty and idle state at Murshedabad.

The puppet King at Allahabad.

All this while the so-called King was living at Allahabad under the supposed guardianship of the Nawab Vizier. He had nothing whatever to do, directly or indirectly, with the government of the empire. The dream of his life was to go to Delhi, and sit on the throne of his fathers; but Lord Clive steadily refused to help him.

The pageant Nawab Nazim.

The Nawab Nazim of Bengal was treated with outward respect, but only as a pageant. Probably he exercised less power outside Murshedabad than one of the Company's native servants. The English provided for the military defence of Bengal, concluded treaties, and made ready for war without the slighest reference to the King or Nawab Nazim. The native administration was left alone; it was superintended by the Mussulman grandee, named Muhammad Reza Khan. This grandee had been appointed Deputy Nawab by Governor Spenser, during the general scramble for money which followed the death of Meer Jaffier. Muhammad Reza Khan exercised real and undivided control over the entire native administration of the three provinces. Clive tried to introduce a check by appointing two Hindu grandees with co-ordinate powers; but, practically, the sole charge of the administration of justice and collection of revenue was left in the hands of Muhammad Reza Khan.

Relations between the Company and the Nizamut.

The sham of a Nawab's government was called the Nizamut. The English were the real sovereigns, but everything was done in the name of the Nizamut. The Court of Directors sent out the most stringent restrictions against any interference with the Nizamut. The people of Bengal were left entirely to the tender mercies of the Nizamut. The sole political duty of the Company was to take over the yearly revenue of the three provinces at the annual Poona at Murshedabad. Out of this revenue the Company paid the stipulated tribute to the King; the stipulated allowances to the Nizamut; the salaries of their own servants, civil and military. The surplus was placed in the coffers of the Company for the purposes of trade.

Experience of native administration.

When Verelst succeeded Lord Clive as Governor of Bengal, he was already alive to the evils of the existing system. He had been supervisor in turn of the three districts ceded by Meer Cossim. He had witnessed the oppression and corruption of native administration. He discovered that his predecessors had shared in the corrupt profits of the native collectors. It was these discoveries that led the Directors to make the remark already quoted, "that an Englishman was unfit to conduct the collection of revenue, and follow the subtle native through all his arts."

Verelst proved by his own conduct that the Directors were mistaken. He largely increased the revenues of the three districts; he planned a way for protecting the cultivators from the oppressions of the zemindars. He induced the Directors to sanction the system inaugurated during the second administration of Lord Clive, under which English supervisors in every district were to interfere more or less directly in every branch of the administration. **Plans of Verelst.**

The so-called Native administration of Bengal was about as bad as could be imagined. It was not native in the proper sense of the word. It was an administration of foreigners. The officials were mostly adventurers from Persia; ignorant of the ways of the people and first principles of government; without sympathies for Hindus; brought up amidst the tyranny, corruption, and anarchy which for centuries had characterised Persian rule. Hindu officials had been much employed by Aliverdi Khan; not out of any regard for the people, but as a check upon the Muhammadans. They were equally as extortionate, but were more easily deprived of their ill-gotten gains.[1] Under such circumstances the zemindars might oppress the ryots; **Evils of the Native administration.**

[1] Meer Jaffier, as already seen, began to squeeze the Hindu grandees, but was stopped by Clive. His successor, Meer Cossim, ruined several by his confiscations. It was a current saying that Muhammadan grandees spent all their gains in profusion and debauchery; consequently when squeezed they disgorged nothing. Hindu officials were more temperate; they absorbed wealth like a sponge; when squeezed they disgorged everything.

the collectors be in collusion with the zemindars; the accounts might be cooked on all sides; there was no one to control the collections except Muhammad Reza Khan. An English Resident was appointed at Murshedabad, but he could do nothing. The Company was King's Dewan; the Nizamut conducted the administration; the constant cry of the Court of Directors was that no one was to interfere.

Ignorance of the English.

The English knew nothing of what was going on, excepting what they could gather during their administration of the three districts ceded by Meer Cossim,—Burdwan, Midnapore, and Chittagong.

Continued monopoly of inland trade.

To make matters worse, the monopoly of the inland trade in salt, betel-nut, and other articles of native consumption, continued in the hands of the servants of the Company. The irregular use of dustucks was prohibited; some restrictions were introduced; a few refractory European interlopers were sent back to England; but the servants of the Company, from Members of Council downwards, derived the bulk of their incomes from the inland trade; and their gomastas or agents continued to oppress the people as in the days of Meer Cossim.

Helplessness of the native administration.

Muhammad Reza Khan was utterly helpless. Meer Cossim, with an army at his back, had been unable to resist the English. Muhammad Reza Khan was necessarily in the hands of the English. His place, power, and wealth depended on the will of the Company's servants. Neither he, nor the native officials under him, could interfere in the trade of their European masters, or exercise the slightest control over the rascalities and oppressions of the gomastas.

The records of Verelst's administration are of the utmost value. His experiences were perhaps larger than those of any other European in Bengal. He was a cautious man but a thoughtful one. He had to solve one of the most difficult problems in the early history of British rule—the obligations of the English both to the native rulers, and to the people ruled. In 1769 he drew up an exhaustive memorandum in which he reviews the rise of British power in India, and the corresponding decay of Native administration. The following extracts furnish a sad picture of the contemporary state of Bengal:— Verelst's Memorandum.

"The ascendency of the English in Hindostan is in the number of those events which are distinguished by a series of fortunate and unforeseen occurrences; not the result of any fixed or connected plan of policy. A colony of merchants, governed by laws, and influenced by principles merely commercial, have acquired a political title and influence over a country, which for extent, populousness, and annual revenue may be compared to many of the most consequential states of Europe; that commerce which was once prosecuted in subjection to a tyrannical government, ever ready to take advantage of our weakness, and to construe the slightest omissions into encroachments, is now but a secondary consideration; and the native authority being too weak to control the power which our agents derive from our name, the rights of the natives have been generally superseded. Substantial natives have declined risking their property in trade under such disadvantages, and the poor and industrious receive but a faint encouragement to their labours. We see, we feel, the increasing Rise of English power and decline of Native authority.

poverty of the country, from the diminution of specie, as well as the slowness and partiality of its circulation. Indeed, from the regulations we have made, examples we have ordered, and the checks we have multiplied, I flatter myself that the equality of commerce will finally be restored, and the spirit of monopoly be destroyed.

Character of the Bengalees.

"But the body of people are in a manner formed to wear the yoke. They possess nothing of the inquisitiveness of the European nations; and the most slender arts are sufficient to obscure their understandings, and fit them for implicit submission. Those among them, who attain to employments in our service, are generally men who have learnt so much of our manners as to corrupt their own, and joining an acute and versatile genius to abundance of low cunning, they scarcely want the consequence of the English name to prompt them to every villany.

Weakness of the Native government.

"Whilst the native government retained its superiority, its tribunals were accessible, and though venality presided at them, yet some show of justice was maintained, and, at times, redress might be procured. The native government is now fallen in the eye of the inhabitants, yet such restrictions have hitherto cramped our proceedings, as to prevent us from taking that intimate part which our present character and dignity require. The dependents of this nominal government have been the only instruments which we could employ either to repress the enormities of our own agents, or to obtain the good opinion of the country people. Their authority is, in general, overawed, their principles too bad to answer the former purpose, and their establishment and conduct too temporary and too weak for the latter, so that the English name has been only all-powerful to do mischief; and a mortifying spectacle of fraud and oppression on the one hand, and imbecility on the other, has been exhibited to us, without the power of interposing.

Mercantile training of the Company's servants.

"In the infancy of our settlement, with all our care and prudence, we could ill defend ourselves from the forged accusations or open attacks of the government; we looked no farther than the provision of the Company's investment; we sought advantages to our trade with the ingenuity, I may add, selfishness of merchants. All our laws were local and municipal, reaching no farther than our own exigencies and conveniencies; all our servants and dependents were trained and educated in the same notions; the credit of a good bargain was the utmost scope of their ambition.

Sudden rise to political power.

"No sooner did we begin to feel our own strength, than our successes followed one another with such rapidity, as to advance us from a state of obscurity or mediocrity, to power, affluence, and national reputation. At length we saw ourselves, though yet under the name of merchants, masters and administrators of a legislative authority: we began to plan, direct, and inspirit every measure of government, whether with regard to foreign treaties or domestic regulations. Wealth flowed in upon us from every side. Our investment was extended: we supported the whole trade of India; and, from our resources, gave security to it in every quarter. But this was rather a temporary thana solid situation; and we soon discovered, that though our acquisitions had been made in so short a space as scarcely to be paralleled, considering their immensity, yet a well-digested system was necessary to introduce permanency in our establishment. The defects and imperfections of which were too apparent to escape our observation. Our dependents, accustomed to apply their talents to present gain, and to extract advantages from the smallest opening, assumed an importance proportionable to our successes, grew immoderate, and disclaimed their dependency on the native government.

Conflicting authority of the English and the Nizamut.

"In this situation we could not retract without exposing ourselves to a second stage of obscurity, perhaps lower than the first. Our circumstances impelled us forward, and the grant of the Dewanny became as much an object of necessity as it was of advantage. Thus we insensibly broke down the barrier betwixt us and government,[1] and the native grew

[1] By the term "government," Mr. Verelst means the Nizamut. By "officers of government," he means the "officers of the Nizamut."

uncertain where his obedience was due. Such a divided and complicated authority gave rise to oppressions and intrigues unknown at any other period; the officers of government caught the infection, and being removed from any immediate control, proceeded with still greater audacity.

Interference forbidden.

"In the meantime we were repeatedly and peremptorily forbiden to avow any public authority over the officers of government in our own names, and enjoined to retain our primitive characters of merchants with the most scrupulous delicacy.

Evil results.

"The consequences are but too evidently exemplified in the decline of commerce and cultivation, the diminution of specie, and the general distresses of the poor; a train of evils which could only have sprung from the above causes, since every advantage of a long and uninterrupted tranquillity has been on our side. Experience must convince the most prejudiced, that to hold vast possessions, and yet to act on the level of mere merchants, making immediate gain our first principle; to receive an immense revenue, without possessing an adequate protective power over the people who pay it; to be really interested in the grand and generous object, the good of the whole, and yet to pursue a narrow and partial end;—are paradoxes not to be reconciled, highly injurious to our national character, dangerous to the best defended establishment, and absolutely bordering on inhumanity.

Obligation of the English to the people of Bengal.

"The people give us the labour of their hands, and in return we owe them our protection; common prudence, as well as the laws of society, require that those obligations should be reciprocal, or the tie must soon be dissolved; for the firmest security of every government is the affections of the people; and for obtaining them, there never, perhaps, presented a more favourable opportunity, or more noble field, than what the English possess in Bengal. The mildness of our government, properly diffused over these provinces, will form so conspicuous a contrast to Mahomedan despotism, that it must bind them to us and our cause for ever.

"I have hitherto considered our interest in this country as built on a precarious foundation, because this cement was wanting to bind it; and, in this point of view, I am particularly happy on the late resolutions which have been taken to appoint English Supra-visors, as an introduction to so desirable an event." Appointment of English Supra-visors.

"But there is a rock, and a dangerous one, which requires the greatest circumspection to avoid. We have stepped forth beyond all former precedent or example. We have the best and most laudable of all arguments to justify our conduct. But it should be remembered, that we have reached that supreme line, which, to pass, would be an open avowal of sovereignty. It should be remembered, that we cannot be more, without being greater than sound policy allows; the interests of our employers at home, no less than our national connections abroad, forbid it. If we were, before the change, cautious of interfering with the native government, and of awakening the jealousy of foreign nations, we ought now to redouble our prudence. The change itself, supposing the greatest forbearance on our parts, has an unavoidable tendency to destroy the name of the Nizamut, by which means, what might have been the happiest event for the Company and nation may become the source of perplexities and jealousies, if not the deprivation of the Company's privileges. Dangers of interfering with the Nizamut.

"There is, however, a middle way, where moderation must guide and continue us; where we may walk with safety, advantage, and consistency without danger of too much confinement or too much liberty. Exteriors should be regarded as essentials. Every order should scrupulously wear the sanction of the native government. Our dependence on its indulgencies, our obedience to its commands, our delicacy to its ministers, should appear most conspicuous in all transactions, either of business or ceremony. I am not ignorant how difficult it is always to preserve and affect that temperate rule of conduct which I mention, when the power and direction of all departments so entirely concentre in your Board, and may be still more difficult to produce a proper conformity in The middle way.

the Supra-visors; for these reasons I am thus earnest in my representations, and am of opinion that the whole weight and vigilance of this Board should be exerted to check the most trifling variation from the line, and to preserve the idea of the native government, its dignity and superiority over all, as entire and unimpaired as possible.

Duties of Supra-visors; training for higher posts.

"Without departing from these maxims, we shall have sufficient opportunities to answer all our views; our power will not be less efficacious in being exercised with prudence. The Supra-visorships will afford you a set of servants capable of succeeding, in their turn, to the first offices; that station will introduce them to a perfect knowledge of the laws and customs of the country; they will form a judgment upon the spot of the dispositions of the people; they will see with their own eyes the prevalent abuses of office, the villainy of agents, and, in short, the true spring of the misery or happiness of the country. Thus much may be advanced with confidence, that if this measure meets with the necessary support and encouragement, there cannot fail being a regular succession of able and vigorous administrators. The service, at present, affords many young men of promising parts and abilities. As the Supra-visorships may be called a nursery for them, in respect to the government of the country, so in like manner their experience in commercial matters, before they reach Council, must bring them acquainted with our commercial interest; and as these are the grand foundation and support of our prosperity, they must be deemed the essential part of their education.

Abuses under the existing system.

"But from what has been said of the characters of the people who are employed directly by us, or intermediately for us, every thinking person must be sensible of one capital defect in our government, that the members of it derive their sole advantages from commerce, carried on through black agents, who again employ a numerous band of retainers. It is notorious that, at times, the agents of the lowest servants have domineered over the ryot and kept the officers of government in a state of awe or subjection; and it cannot be supposed that more respectable names are not equally misapplied. It would be as easy to change the genius and manners of the people, as to prevent the banians, and followers of men in station, from abusing their master's name. Chastisement may deter the oppressor for a moment; but, in such cases the servility of the people must be removed, before oppression can be eradicated. Perwannahs have been recalled and suppressed; excellent effects will doubtless flow from it, but the idea of name and authority will still be held up by rapacious agents for their own ends. The conclusion I draw from it is this, that was it possible to form an administration totally free from commercial views and connections, restrictive laws would and must then have their course; whereas banians and agents, by the spirit with which they act, and the force of their example, will always obstruct their good effects, and propagate a disrespect and delusion of them in others.

"To form such an administration, I not only think possible but easy. I would propose that, from the admission of a member into Council, he put an entire conclusion to his trade; and, in lieu of it, that he receive a certain allowance, chargeable upon the country; which allowance should be augmented in proportion to the improvements made, and its internal prosperity: a method of reward the most honourable that can be devised for those that are to receive it, and the most beneficial to the community, being unencumbered with the consequences, anxieties, and relations of private affairs. The members of administration will have a more undivided attention to the public, and their orders be more thoroughly respected, and more vigorously obeyed."

English Member of Council to cease trading in Bengal.

The wisdom of the foregoing observations will be admitted by all who are familiar with the past and present history of India. They are sufficient to show that, however Mr. Verelst may have been judged by his contemporaries, he was emphatically a man in advance of his time.

Permanent value of Verelst's observations.

The following extract is taken from the proceedings of the Select Committee in connection with the employment of Supervisors; it indicates still more clearly the existing state of the native administration:—

Causes of existing evils.

"The Committee, having endeavoured to trace and assign the true cause of our declining situation, unanimously agree that the following imperfections, in the formation and conduct of the system hitherto pursued, are the grand and original sources thereof:—

Want of control.

"1. The want of sufficient checks in the instruments of government, who are generally adventurers from Persia, educated in the manners and principles of a government where tyranny, corruption, and anarchy are predominant; who are strangers to the customs, and indifferent to the welfare of this country; and who cannot by any vigilance be restrained, or by any severity be deterred, from practising their native oppressions, over a timid, servile, and defenceless people.

Supreme authority lodged in the hands of one or a few.

"2. The delegation of a trust and authority to one, or to a few, which require the abilities and activity of many to execute; an error which is notoriously the cause of those departments being worse administered, but give rise to a complex corruption, which is difficult, if not impossible, to be detected. The avenues of justice are by those means obstructed, and the injured are frequently at a loss where to prefer their complaints, and in whom the right of decision is invested.[1]

Ignorance of the English.

"3. The ignorance of the real produce and capacity of the country, in which we are necessarily kept by a set of men, who first deceive us from interest, and afterwards continue the deception from fear of punishment, and a necessary regard to their own safety.

Host of native dependents.

"4. The numerous train of dependents and underlings, whom the collectors entertain; whose demands, as well as the avarice of their principals, are to be satisfied from the

[1] This paragraph is evidently aimed at Muhammad Reza Khan.

spoils of the industrious ryot, who thus loses all confidence in the government, and seeks protection in other places, where he has better hopes to see his industry rewarded.

"5. The venality which forms part of the genius of the people, and which is known to be openly exercised, or tacitly allowed by government, without drawing any shame or discredit on the guilty, or being thought any peculiar hardship on the injured. Venality.

"6. The collusion of the collectors with the zemindars whom the collector employs as a tool to serve his malpractices, or admits an associate in his fraudulent gains. Collusions of collectors and zemindars.

"7. The oppressions to which the ryot is subject from the multitude of gomastahs and their dependents. Oppression of gomastahs.

"The Committee are convinced that this degree of power without control, of knowledge without participation, and of influence without any effectual counteraction, is too important and replete in the consequences to be vested in any three ministers, or rather one single man; who, allowing him the clearest preference for integrity, ability, and attachment among his countrymen, cannot be supposed superior to temptation; and at least ought not, in good policy, to be trusted so extensively and independently as has been necessarily the consequence of the present system:[1] while the Company are in reality the principals in the revenues of this country, and the most interested in the good conduct of its government, every bar should be removed that tends to preclude them from a knowledge of its real state. In the above causes, and others deducible from them, the Committee discerns, with great regret, the original source and present inveteracy of many of those evils under which these provinces are at present oppressed. Summing up of the case.

"The frequent and peremptory restrictions which the Court of Directors had thought proper to impose on us, and that line of conduct from which no deviation was allowed, and the smallest surveyed with jealousy, have hitherto left us without any choice of measures, freedom of action, or power of reformation. Peremptory order against interference.

---

[1] Here, again, Verelst is alluding to Muhammad Reza Khan.

Sanction of Directors to Supra-visors.

"Their last letter has now offered us the sanction that was so essentially necessary for the welfare and improvement of these provinces, as well as for our own vindication in the pursuit of such plans as we may judge advisable to adopt. By that letter, the Directors seem to approve of the distribution and allotment of the country into farms, and of the appointment of European gentlemen to supervise the different provinces, and to control the conduct of the agents of the country government. From this permission, we have a well-grounded expectation of success to our design of introducing new regulations; and the event will, we are flattered, be the strongest confirmation of the propriety of those regulations.

Necessity for interference.

"We have always acted as far as the nature of the occasion would allow with the most scrupulous regard to the rules prescribed to us by by our employers; and, on our first accession to the Dewanny, chose rather to assume the slow but certain conviction of experience for our guide, than attempt innovations on the precarious foundation of opinion. But now that whole pages of our records are filled with so many incontestible evidences, that great alterations are wanting to form a mode of collection, which may be restrictive to the collector, and indulgent to the ryot, we are happy in finding the sentiments of our employers so aptly correspondent to our opinion, and the necessity of the juncture. Every native of any substance or character in this country has been successively tried in the department of the collections. Fear, reward, severity, and indulgence, have all failed, and ended in a short political forbearance, or additional acts of dishonesty and rapine.

Secret corruption and oppression.

"On an alarm of inspection, or at the annual Poona, they frame accounts to serve the occasion; or by involving them in confusion and ambiguity, waste time till it becomes too late to continue the process against them, without hazarding new losses in the revenue: and thus the culpable not only escape punishment, but often obtain a prolongation of their appointments. Many flagrant grievances reach our ears, but, in a country of such extent, there are, doubtless, many more concealed from us; and, what is equally true under our present disadvantages, they are, and must remain, inexplorable; we can neither redress grievances, nor effect improvements. With regard to the former, our distance, and our too indirect information through ministerial channels, set the offender beyond our reach, and the impossibility of having time and competent knowledge puts the latter out of our power.

Necessity for promoting cultivation, and nature of trade.

"Enough has been said, and more might be produced, to prove that the system, established and now pursuing in this country, is deficient in every particular that is requisite to defend and support the poor from the injustice and oppression of the strong, and to increase its value to its possessors, by promoting the industry of the ryot and manufacturer.

"That although we have seen these evils growing and preying upon the vitals of the country, we have been unable to stop their progress, or afford effectual protection to the people.

"Lastly, that we can never hope to emerge from that uncertainty and ignorance into which this system has thrown us, whilst we sit tamely and will admit of no variation in it.

Prosperous state of the three ceded districts.

"Let us now turn our eyes and attention to a more pleasing scene; to Burdwan, and the rest of the Company's proprietary lands, where we ourselves have been the managers. Plenty, content, population, increase of revenue, without increase of burthen, are now the effects; and form so forcible an argument in the comparative view, that nothing can strengthen, nothing can render it plainer or more convincing.

Administration extended to all of the provinces.

"And here the Committee cannot hesitate in drawing a decisive conclusion—that the same or similar regulations be established throughout the provinces in every distinct district. The same beneficial consequences to the country and Company may be expected from them, and by an increased security of the property of individuals, as also by an encouragement to cultivation and commerce, they may give a new flow to the circulation of specie, which is become so limited as to affect every rank and profession.

Extent of the work.

"The Committee are sensible that much application, integrity, good conduct, and time will be necessary to retrieve the desolations of the native collectors; to raise the sinking heart of the ryot from despair to confidence and hope; to re-people and settle the deserted and uncultivated tracts, and to take every advantage of the abundant fertility of the lands.

Imperfect knowledge.

"The progress towards this desirable change must be gradual. We have yet but an imperfect knowledge of the soil, the productions, the value, the capacity of the various provinces, and sub-divisions of the country. This, however, is the foundation on which, and which only, we can build with success and direct our grand design with judgment; and to acquire this knowledge should therefore be our first care, by means of the minutest local investigation, for none other can give us an authentic record to refer to on every occasion as an established authority; nor can we judge of the lenity, rigour, or propriety of any of our resolutions respecting the country, without such a work completely and accurately executed.

Relations between the Supravisors resident at Murshedabad.

"The Committee concurring in the necessity of pursuing the above work in the most effectual manner, that when perfected they may proceed in the important business before them; and being farther induced by the opinion of the Court of Directors, expressed in their last letter of the 11th November 1768, agree unanimously to the following resolutions:—

"That, in every province or district, a gentleman in the service be appointed, with or without assistance, in proportion to the extent of the district, whose office or department is to be subordinate to the resident of the Durbar."

Native administration of justice.

The instructions to the Supervisors have become obsolete, but the following remarks which refer to the native administration of justice are interesting and suggestive:—

"It is difficult to determine whether the original customs or the degenerate manners of the Mussulmans have most contributed to confound the principles of right and wrong in these provinces. Certain it is, that almost every decision of theirs is a corrupt bargain with the highest bidder. The numerous offences which are compromised by fines have left a great latitude for unjust determinations. Trifling offenders, and even many condemned on fictitious accusations, are frequently loaded with heavy demands, and capital criminals are as often absolved by the venal judge. Your conduct in all capital offences should be to enforce justice where the law demands it, checking every composition by fine or mulct; and where any disputes arise in matters of property, you should recommend the method of arbitration to any other; and inculcate strongly in the minds of the people that we are not desirous to augment our revenue by such impositions, but to acquire their confidence by the equity and impartiality of our proceedings, and by our tenderness for their happiness. The arbitrators should be men chosen by the parties themselves, and of known integrity, and whose circumstances may suppose them exempt from venality, and promise best to insure their rectitude. In capital crimes, the sentence should, before execution, be referred to me, and by me to the ministers of the Nizamut, that they may ultimately approve or mitigate it, according to the peculiarity of the case. You are further to observe, that the want of regular registers of all causes and determinations have encouraged the natural propensity of the native judge to bribery and fraud by making him easy with respect to any future prosecution on a re-hearing of the cases which have been thus partially determined. Whereas, whilst a reference to records is always open, he must live in perpetual fear of detection. One of these registers should be lodged in the principal cutcherry of the province, and an authenticated copy transmitted to Murshedabad. As to suits on account of revenues, these will, we are flattered, be much obviated in future by the happy consequences of our possessing a real, local, and undisguised knowledge of the country; which we promise ourselves from the investigations above mentioned, and from your diligence and exactness in the performance of the several duties.

"For the ryot being eased and secured from all burthens and demands but what are imposed by the legal authority of government itself, and future pottahs [1] being granted him, specifying that demand; he should be taught that he is to Leases to ryots.

[1] Leases.

regard the same as a sacred and inviolable pledge to him, that he is liable to no demands beyond their amount. There can, therefore, be no pretence for suits on that account; no room for inventive rapacity to practise its usual arts: all will be fair, open, regular. Every man will know what he can call and defend as his own; and the spirit of lawless encroachment subsiding, for want of a field for exercise, will be changed into a spirit of industry; and content and security will take place of continual alarms and vexations.

Other reforms. "The instance where venal, ignorant, and rapacious judges avail themselves of a crude and mercenary system of laws of the prevalance of licentiousness and the force of reigning habits and customs, have been already mentioned. I can only repeat, that it is your part to endeavour to reform all these corruptions which have encroached on the primitive rights of both the Mahomedans and Hindoos; particularly by abolishing the arbitrary imposition of fines, and recommending all in your power the more equitable method of arbitration.

Control of Kazis and Brahmins. "The officers of justice and Kazis who are established by the Mahomedan law, as also the Brahmins, who administer justice among the Hindoos, in every village, town, and quarter, should all be summoned to appear, produce their Sunnuds, or authority for acting, and register them. Records, of whatever cases are heard and determined, are to be sent to and deposited in the Sudder Cutcherry of the province, and monthly return thereof forwarded to Murshedabad.

Registration of sunnuds. "The register of Sunnuds is intended to deter any from exercising a judicial, because lucrative function, who may not be legally appointed by government, if a Mahomedan, or fairly elected by his caste, if a Hindoo. And the depositing of all cases and determinations, added to the other regulation, will figure to the several officers a vigorous and observant power, watching all their actions, and, in case of abuses, direct you at once to the culpable.

Forfeit of caste. The peculiar punishment of forfeiting castes, to which the Hindoos are liable, is often inflicted from private pique and personal resentment amongst themselves; and requires to be restrained to those occasions only where there may be a regular process, and clear proofs of the offence before the Brahmins, who are their natural judges. But when any man has naturally forfeited his caste, you are to observe that he cannot be restored to it without the sanction of government, which was a political supremacy reserved to themselves by the Mahomedans, and which, as it publicly asserts the subordination of Hindus, who are so considerable a majority of subjects, ought not to be laid down; though every indulgence and privilege of caste should be otherwise allowed them.

The following evidence about the oppressions of the zemindars may be regarded as trustworthy:— Oppressions of zemindars.

"The truth cannot be doubted that the poor and industrious tenant is taxed by his zemindar, or collector, for every extravagance that avarice, ambition, pride, vanity, or intemperance may lead him into, over and above what is generally deemed the established rent of his lands. If he is to be married, a child born, honours conferred, luxury indulged, and nuzzurannas, or fines, exacted, even for his own misconduct, all must be paid by the ryot. And what heightens the distressful scene, the more opulent, who can better obtain redress for imposition, escape, while the weaker are obliged to submit."

The drain of silver out of Hindustan was producing the most lamentable results. The following extracts from a dispatch to the Court of Directors will throw some light on the subject:— Drain of silver; its causes.

"We have frequently expressed to you our apprehension lest the annual exportation of treasure to China would produce a scarcity of money in the country. This subject becomes every day more serious, as we already feel, in a very sensible manner, the effects of the considerable drain made from the silver currency. Experience will ever yield stronger conviction than the most abstract and refined reasoning.

"Whatever sums had formerly been remitted to Delhi were amply reimbursed by the returns made to the immense Non-return of specie.

commerce of Bengal, which might be considered as the central point to which all the riches of India were attracted. Its manufactures found their way to the remotest part of Hindostan, and specie flowed in by a thousand channels that are at present lost and obstructed. All the European companies formed their investments with money brought into the country; the Gulphs[1] poured in their treasures into this river; and across the continent, an inland trade was driven to the westward to the extremity of the kingdom of Guzerat

Vast exports of silver.

"How widely different from these are the present circumstances of the Nabob's dominions! Immense treasures have lately been carried out of the provinces by Meer Cossim, which may possibly be reserved as a fund to excite future troubles. Each of the European companies, by means of money taken up in the country, have greatly enlarged their annual investments, without adding a rupee to the riches of the province. On the contrary, the increase of exports to Europe has proved so great a restraint upon the industry of private merchants, that we will venture to affirm the balance from Europe, in favour of Bengal, amounts to a very trifling sum in specie. We know of no foreign trade existing at present which produces a clear balance in money, except that carried on with the ports of Judda, Mocha, and Bassora, from whence not fifteen lakhs[2] in bullion have been returned in the course of four years.

Threatened ruin of Bengal.

"When the provinces of Bengal, Behar, and Orissa came under your jurisdiction, they were much sunk in opulence, population, and manufactures, from their ancient importance. The almost continual irruptions of the Mahrattas, under the government of Alliverdy Khan, and the avarice of the ministers under the supineness of Seraj-u-doulah, the necessities of Meer Jaffier, and the iron hand of the rapacious and bloodthirsty Meer Cossim, struck equally at the property of the rich, and industry of the poor: and while it reduced the one to indigence, compelled the other to seek

[1] The two Gulphs of Mocha and Persia.

[2] 187,500*l.*

safety in flight. If to these we add, first, the immense amount in specie and jewels to the value of between three and five crores of rupees [1] secreted or carried off by Cossim after his several defeats had obliged him to relinquish all hopes of a reinstatement: 2ndly, the royal tribute of twenty-six [2] lakhs and the expence of about twenty lakhs for a brigade, both paid annually out of the provinces, and consequently out of the sphere of our immediate circulation: 3rdly, the annual amount of our own, and the other nations' investments, for which no value is received into the country: 4thly, the large exports of bullion to China and the different presidencies during the three last years: and lastly, the unavoidable misfortune and capital drain, the immense sums paid into the cash of foreign nations, for bills on their respective Companies. I say, the aggregate of these several exports must appear inevitable and immediately ruinous to the most flourishing state, much less be deemed tolerable to a declining and exhausted country! Yet it is in this situation the Court of Directors, and the nation in general, have been induced to expect prodigious remittances in specie, from a country which produces little gold and no silver; and where any considerable imports of both have, for a series of years, been rendered necessary to the trade of foreign Companies, by the general demands for draughts on Europe."

It appears from another calculation that during three years the exports of bullion from Bengal exceeded five millions sterling, whilst the imports of bullion were little more than half a million. Meantime the rupee rose to an exchange value of two-and-sixpence. Rise in the value of rupees.

The views of Verelst on the political situation of Bengal as regards the native powers in Views of Verelst on foreign affairs.

[1] Between 3,750,000*l.* and 6,250,000*l.*

[2] 325,060*l.*

Hindustan may be gathered from the following extracts:—

Prostration of the Moghul empire.

"The first and great cause of our security is the general indigenee of the Moghul empire. The invasion of Nadir Shah gave the first stroke to its power and opulence, but it fell not so heavily as is commonly imagined. It gave a mortal wound, it is true, to the overgrown wealth and arrogance of the Moghul grandees; but, as the blow was not pursued, its effect was not immediately felt beyond the capital. The eruption of the Mahrattas ensued, their wide-extended ravages laid desolate almost everything on the south side of the Ganges, from near the frontiers of Behar on the east, to Sirhind on the north and west. Their undistinguishing rapine plunged cities and countries in one common ruin, and the empire must have sunk under their oppression, or fallen a prey to their ambition, if the defeat at Paniput had not put a period at once to their power and devastations.[1] The expeditions of Ahmad Shah Abdali succeeded, which, though neither so extensive, destructive, or bloody as those of the Mahrattas, still conduced greatly to exhaust a declining state; and, though his sphere of action was chiefly confined to the Panjab and confines of Dehli, yet the vast sums he levied must have been severely felt throughout a country which produces no silver, and but very little gold. So large a decrease of specie naturally produced a decay of trade, and a diminution of cultivation; and, though these evils have, in some measure, been palliated in our provinces by the annual imports of bullion, yet in the most flourishing interior parts, such as Benares, Mirzapore, &c., the fact is notorious, and beyond dispute.

Weakness of Native powers.

"The natural consequence of these circumstances has been, that the different native powers find their finances narrow, and their treasures unequal to the maintenance of a respectable army, or the prosecution of a war of any duration. Whenever, therefore, they are urged by ambition or necessity to

[1] The Mahrattas were defeated by the Afghans under Ahmad Shah Abdali in 1761.

enter on any expedition, they assemble new levies for the purpose with the most unreflecting precipitancy; they risk everything on one campaign, because they have seldom resources for a second; and come to an engagement at all events, because the consequences of a defeat are less terrible than those which must ensue from the desertion or sedition of an ill-paid and disaffected army. As their troops, then, are chiefly raw men and aliens, they are without attachment to their general, or confidence in each other: a variety of independent commanders destroys all subordination and authority; and the certainty of beggary and starving from the common accidents of war, throws a damp on the most ardent bravery.

"These circumstances, I apprehend, gentlemen, have been very principal sources of our repeated victories over these immense Asiatic armies, which have fled before a handful of your troops; and these will, I trust, either deter others in future, or ensure success against any who may be desperate enough to brave a force like ours, so strengthened by discipline, and rendered formidable by uninterrupted successes. English victories.

"A second, and no less powerful reason for the security of our situation, is the discordancy of the principles, views, and interests of the neighbouring powers; and which must ever defeat any project of accomplishing, by an association, what the wealth or power of a single one must prove unequal to. The majority of the present princes of Hindostan have no natural right to the countries they possess. In the general wreck of the monarchy, every man seized what fortune threw into his hands; and they are, therefore, more studious to secure what they have already obtained, than to grasp at new acquisitions. Hence, the principal disturbances which have lately happened in Hindostan (Shuja-u-daula's invasion of Bengal excepted) have been accidental broils raised by the Mahrattas, Sikhs, and Ahmad Shah Abdali, whose views were rather extended to plunder than to territorial possessions. Conscious that the maintenance of their usurped authority depends on their preventing any of the members from being too much depressed, or too much elevated, they Discordancy of Native princes.

are become jealous and suspicious of each other, and ever ready to throw in their weight against any one whom they see rising too high above the common level. For this reason, they at first looked on our successes with an evil eye; still our generosity to Shuja-u-daula, our attention to our treaties and public faith, and, above all, our moderation in not pursuing our victories, begot a confidence in us they had not in their countrymen, and made them rather ambitious of our friendship than jealous of our power.

English holding the balance in Hindostan.

"Thus circumstanced, it will always be easy for a watchful and active administration on our side to hold the general balance of Hindustan, and crush every combination in the bud, by spiriting up some neighbouring power, who may be either ill-disposed, or at least not favourable to the confederates. A very little acquaintance with the disposition of the natives will shew their ardour for change, where they have a prospect of support; and the situation of Allahabad, and the station of a brigade there, renders this plan still more practicable. Its situation makes it, in some measure, the key of the surrounding territories; and its vicinity to the several countries of Shuja-u-daula, the Rohillas, Jauts, and Mahrattas, enables us to penetrate their views with more certainty, and in case of necessity, to enter any part with our army in ten or fifteen days, where we can have either an ally to support, or an enemy to punish. It is for these reasons, we have been obliged to retain a brigade out of the provinces. Our repeated resolutions in Committee will, I doubt not, evince our earnest desire to fulfil your orders on this head, and the necessity itself excuses us for keeping it there as long as these reasons shall subsist.

Character and situation of native powers.

"Such, gentlemen, seem to be the general causes of our present security here; but they receive additional strength from the particular characters and situations of the several potentates themselves.

The King Shah Alam.

"The King Shah Alam, acknowledged emperor of Hindustan, retains little of the authority or dominions of his ancestors, but what he has derived from us. The provinces of Korah and Allahabad yield him a revenue of about twenty-seven lakhs[1] per annum, at a rack-rent; this is almost exhausted, to support rather the name than the substance of an army, whilst the Bengal tribute defrays the expences of his court and household, and enables him to live in an affluence, if not with a splendour, he never before enjoyed. His abilities are rather below mediocrity, and his character seems rather calculated for private life than a throne. He is religious as a man, affectionate as a father, and humane as a master; but as a prince he is weak, indolent, irresolute, and easily swayed by the counsels of self-interested men: I cannot, however, think we have anything to apprehend from these dispositions; the remembrance of what he experienced, when dependent on Shuja-u-daula, has created in him such a diffidence of Hindustan connexions as will effectually prevent him trusting himself to any of them again; and, at the same time, he probably entertains a distant hope that the hand which has already raised him to his present independence, may one day be extended to restore him to his throne and right.

Anxiety of the King to go to Delhi.

"The King has lately affected great earnestness to undertake his favourite expedition to Dehli. But the lowness of his finances threaten his project with a very sudden abortion. The weakness of his disposition is no less evident in the administration of his domestic affairs, than in the formation of his political schemes. Perpetual changes of his ministers and confidants have bred an uncertainty and distrust in the minds of all his adherents, which has checked public spirit, and produced a general turn to selfish pursuits. With a treasury so ill supplied, and a court so ill affected, it is more than probable, if he should advance, that he will be preyed on by his own servants; and being awakened from his delusion by a scene of beggary and contempt, will ultimately take protection in our provinces.

"From these conclusions it was I formed my opinion

---

[1] 337,500*l.* The King drew the revenue of Korah and Allahabad in addition to the tribute which he drew from the English in Bengal.

some months ago, when I acquiesced in His Majesty's requisition of two battalions; and all circumstances since have served to corroborate that opinion. An occasion of demonstrating the sincerity of our professions, without subjecting us to any apparent inconvenience, were too inviting advantages to be neglected, and may be derived from our connections with his Majesty.

Necessity for retaining the King at Allahabad.

"As the necessity of retaining His Majesty under our influence, or separating ourselves entirely from him, is a maxim in our system, and as the former seems most probable, we should be careful how we allow strangers to assume the management of his councils. Our conduct towards him is plain. We must either contrive to guide him at a distance, or so to palliate, that, if unsuccessful, he may consider us as his protectors, our provinces as the place of his refuge.

Superior advantage of the King removing to Bengal.

"All things, at present, seem tending to the latter, and it is an event most to be wished; but I had rather His Majesty should make the proposition, than that we should give the invitation. Disappointment may correct his impatience, and difficulties may teach him prudence. The treachery of Hindustan professions will prepare him better for the frank, plain declarations of his English allies; and there is the greatest reason to believe he will return to us with repentance.

Shuja-u-daula, Nawab Vizier of Oude.

"The Nawab Shuja-u-daula is our next ally; and, if gratitude can be any tie on an Hindustan heart, we have every reason to consider him as connected with us by the most indissoluble bonds. His dominions, except the zemindary of Bulwant Sing, lie on the north of the Ganges, and extend to the hills; and, though they are more thinly peopled than is common in this country, have been so much improved by his late regulations in them, as to produce annually near one crore and twenty-five lakhs of rupees.[1] His increase of strength has kept pace with his increase of revenue. He has near eleven battalions of sepoys of all sorts, a good body of horse, and has made considerable additions to his artillery and magazines; but, as his whole revenue can never support a

---

[1] 1,563,500*l*.

force which can be really formidable to us, so it will always be in our power to direct the force he has to such purposes as may best conduce to the interest of the Honourable Company and the general peace. The Nawab's education, and perhaps disposition, have led him to be vain, aspiring, and impatient. He is active, but desultory; his judgment rather acute than sound; and his generalship and policy more plausible than solid. From pride, or jealousy, he is afraid to employ men of abilities or rank in the several departments of his government; he plans, directs, oversees, and executes everything himself; so that the multiplicity of business, and his daily increasing infirmities, oblige him to leave his best designs imperfect and crude. His ambition, it is true, is always inciting him to form new projects, but his volatility induces him to be continually abandoning some, and his impetuosity often renders the remainder abortive. In a word, from a most careful review of his character and conduct, he seems a much proper instrument to accomplish the Company's main point, the maintaining themselves the empire of Hindustan, than an enemy who, from his strength or situation, could give them any material uneasiness or trouble."

Mr. Verelst contemplated a measure, as regards the Nizam of Hyderabad, which reads somewhat strangely in the present day. The Nizam had proved refractory. He had joined Hyder Ali of Mysore in his war against the English at Madras. Verelst proposed to punish him, and set up another Nizam in his room. He proceeded after Moghul forms. He procured a grant from the King at Allahabad of the whole of the Nizam's dominions. The name of the person to whom the grant was to be made was left blank. The grant was sent to Madras. The English at Madras were told to depose

Proposed dethronement of the Nizam.

the Nizam, and set up another in his room. They were at liberty to make their choice, and then to fill up the blank in the grant with the name of the new Nizam. The measure is fully explained in the following extract from a general letter[1] :—

Grant of a blank firman to the English for the Subahdarship of the Dekhan.

"By letters some time since received from the gentlemen at Madras, it appears that they laboured under great difficulties in the nomination of a Subah to the Moghul province of the Dekhan, in case Nizam Ali should, by an obstinate perseverance in his unjust measures, oblige them to deprive him of his government; and they were even pleased to request our opinion in a matter of so great importance. We expressed ourselves with that unreserved freedom which we wish may mutually subsist between the two Presidencies; and judging it expedient to secure the King's firman for the nomination of some other person, our President was desired to apply for the same to His Majesty, who has been pleased to comply with the request; and in a letter lately received from him, he promised to despatch a blank firman within five days of the date thereof, to be filled with the name of any person we may judge most proper for the security and lasting tranquillity of your possessions on the coast. This is a power we should be loth to avail ourselves of, excepting in the case of the utmost necessity; and such we fear this will prove, if we can form our judgment from the present situation of affairs."

Regrets of Verelst.

Verelst was so convinced of the expediency of this measure, that a year afterwards he expressed his regret that it had not been carried out. The passage is worthy of extract :—

"I could have wished the gentlemen on the coast[2] had been more deeply impressed with this idea, so that the reinforce-

[1] Despatch to the Court of Directors, dated 3rd February 1768.

[2] The presidency of Madras, on the coast of Coromandel.

ments sent from Bengal, instead of being scattered and dismembered, might have struck the important blow we meditated against the Subah.[1] In this case, Hyderabad, weak and defenceless, must have fallen an easy prey before the Nizam could have even received intelligence of the expeditions; and, as the capture must have more universally enforced a conviction of our power, so the generous restitution of it to a repenting enemy, must have highly exalted our moderation and disinterestedness."

The measure, however, was contrary to the policy of the Directors. They expressed their disapproval in the strongest terms. They ordered the grant to be cancelled. Directors cancel the firman.

Verelst left Bengal at the end of 1769. He was succeeded by Mr. Cartier, who in his turn gave place to Warren Hastings. The administration of Warren Hastings opens up a new era in Indian history, into which it is impossible to enter in the present volume. Departure of Verelst.

It has been seen more than once that within two or three years of the battle of Plassey, the English entertained the idea of going to Delhi. Possibly the attempt might have proved a success, and even at this early period the English might have established a paramount power in Hindostan. But the course of events prevented the enterprise. Indeed, an Anglo-Indian empire under the existing system would have been productive of evil rather than of good. The appropriation of revenues for trading purposes, without regard for the people who Possibility of an English empire over Hindostan.

---

[1] Nizam Ally, Subah of the Dekhan.

paid it, was bad enough in Bengal; it would have been fatal to the good name of the British government had it ever been extended into Hindostan.

Failure of the scheme of Supravisors.

It was destined that Bengal should be the school of English administrators; that the English should not become masters of an Indian empire until they had learned how to rule it; and this result was not effected until a later generation. The measure of appointing Supravisors was a move in the right direction, but it proved a failure. An Englishman placed alone in a large district, surrounded by native influences of the worst character, was helpless to contend against the general corruption, and was often tempted to share in the spoil. Such appears to have been the fate of Verelst's Supravisors.

INDEX.